Maria Pia

Queen of Portugal

By Sabrina Pollock

Epilogue by Arturo E. Beéche

EUROHISTORY.COM

ISBN: 978-0-9854603-7-2

ISBN: 978-0-9854603-7-2

First Edition – April 2015

Published by:

Kensington House Books
a division of Eurohistory
6300 Kensington Avenue
East Richmond Heights, CA 94805 USA
Telephone: (510) 236-1730
Fax: (510) 778-8465
Email: books@eurohistory.com
URL: http://www.eurohistory.com

Cover design by Arturo E. Beéche and David W. Higdon
Editing by Arturo E. Beéche & David W. Higdon
Layout & Design by Arturo E. Beéche
A proud product of the USA

To my Grandmother, Reba Stone Polson,

the first writer in our family!

Table of Contents

Acknowledgements		*i*
Introduction		*iii*
Chapter I:	*Childhood*	*1*
Chapter II:	*Portuguese Interlude*	*9*
Chapter III:	*The Red Queen*	*19*
Chapter IV:	*The Spanish Crown*	*35*
Chapter V:	*Daily Life*	*46*
Chapter VI:	*A Death in Rome*	*59*
Chapter VII:	*The Death of Ferdinand*	*64*
Chapter VIII:	*The Marriage of Carlos*	*71*
Chapter IX:	*The Turbulent Eighties*	*78*
Chapter X:	*Breaking Point*	*85*
Chapter XI:	*Luis "the Popular"*	*95*
Chapter XII:	*The Long Widowhood*	*103*
Chapter XIII:	*Regicide*	*115*
Chapter XIV:	*Revolution – Exile and Death*	*128*
Epilogue:		*140*

Family Trees: *The Royal House of Savoy* *152*
The Coburg and Braganza Dynasties *154*
Endnotes *156*

Bibliography *164*
Index *169*

Illustrations: *Between Pages 70-71**

(*) All illustrations provided by the Eurohistory Royal Photographic Archive and Ms. Sabrina Pollock

Acknowledgements

I gratefully acknowledge the permission of her Majesty Queen Elizabeth II to publish certain letters from the correspondence between Queen Victoria and the Portuguese royal family held in the Royal Archives in Windsor Castle. I also wish to thank the Fürst of Hohenzollern for his permission to quote from the correspondence between the Portuguese sovereigns and Prince Leopold of Hohenzollern-Sigmaringen held in the Sigmaringen State Archives; I am particularly indebted to Dr. Volker Trugenberger, the Sigmaringen archive director, for his gracious assistance.

I am likewise indebted to Marina Tabares Dias for her invaluable help at the Torre do Tombe (Institute of National Archives) in Lisbon, Portugal. Not only for her thought provoking insight into the Portuguese royal family, but she was also instrumental in helping to decipher Queen Maria Pia's handwriting, which is extremely difficult to read.

A very special thank you must go to Larry Russell and Arturo E. Beéche for their patronage. Their support allowed this book to become a reality.

Books cannot be financially viable without the help of those who sell and market them. With that in mind, I would like to acknowledge the support of the following well-respected resellers: Ted Rosvall (Rosvall Royal Books), Annet Bakker (Hoogstraten English Bookstore), Nicolas Fouint (Librairie Galignani) and Jeannie Pittard-Whitmarsh (MAJESTY).

Finally, I wish to thank Dave Higdon, Greg King, Henry Wong, Katrina Warne, Dr. Mary Houck and the rest of staff at the European Royal History Journal (EUROHISTORY). Their endless encouragement and support in all my writing endeavors has been invaluable.

Sabrina Pollock
Lexington, Kentucky

Introduction

Very little information is available on Queen Maria Pia of Portugal in English, but the few mentions of this Queen in cumulative works on royalty intrigued me as she is presented as a mass of contradictions. She had a temper, but was not a scold. She was as extravagant as she was charitable. She was intimidating; she was emotionally fragile. The list goes on and on.

Delving into Portuguese works on the House of Braganza I devoured whatever information I could on Maria Pia. These secondary sources led to the fascinating anecdotes that precede all historical figures through the ages such as *"Luis does not please me"* and *"if I were King, I would have you shot."* But as titillating as these statements are, the more research I did the more I realized these were merely exaggerations more than the actual truth.

Luckily, in time I was able to go to the original source so to speak as I was able to consult Maria Pia's correspondence housed in archives in Portugal, Italy, Great Britain, and Germany. Maria Pia's handwriting, however, does present a challenge to researchers. For such an extravagant queen, Maria Pia was surprisingly an early believer in conserving paper, which was quite expensive at that time. Determined to get the full worth out of a single sheet of paper, the Queen was in the habit of filling every square inch by writing vertically over the horizontal lines she had already set down. Needless to say this makes her letters extremely difficult to decipher and translate. Her own son once even complained at the difficulty of trying to figure out what she had written, imploring his mother *"for the love of God, do not cross your cherished letters three times over, because I can almost not read them."* Made aware of her almost illegible handwriting Maria Pia apologized, admitting she had written her letter while lying down. I can only conclude she wrote all her correspondence while lying down!

I have done my best, but unfortunately I was unable to decipher all of her letters. In the ones I have been able to decipher, any mistakes made in the translations are my own. Hopefully, one day all her correspondence will be transcribed and an even broader understanding of Maria Pia will be available to future historians. But what I was able to discover and present here will hopefully put an end to the many misconceptions concerning this Queen.

It has been said Maria Pia disliked her husband. While it is true she could be frustrated by Luis' inability to be a firm king instead of a man of action like her Savoy relations, she had a great fondness for her husband as her correspondence attests to and their marriage survived despite its infidelities. Dismissed so often as merely a decorative consort, Maria Pia was far more involved in politics than I had previously been led to believe. Indeed, during her son's reign Maria Pia can rightly be called Carlos' best secret political weapon. But the most disturbing accepted norm concerning Maria Pia is the assertion she was insane at the time of her death. While she did suffer a nervous breakdown in the aftermath of her son's assassination, all evidence points to Maria Pia having fully regained her mental faculties and when she died in exile in 1911 she was of perfectly sound mind.

I have a great admiration for Maria Pia and all the more so since she has been judged so harshly and incorrectly in the past. Condemned for her extravagance, it is important to note Maria Pia was no more extravagant than the many other royal consorts of her day, including her own sister-in-law Margherita, the first queen of Italy, and the French Empress Eugenie. While most of Maria Pia's extravagance derived from her age-old traditional belief on how a queen should present herself suitably in her public role, in her private life Maria Pia broke with tradition. Unlike most women of her era and station Maria Pia was a very hands on mother. Indeed, her love and loyalty to her children and to her extended family are one Maria Pia's most admirable qualities, and this love was matched only by her loyalty and devotion to her country of adoption.

People's opinions will no doubt continue to vary on Maria Pia's strong willed character, but no one can deny she endured more than her fair share of tragedies or the courageous defiance in which she faced her many trials and tribulations. Above all everyone can agree that ultimately Maria Pia was a survivor.

Chapter I

Childhood

On October 16, 1847 at the Royal Palace in Turin a second daughter was born to Prince Victor Emmanuel, the Duke of Savoy, heir to the kingdom of Sardinia, Piedmont and Savoy, and his wife the Austrian Archduchess Marie Adelaide, who was also his first cousin, being the daughter of his paternal aunt Elisabetta of Savoy-Carignano and Archduke Rainer, the Viceroy of Lombardy. In honor of her godfather, Pope Pius IX, the little princess was given the name of Maria Pia, the feminized version of Pius. At her christening, over which her godfather presided, the proud parents were presented on their daughter's behalf with the golden rose, a sacred ornament made of pure gold, which from the beginning of the Seventeenth Century was given only to Catholic queens, princesses, and eminent noblemen as a token of special reverence.

Although happy with the birth of their second daughter, the young couple's choice to honor the Pope through their newborn was a source of dissatisfaction to their anticlerical subjects. Only a few days old, Maria Pia was already at the center of a controversy. Offering what comfort he could, the Princess's maternal grandfather wrote that he hoped, *"the names of Maria and Pia will lend luck and that she will be of a consolation to her parents as her mother was to us."*[1] As it turns out her given name would be of no real significance in bringing luck to the Savoys, particularly pertaining to the little Princess herself, as Maria Pia was to endure more than her fair share of tragedies throughout her life.

At the time of Maria Pia's birth the royal nursery was already full. There was the four-year-old Princess Clotilde, affectionately known as *Kekina*, the eldest of the Savoy children, and the Princes Umberto, Amedeo, and Oddone, ages three, two, and one respectively. Unfortunately, Oddone suffered from a curvature of the spine, and he would never be strong, while there was increasing worry over their mother's own delicate health. Maria Pia was Marie Adelaide's fifth pregnancy in as many years, and shortly after the Princess's birth her maternal grandfather Archduke Ranier warned his son-in-law that such frequent pregnancies were *"spoiling too early the health of our Adele* [sic], *so dear."*[2]

Victor Emmanuel heeded his father-in-law's sound advice. Consequently, there was a four-year interval before there was another arrival to the nursery on January 2, 1851. For the first time, Maria Pia was the elder sister, and she was delighted with her little brother Charles Albert, who was named in honor of their paternal grandfather. Sadly, this beloved little Prince was to die shortly after his third birthday.

Unfortunately, this was not the first death within the House of Savoy, and as the youngest of the surviving royal offspring Maria Pia, unlike her elder siblings, would never be able to cherish the memory of running into their grandfather Charles Albert's bedroom in the early hours of the day to hop on his bed to bid him good morning and then refuse to leave until he gave them the caramels and milk chocolates he reserved in his bedside table for just such occasions. When she was not yet two, Charles Albert, the King of Sardinia, Piedmont and Savoy, abdicated his throne in favor of Maria Pia's father, Victor Emmanuel. It had been Charles Albert's lifelong dream to drive the hated Habsburgs from the northern provinces of the Italian states, in order to create a united nation under Italian rule, but he had suffered humiliating defeats at the hands of the Austrians in the regions of Custozza and Novara. It was believed the younger, more vigorous son could succeed where the father had failed. After his abdication on March 23, 1849 the ex-King voluntarily went into exile where he would ironically die just four months later on July 28, 1849 in Oporto, Portugal, the country over which his granddaughter would one day reign.

Their parents' elevated status made little change in the Savoy children's upbringing. When she was not occupied by her queenly duties, Marie Adelaide supervised her daughters herself until they were of the age five at which time they were given into the care of a governess, one Marchesa Pes di Villamarina, affectionately called "Nonna Pes" by her charges. Under the direction of the pious queen particular emphasis was given to lessons on religion and morality, but Maria Pia and Clotilde were also taught French, German, history, geography, and the traditional feminine courses of painting, sewing, dancing, and good manners.

Maria Pia was a decent, but not outstanding, pupil. Although bright, she was too restless and impulsive to apply herself diligently to her studies. The Princess particularly struggled with mathematics and learning foreign languages, even Italian: the Royal Family spoke the Italian dialect of Piedmontese, which Maria Pia proudly maintained was its own separate language. When corresponding in French a few words in her native language would inevitably be scattered throughout. The only subject Maria Pia excelled in was the arts as she had a gift for drawing and an ear for music.

Military tutors taught Maria Pia's brothers separately, at Castle Moncalieri located a few miles south of Turin. Maria Pia and Clotilde were only allowed to see their brothers once a week, but the siblings made the most of their visits, and they developed close bonds that lasted throughout their lives.

This fellowship among the siblings, however, would not extend to their father's by blows. While Victor Emmanuel admired, even cherished his saintly, delicate wife, he was of an earthier nature, immensely fond of women, and even more if they were common. Shortly after he came to the throne Victor Emmanuel began the most serious of his affairs with Rosa Vercellona, the teenaged daughter of the commander of the garrison at the Savoy Castle Racconigi. This well developed girl, said to possess a fearsome temper, captivated Victor. At first the two met furtively, aided by Victor's adjuvant, but when residing in Montcalieri, the King could spend the better part of the night with his "Rosina," enabled by the use of a secret tunnel located – quite insultingly given his intent – adjacent to a closet that functioned as a retreat for his wife's evening prayers.

Over time the enamored Victor Emmanuel made little effort to conceal his mistress or their offspring from Marie Adelaide. He would proudly boast the mixture of royal and common blood was good, remarking with a complete, if insensitive, frankness that Rosina's children were more beautiful than the Queen's.[3] He was an affectionate father to his illegitimate children and delighted in their presence. When Victor spent his summer months at the Stupinigi Castle with his wife and royal offspring, Rosina and their two surviving children would be lodged in a smaller establishment at the further end of the castle's park. In such close proximity it was inevitable for the two families to meet. One day while walking hand in hand with his mother the heir Umberto spotted Rosina's children and exclaimed, *"Those are also Papa's children!"*[4] On another occasion Marie Adelaide came across Rosina's eldest child at play. The Queen kissed the boy tenderly, but she could not hide her tears. Sadly, she would be dead shortly thereafter.

Her husband's affairs had taken their toll on Marie Adelaide's mental and physical well-being. But it was Marie Adelaide's frequent pregnancies that reduced her to a shadow of her former self. In her gradual decline she began to lose her hair and then her teeth. She constantly felt feverish, and was always off balance as one of her legs was unable to support her full weight. The Queen lost her youthful good looks, becoming pale and emaciated with a face full of premature wrinkles. Sinking into depression, she became disinterested in her surroundings, ceasing to dress up, languishing instead in a bathrobe with curl rollers in what little hair she had left.

Marie Adelaide's death finally came in the year of 1855, but hers would be only one in a series of deaths inflicted upon the Savoys, and at the tender age of seven Maria Pia would lose in a span of five months her grandmother, her mother, an uncle, and newborn baby brother. The year had begun happily enough when in early January the Queen gave birth to her sixth son (a fifth son had been stillborn in 1852), who was named Victor Emmanuel after his father, but the fragile Marie Adelaide – weakened from the birth – contracted typhoid fever. It would be the Queen Mother, Maria Teresa, however, who was the first to succumb to the disease on January 12, 1855. For their own protection Maria Pia and Clotilde were taken from the Royal Palace to stay at Montcalieri with their brothers. It was here that they learned their mother had died on the evening of January 20.

That she had not been present at her mother's deathbed weighed heavily upon Maria Pia's sensitive eleven-year-old sister Clotilde. Years later she would assert, *"I don't think she realized she was going to die; otherwise she would have sent for me."*[5] But even if Marie Adelaide had sent for her offspring it is not known if Victor would have permitted their presence in the death chamber as the Queen was delirious in her final hours, convinced that her eldest daughter was walking on the cornices of the room. Hearing their mother's ravings could have proved quite distressful for them, particularly for Clotilde who was one of the focal points of her mother's delusions, and their father's main concern during those trying days was to preserve his children's health; he would not even allow them to accompany their mother's funeral procession, for the journey would entail a long, hard drive in a horse drawn carriage over the frozen, mostly uphill, roads to the Basilica of Superga, the traditional resting place of the Savoys.[6]

The two Princesses had hardly been informed of their mother's death when they were told their father's younger brother, Ferdinand, the Duke of Genoa, had also died. The Savoy children had had barely enough time to comprehend their losses when they were given even further cause for bereavement at the death of the five-month-old Victor Emmanuel on May 17, 1855.

Most historians have asserted that the seven-year-old Maria Pia was too young to fully grasp the terrifying irrevocableness of death.[7] Given her mother's depression and withdrawal from her surroundings towards the end of her life, Marie Adelaide perhaps did not make as a strong impression upon her youngest daughter as she had with her eldest. Regardless of how deep of a bond had existed between the two the lack of a mother's presence did indeed leave its mark upon Maria Pia's childhood. And this tragedy was compounded by the fact that her remaining parent made no effort to compensate for the loss.

Victor Emmanuel now left his daughters to reside at Moncalieri, bringing his sons back to live with him at the Royal Palace. However, despite living under the same roof with the Princes, Victor Emmanuel was an inattentive father. Of his legitimate children only his eldest Clotilde, who most resembled their sainted mother in character, had a firm place in his heart. What little attention the King deemed appropriate to spare to his royal offspring was given solely to Clotilde, who alone was given the honor of being invited to dine with their father. While the conscientious Clotilde was sensitive to the slight inflicted upon her siblings by Victor Emmanuel, her apologetic explanations that it was not her intention to deprive them of having dinner with Papa did little to soothe the hurt. So along with being denied a mother's love, Maria Pia had the misfortune of knowing she was always second best to Clotilde in her father's affections.

Thus the only positive male affection and attention Maria Pia received in her formative years came from her elder brothers. She in return idolized them, which would have repercussions in her future relationships with the male sex.

Unfortunately, the King was not the only one to favor Clotilde over Maria Pia. Marchesa Pes di Villamarina, "Nonna Pes," loved both her charges, but she found the calm, docile elder princess easier to rear than the high-spirited Maria Pia, who chaffed under their strict upbringing with its constant supervision and moralizing lectures. The little Princess was never left unsupervised, not even when reciting her prayers three times a day. When dressing, a maid along with one of her governess's assistants had to always be present but during the process Maria Pia was not allowed to say a word to the maid.

Along with her more rebellious nature, Nonna Pes found Maria Pia to be less devout and humble than the pious, self-effacing Clotilde as perfectly demonstrated by the sisters' childhood dreams for their future. While Clotilde fervently prayed never to become a queen, this was exactly what the vivacious Maria Pia aspired to be. Although the Marchesa judged Maria Pia negatively for her ambition, it is perhaps not a surprising desire on Maria Pia's part for as a daughter and granddaughter of queens it would have been natural for her to want to follow in their footsteps.

Maria Pia's health was also a cause of concern to her governess. She suffered from the heat and debilitating headaches, which she would be subject to all her life, and a defect was eventually discovered in the Princess's posture.[8] Forced to wear a brace, in time Maria Pia defeated this minor disability, but according to oral tradition amongst the Savoys the little Princess had developed the nervous habit of constantly adjusting her clothes to disguise the brace and her poor posture.[9]

While Maria Pia had her faults, perceived or otherwise, she also had her positive attributes. The Marchesa admitted the Princess was charming and sweet, with a strong sense of justice and conducted herself with a delightful informality with her loved ones. Realizing Maria Pia disliked standing on ceremony with her suite, Nonna Pes addressed her youngest charge accordingly by *"tossing aside all etiquette because I love you as a child of my heart....I speak to you with an open heart, knowing your heart prefers tokens of love to ceremonies."*[10]

Maria Pia's physical countenance, her troublesome posture notwithstanding, was proving to be just as pleasing. The red haired, blue-eyed Princess was the acknowledged beauty of the family. Having inherited their father's coloring and their mother's sweet but melancholy smile, the Princess's brother Umberto asserted, *"All the good looks of our father and mother meet in Maria Pia."*[11] Her father, however, in his usual blunt manner was far less flattering when describing his legitimate children's physical tributes, and Victor Emanuel once paid the adolescent Maria Pia the backhanded compliment of conceding, *"Maria has become beautiful or if possible at least less ugly."*[12] Maria Pia's subsequent actions demonstrate that she was perhaps inclined to agree with Victor Emmanuel's opinion instead of her brother's sentiments for the precocious Princess would instruct her servants to hide unflattering photographs of herself as a small child, which showed her problematic posture.

Despite Maria Pia's acknowledged good points Clotilde remained the golden child. When comparing Maria Pia's more volatile temperament to that of the staid Clotilde, the youngest Princess always came up short in the eyes of her father and governess. Consequently, Nonna Pes was always exhorting Maria Pia to be more like her sister, such as in the missive where she assured the little Princess that if she behaved in a gentler manner then she would receive more love.[13] Maria Pia could not compete with her saintly sister and as shown by her governess's edict obviously felt unloved at some point in her childhood.

The hurt over this favoritism did not fail to take its toll on the relationship between Maria Pia and the Marchesa. While Maria Pia would always be grateful to her Nonna for the care she received, the Princess eventually withdrew emotionally into herself, learning to conceal her innermost thoughts from her governess to avoid criticism and constant comparisons to her sister. *"She is particularly kind and tender to me,"* the Marchesa subsequently noted of her youngest charge's behavior, *"but she has a tendency...not to confide in me."*[14]

Clearly, Maria Pia longed for someone to love her for who she was and not for what they wanted her to be. Yearning for this acceptance, Maria Pia eventually turned to her painting tutor, Virginia Panizzardi, and to Nonna's assistant Camille de Foras, who appreciated the inquisitive and spontaneous nature of the little Princess; soon the two entered into an intense relationship. Letters exchanged between Maria Pia and Camille show the deep emotional bond they developed and in this one particular letter written by Camille during an absence shows how physically demonstrative Maria Pia was with those she loved: *"Let us imagine now, Madame, that we are in your salon at Turin and you allow me to install myself at the foot of one of those large easy chairs where you often gave me the pleasure of sitting you on my knees. It puts me in the mood again for one of the gentle caresses of my Princess...I...hope that you save some for me on my return and that you deign to repay me for all those of which I am deprived at this moment."*[15]

Sadly, on the cusp of her adolescence Maria Pia would lose Camille, when she became engaged in 1858. The remaining royal household feared the effect that Camille's departure would have on the emotional Princess, but showing a growing maturity Maria Pia surpassed their expectations by not giving in to her melancholy. Instead, she channeled the sadness of her loss into a greater dedication to her studies.[16]

Still, a strong bond remained between the two, and they continued to stay in touch. *"Not an hour goes by that I do not unite my thoughts with all that you do, my beloved little princess, recalling your soft caresses, your cries of laughter, your questions, and a thousand other things constantly presenting themselves to my memory,"* Camille reminisced.[17]

In response the now adolescent Maria Pia acknowledged she owed much of the happiness she had found in her childhood to Camille, one of the few adults in her life to love her unconditionally. *"I am very grateful you think about your little Maria who loves you, who hasn't forgotten the pleasant times that she spent with you for which she is in your debt,"* she wrote in thanks. *"My dear those times haven't faded from my memory, they are so beautiful to me."*[18]

The following year in 1859 the eleven-year-old Princess suffered the loss of another constant companion when her father, in exchange for French aid, consented to a match for the fifteen-year-old Clotilde that can only be described as a sacrifice. It was agreed that if the French fought against Austria in the Italian war of independence then Victor Emmanuel would cede Nice and Savoy to Napoleon III; the French Emperor had an additional condition of his own. He wanted a wife for his notorious womanizing cousin Prince Jerome Bonaparte, better known as "Plon-Plon." At the age of thirty-seven Plon-Plon had thus far escaped the institution of marriage, but not from any lack of effort on his part. He was the rejected suitor of Princess Stephanie of Hohenzollern-Sigmaringen, the future consort of King Pedro V of Portugal; Princess Mary Adelaide of Cambridge; his own cousin's wife the Empress Eugenie; and of Clotilde and Maria Pia's widowed aunt, the Duchess of Genoa.

Well aware of her suitor's dubious moral character to the amazement of those around her (*"But who told her? We don't know!"* was the reaction of her bewildered entourage[19]), the usually tractable Clotilde for once had sufficient sense of self-preservation to delay negotiations, and Victor Emmanuel refused to pressure his favorite daughter. The King left this task instead to his Prime Minister, Count Camillo Cavour, who was one of the true geniuses behind Italy's Risorgimento. *"In a word,"* grumbled the war hungry Cavour, *"he wants me to play the part of the tyrant, reserving for himself the role of the noble, affectionate father."*[20] But selflessness was the foundation of Clotilde's character and, eventually to Cavour's satisfaction, *"true to the sense of duty which stamped the House of Savoy,"*[21] she willingly complied.

When Maria Pia was informed of her sister's upcoming marriage, she with her brother Oddone, who was particularly attached to Clotilde, cried bitter tears at the thought of her departure. Fortunately, Maria Pia had not allowed the overt favoritism of Clotilde to sour her relationship with her sister, who despite her own young age had done her best to mother and nurture her younger sister, and Maria Pia would remain as devoted and protective of Clotilde as she would be with her brothers. However, when the prospective bridegroom arrived in Turin, only the fourteen-year-old Umberto dared to show his dislike of the impending nuptials. In the festivities leading up to the wedding Umberto, forced to attend the theater with Plon-Plon, showed his displeasure by twice refusing the loan of the Bonaparte prince's opera glasses.

But her siblings' resentment could not stop the wedding, and on January 30, 1859 Clotilde and Plon-Plon were married in the chapel of the Holy Shroud in Turin, though there would be some doubts as to the validity of their vows. The agnostic Prince paid little attention throughout the ceremony and had to be prompted to give his consent to the marriage and again reminded to perform the ritual of putting the ring on Clotilde's finger. Irritated by his son-in-law's antics, a concerned Victor Emmanuel had asked one of the officiating clergy, *"But are they really married?"*[22]

"I certainly hope so, Your Majesty," was the amused priest's reply.[23]

Indeed, they were married for better or for worse. Politically the match proved for the better for the House of Savoy as Victor Emmanuel, with the help of the French, was able to wrest the Italian states of Parma, Modena, and Tuscany from Austrian control as well as the province of Romagna, which broke away from the Papal States during the war, an action that earned the King his first excommunication from Maria Pia's godfather. Personally, however, the union proved for the worse. Plon-Plon would have been a disappointing example of a suitor under any circumstances, and Maria Pia must have wondered what kind of a husband awaited her. However, given her sister's marriage Maria Pia would have realized that she'd have to reconcile her dreams to her father's political needs.

Maria Pia did not have long to wait for a husband to materialize, for just two years later when she was only fourteen the new King of Portugal, Luis I, asked for her hand. Maria Pia doubtlessly felt relief and excitement at this proposal for unlike her brother-in-law Luis at the age of twenty-three was a young man, and in marrying him her childhood ambitions would be realized. But in becoming a Queen Maria Pia would have to leave her childhood behind, and it was a childhood made all the more striking by its traumas and its mere brevity.

Chapter II

A Portuguese Interlude

Portugal, the westernmost country of Europe, occupies only one-fifth of the Iberian Peninsula. Isolated from the remainder of continental Europe by its neighbor Spain, which formed the country's northern and eastern borders, in the middle ages Potugal naturally turned its attention to its western and southern borders; the Atlantic Ocean. The tiny nation reaped the benefits and by the 1500s Portugal had become the leading maritime power, possessing the greatest sea-born empire the world had yet seen.[1] But maintaining their early glory was a feat the Portuguese could not uphold. Costly wars to preserve their independence from Spain, natural disasters, and extravagant rule depleted the once mighty kingdom. The rise of Napoleon I further threatened the nation's sovereignty.

By the early 1800's Portugal alone on continental Europe had withstood the Bonaparte upstart.[2] But in 1807 when Napoleon's troops led by Marshal Junot crossed their frontier the Braganzas, following the counsel of their oldest ally Great Britain, fled from the invading army. The Royal Family sailed to their greatest colony of Brazil; there, most became so comfortable that they would remain for some years even after the defeat of Napoleon. It was not until 1820, fourteen years after their harrowing flight, that the Braganzas – with the exception of King John IV's eldest son Pedro, who was left behind as Brazil's regent – were finally induced to return to their homeland.

However, in their sovereign's absence the Portuguese government had tired of the notion of the divine right of Kings; on his arrival King John had to swear to abide by a as of yet unwritten constitution. His scheming Spanish Queen Carlota found such impertinence unacceptable, and plotted to replace her husband with their second son Prince Miguel. The ambitious Prince Miguel, who would never forgive the disrespectful cries of "Liberty" shouted by the Masons upon their arrival, readily fell in with his mother's intrigues. On April 30, 1824 the twenty-one year old Miguel's troops imprisoned King John in the Royal Palace at Bemposta, but the diplomatic corps and the British envoy were able to secure the King's safety. Miguel's father sent the unabashed young Miguel into exile to Vienna.

When John died two years later in March of 1826, his eldest son Pedro became King of Portugal and Brazil. But Pedro had no desire to leave Brazil and he abdicated the Portuguese throne in favor of his eldest daughter, the seven-year-old Maria da Gloria. His abdication was conditional, however, upon the betrothal of his daughter to her uncle Miguel and the acceptance by the Portuguese of a constitution similar to the one he had implemented in the now independent Brazil.

Miguel returned from exile to become Regent in Portugal, but he soon tired of playing second fiddle to a little girl still in short petticoats. As the majority of the Portuguese considered their absentee child Queen a foreigner due to her Brazilian birth and viewed her father Pedro with even more suspicion as he had deprived the country of their greatest colony, they readily accepted the handsome and charismatic Miguel as their sovereign when he usurped the Crown in April of 1828. Only the liberals were truly dissatisfied. In the meantime, Pedro's relations with the Brazilians had so deteriorated that he decided to cut his losses in 1831. Pedro abdicated the Brazilian Crown in favor of his only legitimate son and namesake, and proceeded to raise an army of mercenaries to reclaim his daughter's throne, thus plunging the already bankrupt Portugal into civil war.

In the war of the brothers the eldest emerged victorious in 1833, and Miguel was once again sent into exile, this time with nothing more than the clothes on his back. The victor, however, would not live to enjoy his triumphs. Success had been achieved at the price of Pedro's health, and to compound his illness he was not well received by the populace, who blamed him for the improvised state of the nation. Pedro was stoned twice while driving through the streets of Lisbon and he was hissed at in his box at the opera. He had no choice but to retire to his bed at the Queluz Palace where he died from tuberculosis at the age of thirty-five on September 24, 1834.

Before his death Pedro made arrangements for his fifteen-year-old daughter Maria to marry her step-uncle Prince Augustus de Beauharnais, Duke of Leuchtenberg, the brother of Pedro's second wife Amelia. Ironically, the Beauharnais siblings had connections to the Braganzas' old enemy, being the children of Eugene de Beauharnais, the stepson of Napoleon I. But one can presume on Maria's behalf that it was infinitely preferable to marry a step-uncle, whatever his heritage may be, than her actual uncle.

Maria and Augustus were married by proxy in Munich on November 5, 1834. A month later on December 2 they ratified their vows in person in Lisbon. The future looked bright for the young Queen and her handsome Prince Consort, who had impressed his wife's ministers with his ability to speak Portuguese, which he had learned when visiting his sister and brother-in-law in Brazil. The young couple happily planned for the future, with Augustus remolding the Ajuda Palace, a structure that was originally erected in 1794 but had remained largely unfinished due to the Braganza's flight to Brazil, for his wife. However, a mere three months after his arrival Augustus developed a throat infection, which would prove fatal. When it became apparent there was no hope for recovery, an inconsolable Maria had to be removed from the sickroom. On March 27, 1835 the Prince Consort died in the arms of his sister, the ex-Empress of Brazil.

Maria's friend and contemporary Princess Victoria, the heiress to the British throne, was shocked by the unexpected tragedy. In her journal Victoria recorded with dismay, *"It is a most lamentable and dreadful event. His Royal Highness was in his 25th year, and in the flower of his age. Young, amiable, good and well-meaning; for since his arrival at Lisbon he had won the hearts of many by his affability and good nature. He caught a cold, which he neglected and it ended in the quinsy. It was really quite dreadful for the poor young queen, who is now left a widow at the early age of 16! Her Majesty completed her 16th year on the 4th of this month. It is likewise dreadful for his amiable and accomplished sister the young Empress-widow, who is still in mourning for husband, Dom Pedro; and also dreadful for his mother, the Duchess of Leuchtenberg. Not two months ago he was seen leading his young bride from the altar, and now all that prospect of happiness is cut off!"*[3]

Despite the brevity of their marriage Augustus would never be truly forgotten by his young widow. For the rest of her life Maria could never bring herself to return to the Ajuda Palace. This residence that had once held such promise, now only brought painful memories to the Queen.

Maria, however, would not be allowed a normal grieving process. The sudden death of the Prince Consort left Portugal in an extremely vulnerable position. The specter of Miguel reared its ugly head within the Queen's cabinet, and to safeguard Maria's reign it was determined that Her Majesty should remarry to produce heirs as soon as possible. With indecent haste Maria was told just ten short days after her husband's death that for the preservation of the monarchy she must begin negotiations for a new marriage. It was a brutal task to ask of the teenage Queen who had already seen too much death, but she bravely arose to the occasion.

There were many eligible catholic princes for Maria's hand, but her stepmother Amelia was determined to keep the Portuguese throne within the Beauharnais family and it was her wish that Maria marry her and Augustus's younger brother Maximilian. The Queen, however, felt this would be in poor taste, and she dismissed Maximilian as having a face like a fried potato! Other candidates included Prince Carignano, a cousin of the King Victor Emmanuel, and the Duke of Nemours, a son of French King Louis Philippe, another Prince that Maria found distasteful. In private she suggested his brother the Prince of Joinville as an alternative.[4] But negotiations with the French were not successful, and it was King Leopold of Belgium who triumphed when Portugal accepted his candidate, the nineteen-year-old Prince Ferdinand of Saxe-Coburg & Gotha.

Ferdinand was Leopold's nephew, the son and namesake of Leopold's brother Ferdinand and his wife Antonia Kohary, an Austrian heiress. For the sake of her fortune Ferdinand (senior) had agreed to raise their children in the Catholic faith, which now rendered his son eligible for marriage with the Catholic queen. Leopold quickly took his nephew in hand, writing down for him *"everything which he ought to know about the organization of a government in general and what will be necessary in specific to carry on successfully the government in Portugal."*[5] Fortified by a few weeks of tutelage under his Uncle in Brussels, Ferdinand set sail for Lisbon.[6]

In route to Portugal Ferdinand stopped in London to visit with his cousin Victoria. Victoria, ever the admirer of a handsome man, was clearly attracted to the Prince finding *"something quite beautiful in his expression when he speaks and smiles and he is so good."*[7] A courtier was agog at the cousins' obvious affection for each other.[8] He commented: *"What would I give to hear of their elopement in a cab!"*[9] Of course this was impossible due to Ferdinand's religion as heirs to the

British Crown were barred from marriage with a Catholic, and besides Leopold had already handpicked his protestant nephew, Albert of Saxe-Coburg & Gotha, to wed his niece.

It did not take long, however, for word of this warm relationship to reach Lisbon, and a jealous Maria fired off a forceful letter in which she ordered Ferdinand to stop being so charming with his cousin. A crisis was averted when Ferdinand wrote to his fiancé in reassurance, asserting his intentions toward her remained unchanged.

Despite this near setback the wedding went on successfully, and the grieving Maria cheered considerably in gaining such an attractive husband. But unfortunately her remarriage was not popular with her countrymen. Ferdinand was held in low esteem, mainly due to his immediate meddling in state affairs, but his illustrious relations gave even further cause for concern. With a cousin to inherit the throne in Great Britain and an uncle ruling in Belgian, Ferdinand was naturally perceived as nothing more than a tool for their collective countries' ambitions.

Ferdinand's family surname was also a source of derision for his subjects, as the German words Saxe, Coburg, and Gotha punned in Portuguese means black tooth tartar, scurvy, and gout, far more elements than any one man should have to suffer from![10] The Portuguese may have found merriment in the Saxe-Coburg & Gotha surname, but the influx of new blood would prove to be very beneficial to the House of Braganza. Maria and Ferdinand had a highly prolific marriage, with Maria carrying eleven pregnancies to full term. Unfortunately, four of her pregnancies resulted in stillbirths and of her eleven children only seven survived: Pedro, Luis, Joao, Maria Anna, Antonia, Fernando, and Augusto. The arrival of the Princes and Princesses, however, did have a stabilizing effect on the country as now the people had true Portuguese royals to love.

Maria and Ferdinand were devoted to their children and supervised their education carefully, ensuring that their schooling covered all spheres of the arts and sciences, free of privilege and in close touch with reality.[11] Their eldest, Pedro, proved their most talented pupil; he was resolved never to pass a paper without being able to read and understand it.[12] As the heir Pedro naturally received the most attention from his parents, but Maria determined that her next eldest son Luis, affectionately known as Lippi (a nickname derived from the first two of his proper names, Luis Filipe), would have a naval career. Luis had impressed his mother as a small child with his aptitude for swimming, and fortunately given his designated profession the Prince developed a lifelong love for the sea.

After 1847 not one of Maria's pregnancies was successful, and doctors warned her to stop having children, but with her typical strong will the Queen determined, *"If I die, I'll die at my post!"*[13] In November of 1853 Maria, worn out by childbearing, died bringing forth her last stillborn child, leaving behind a devastated Ferdinand. They had lived together happily for seventeen years, and although Ferdinand loved his children he could not find their affection compensation for the loss of a wife's love. *"I have my children whom I love,"* he confessed to his cousin

Victoria, now Queen, *"but a woman who loves you is not replaced."*[14]

Ferdinand, however, was not suited to the single life, and as a young widower who was still *"a beautiful figure of a man,"*[15] Ferdinand would find that a woman's love could be replaced not by one but by many. He became quite fond of chorus girls, to the irritation of his proper eldest son Pedro, who complained, *"this flood of beau monde, I find very annoying, but it is one poor Papa likes immensely."*[16] Once when Ferdinand returned to the Necessidades Palace after a late night of carousing he was shocked to have the palace door opened by Pedro. In response to his father's astonishment the young King had admonished, *"I came to open the door because I don't want the servants to know the hours Your Majesty returns home."*[17]

In spite of his son's annoyance Ferdinand continued to enjoy lightweight dalliances until 1860 when his heart was recaptured by an opera singer, one Elise Hensler, the daughter of an Austrian tailor who had immigrated to the United States. Pedro would find the intensity of his father's feelings for Elise to be even more of a menace, and out of consideration for his son Ferdinand was not able to pursue the relationship as actively as he wished. Elise probably saw no real future with Ferdinand and keeping her options open maintained another lover. She was known to spend the night at the palace with Ferdinand and then leave to sail across the Tagus River to where her other lover was waiting.

Part of Pedro's intolerance for his father's affair stemmed from the rumor that Ferdinand had fathered a daughter with Elise, which proved false as her daughter was the product of an affair with an Italian aristocrat, and she had previously bore two other illegitimate children with Miguel Angelo Pereira, an Oporto musician.

While the relationship with his eldest son was tense and conflicting, Ferdinand's relationship with the Portuguese had improved. Ferdinand had lost his early stiffness, and consequently he had weathered through his early unpopularity. Now, Ferdinand ruled as regent among universal approval for his son until Pedro reached his majority at eighteen. This regency allowed Pedro with his brother Luis to travel throughout Europe to complete their education. The two Princes were well liked everywhere, but it was in England where they made the strongest impression. Queen Victoria and Prince Albert became quite fond of these cousins, Pedro in particular. In this studious Prince they saw everything they had tried to achieve in their own heir Albert Edward, but had failed to accomplish. Albert grew so attached to Pedro during their visit that he came to resent Luis' presence as he felt Lippi took up too much of his brother's time.

At eighteen Pedro took over his duties as King, and he relied upon Albert, whom he respectively called Uncle, for fatherly advice, counsel Prince Albert was only too happy to give. Such was his confidence in Albert that in April of 1858 Pedro married by proxy sight unseen the Princess Stephanie of Hohenzollern-Sigmaringen, the German bride chosen for him by his confidant, who believed that the Princess would offer Portugal *"views of life…which will not be those of other old Catholic houses."*[18] Fortunately, Albert's faith in Stephanie was justified as she became devoted to her adopted country, greatly concerned with its poor and sick.

Albert was just as certain that Stephanie would be an exemplary wife, asserting, *"She is good, simple, and unassuming, and has an expression in her eyes…a kind of selflessness and trustful entreaty, to which one would fain tender knightly service and protection. She will be sure to please Pedro."*[19] And again his assumption was proven correct as Pedro would shortly confirm, *"Could I ever forget, dear Uncle, the part you have taken in my happiness, which is so great that I can hardly concentrate?"*[20] What had begun as an arranged marriage evolved into a union of love on both their parts. *"We are so happy together that we do nothing but kiss and tell each other the nicest things,"* the new Queen confided to her mother.[21] *"To me, he is so excellent, always thoughtful…so full of regards, so tender!...I can't thank God enough for my happiness."*[22]

But there were troubles within the family that Stephanie had joined, and she had been immediately put right into the middle of the battle of wills between Pedro and his father, whom she found to have a difficult personality. The Queen wrote to mother of her concerns: *"If the two principle persons* (Pedro and Ferdinand) *could be put into agreement, of a more perfect form, everything would go better…but I encounter here a great obstacle, in which, more or less, everything ends because of clashes. I guarantee you, dear mother, that when my father-in-law is not present, my husband is another man, much freer in spirit and actions, kinder to everybody and even more cheerful. Nevertheless, he prefers that father is present, in order to maintain family unity…* (But) *being that he* (Ferdinand) *is used to…being first…he naturally maintains these habits in his manners and in his behavior…I have a good opinion of him, and much respect, but there are moments in this situation that can be very annoying for the daughter-in-law, who's duty is to be the lady of the house, the center of the family. But to…carry out this role, I would have to sacrifice the calmness and unity of the family, because… I find him very demanding in matters which, in my opinion, he does not have the right to be."*[23]

Stephanie would find her husband's siblings much easier to get along with. She treated her young sisters-in-law Maria Anna and Antonia like daughters, and of her brother-in-laws she found Luis, in particular, to be good-hearted but shy. This shy Prince, however, following in the footsteps of his father, was becoming something of a ladies' man much to the displeasure of his eldest brother. When Pedro learned of Luis' affair with Maria Oliveria, a daughter of a shoemaker, the King gave his brother the command of the ship *Bartolomeu Dias*, in the hopes of removing him from temptation. But the enamored Luis always returned from his journeys to his lady love. Inevitably, it would be Maria who ended the affair. During one of Luis' voyages Maria married her cousin and five months later presented her husband with a full-term baby boy whom he accepted with ill grace.

In the meantime, however, Pedro found sympathetic ears in Prince Albert and Queen Victoria, who were just as determined to keep their sons chaste until marriage. The King never hesitated to air his grievances against his brother in his correspondence with the Royal couple. *"Lippi has acquired ways that would not give credit to any salon,"* Pedro vented early in 1859. *"At the same time my father encourages him in the search of pleasure...* [In addition] *to all this he has an enormous appetite...and worse one for cigarettes."*[24] In April of 1859 Pedro requested the aid of the British monarchs to delay Luis in London as much as possible so that Victoria could impart into the wayward Prince a degree of modest feeling. In a letter that Luis himself hand delivered to Prince Albert, Pedro appealed: *"Lippi knows nothing about this subject and must not know it. I have not even said a word to my father... The beloved Queen is perhaps the best person to smooth some of his edges."*[25]

The King actually loved his brother tenderly, but in his determination to improve Luis's ways Pedro was unduly harsh in his judgment of Lippi. For the intellectual Prince had shown qualities of loyalty and justice when dealing with his subordinates under his command, characteristics that would suit Luis well for his future role.[26] But for the time being Luis was at his liberty, conducting a career he loved, while Pedro's preoccupation with improving his heir's knowledge and moral outlook was soon to take a backseat to graver matters.

On July 13, 1859 Stephanie was unexpectedly stricken with diphtheria, dying just four days later. She had thought of other's needs right up until the end, asking her husband's family to assure her mother that her happiest moments had been spent in Portugal, and finally to console Pedro. And the widowed Pedro would be in dire need of consolation. Upon realizing that his beloved wife of just fourteen months was dead, a grief stricken Pedro had gone into shock for two days. Such was the King's sufferings that even daylight wounded his sensibilities.[27] Another eventual manifestation of his grief was insomnia. When Pedro was finally able to fall into a broken sleep, he was only to awake crying. *"God has taken a pure, lovely angel to him,"* lamented Queen Victoria. *"She was too good for this world, poor dear Pedro! He had found an angel to cheer his hard trying life – his melancholy character – and now in a moment snatched from him! It is too dreadful!"*[28]

In time Pedro threw himself passionately into the duties befitting his position, which he wished above all to fulfill suitably.[29] There were some members at court, however, who felt the King needed a wife to help him carry out these obligations. For a time there was even talk of the adolescent Princess Maria Pia of Savoy as a potential bride, but Pedro refused to contract another marriage instead remaining faithful to the memory of his Queen. The court would have no choice but to except Pedro's unequivocal stance for it would seem with four brothers to carry on the Braganza line the dynasty was assured for years to come. Sadly, no one could have foreseen that Stephanie's death would be just the first of many.

In September of 1861, three years after the Queen's death, Infanta Antonia wed Stephanie's elder brother Prince Leopold of Hohenzollern-Sigmaringen. Antonia's brothers Luis, her favorite, and Joao escorted her to her new home in the German states, just as Luis had done two years previously when her elder sister Princess Maria Anna had married Prince George of Saxony. The two Princes would also use a portion of this trip to broaden Joao's education by touring Europe, including a visit to their royal cousins in London. While they were in France, Luis and Joao learned their brothers Fernando, Augusto, and Pedro had contracted typhoid fever. Napoleon III, himself, personally broke the news that their brother Fernando had succumbed to the deadly fever. Luis and Joao quickly departed for Portugal and when they first arrived in Lisbon on November 14 they thought the flags flying at half-mast were for the anniversary of their mother's death. It was only when the Duke of Loulé, the Prime Minister and the Princes' great uncle by virtue of his marriage to Princess Ana de Jesus Maria, the youngest daughter of King John VI, addressed Luis as *"Your Majesty"* that they realized Pedro was dead. *"I have lost at one stroke,"* a despondent Luis replied, *"the two things which I most prize in this world – my brother and my liberty."*[30] Fernando had predeceased Pedro and while Augusto eventually recovered, his physical and mental capabilities would never be the same.

The Portuguese were shocked by the rapid deaths in their Royal Family and it was believed not enough had been done to save their lives. It was quickly rumored that poison was at work and suspicion fell on the Duke of Loulé, who was felt to be overly ambitious for his children. Riots broke out in Lisbon with cries of *"Death to Loulé"* in the streets.[31] The populace was only reassured when the results of the royal autopsies were made public.

The deaths within the Braganza Royal Family also struck London particularly hard. Queen Victoria, who learned of the demise of the Braganza brothers before Luis and Joao docked, could only console herself with the thought of Pedro being reunited with his wife in heaven. She wrote along these lines when she poured out her grief to her Uncle Leopold:

"My beloved Uncle, – I hardly know how to write, for my head reels and swims, and my heart is very sore! What an awful misfortune this is! How the hand of death seems bent on pursuing that poor, dear family!...Poor Ferdinand, so proud of his children – of his five sons – now the eldest and most distinguished, the head of the family, gone, and also another of fifteen, and the youngest still ill! The two others at sea, and will land tomorrow in utter ignorance of everything, and poor dear, good Louis [sic] *(whom I thought dreadfully low when we saw him and Jean* [sic] *for an hour on Friday) King! It is an almost incredible event! A terrible calamity for Portugal, and a real European loss! Dear Pedro was so good, so clever, so distinguished! He was so attached to my beloved Albert, and the characters and tastes suited so well, and he had such confidence in Albert! All, all are gone! He is happy now, united again to dear Stephanie, whose loss he never recovered."*[32]

Sadly, the hand of death had not finished with the brothers. Prince Joao, too, contracted typhoid dying by the end of the year as did an exhausted Prince Albert. To safeguard their new King the Lisbon municipality implored Luis to leave the deadly Necessidades Palace. He obeyed and on Christmas night the King was escorted by thousands of his subjects bearing torches to the Caxias Palace on the Tagus.33 Bowing to his people's continued superstitions concerning the Neccessidades Palace, Luis made preparations to move into the Ajuda Palace, uninhabited since his mother's first marriage.

There he led a lonely existence. The death of Joao, the brother closest to him in age accepting Pedro, so soon after that of the revered Pedro, himself, left a huge void in Luis's life that could not be filled by the one other surviving brother, the fourteen-year-old Augusto. *"Today I have one brother close to me, that keeps me sufficient company,"* Luis would admit, *"but who can not substitute the King and my brother Joao. Pedro my elder brother, not only was a brother, for me he was my best friend, my second father. Joao, my companion from infancy, I saw him die without being able to save him."*[34]

Luis, however, did have one companion in his bereavement: Queen Victoria. The grieving widow was finally able to bestir herself at the beginning of the following year to commiserate with the despondent King: *"My poor dear Luis! God has subjected to our two poor families a trial in a manner so horrible…that I don't know how to write to you! Only two and a half months ago we 4 – you, my angel, my adored Albert, poor dear Joao, and I – were together in the same room – and those two that were sitting next to one another - those two in perfect health contract…that horrible fever – and we are left alone!"*[35]

The solitary existence of the King was a cause of grave concern in Portugal. For the preservation of the Braganza dynasty it was expedient for Luis to marry. Nostalgic for the happier, carefree days he had spent as a teenager with Pedro in London Luis wrote to Queen Victoria on March 16, 1862 requesting the hand of her second daughter Princess Alice, with whom he had maintained a correspondence and loved like a sister. But the Queen declined on the grounds of religious differences, and besides her "angel" had wanted Alice to wed the future Grand Duke of Hesse and By Rhine. Victoria instead recommended Princess Marie of Hohenzollern-Sigmarigen, the younger sister of Stephanie. Her parents, however, having already lost one daughter to Portugal, would not lose another, and they refused to consider Luis's discrete inquiries. Despite this rejection Luis still consulted the Queen in his pursuit for a wife, and eventually Luis's options for a bride were narrowed down to two Catholic Princesses, the Archduchess Maria Teresa of Austria, another of Victoria's suggestions, and the fourteen-year-old Princess Maria Pia of Savoy.

Within the Portuguese cortes the Italian Princess was highly favored. The strict conservatism of the Habsburgs was feared, recalling the days of Miguel, while Maria Pia was the daughter of a liberal King. And it didn't hurt that Maria Pia was reputed to be beautiful and well developed for her age. In addition Luis's good friend from his sailing days, Prince Oscar of Sweden and later King, and his minister the Marques da Bandeira, endorsed her candidacy.

Although he had reservations concerning the great youth of Maria Pia, Luis, too, initially favored a union with the daughter of the Italian King, whom he admired for his fight with the conservative Roman Catholic Church. But Maria Pia had one determent in her path; she did not have the approval of Queen Victoria. Albert had not trusted Victor Emmanuel and the widowed Victoria held her deceased husband's views as sacred. *"I confess that this alliance would not have pleased my angel who always guides me on all things,"* the Queen wrote in caution.

"The politics and still more the character of the father we dislike."[36] Under the influence of Queen Victoria, Luis eventually became leery of the tarnished image of Maria Pia's excommunicated father, and in May of 1862 he decided in favor of Maria Theresa. According to the Marques da Bandeira, *"The King said to me that he has decided to marry the Archduchess, the elder daughter of Archduke Albert, that he had taken into consideration the age of the Princess and the advice of Queen Victoria and King Leopold; besides the youth of the daughter of Victor Emmanuel the prince* [sic] *is badly looked at by most sovereigns, for his behavior with the King of Naples* (his kingdom had been a casualty of the Italian Risorgimento)*…It is agreed to say, when it is necessary, that the given preference for the princess of Austria over the Italian comes from the difference of age."*[37]

However, when Luis approached the Archduke for his daughter's hand he had quickly declined, citing his seventeen year old daughter's incomplete education as the reason: *"I consider the total achievement of the education of a young Princess… essential for much happiness in a marriage,"*[38] Archduke Albert had written contritely, but decisively, on June 6. The Archduke's subsequent actions, however, would prove that this was nothing more than an excuse to hide behind as he would consent to a betrothal for his youngest daughter when she was a mere sixteen. More than likely it was the rash of deaths within the Braganza Royal Family that scared off the Archduke. Maria Pia was Luis's last resort.

On June 18 twelve days after the Archduke's refusal Luis wrote to the Italian King, asking Victor Emmanuel for his daughter's hand. In his letter Luis wisely appealed to their solidarity as liberal monarchs: *"Acceding not only my own wishes, but above all the well wishes expressed by my people, dares me to write Your Majesty concerning a subject that at the moment occupies all of my attention. It is the question of my marriage. No other marriage would correspond better with my desires, or that of my people than marriage with Your August daughter Princess Maria Pia of Italy. Allies bonded by fraternal liberty, two peoples' desire to see two families united by indissoluble bonds…I esteem you Sir, but I will esteem you… more, if one day the title of Sir translates to the sweet name of father."* Referring to his difficulties in securing a wife, Luis concluded, *"There has circulated many rumors concerning my marriage, but I leave them to go around while nothing will be determined or entered into. There is not a catholic princess of whom that hasn't been spoken of. I have made my choice, I lack only your consent to my request."*[39]

Fortunately for Luis, but rather callously in regards to his daughter, Victor Emmanuel had no reservations in uniting Maria Pia with the recently decimated Royal Family. Nor did the Italian King pay any lip service to the notion of a finished education, as the plebian Victor Emmanuel placed little value on schooling, complete or otherwise, for his children. His only concern it would seem was that his daughter would become a Queen. The new Queen of Portugal was to be the young Princess of Savoy.

Chapter III

The Red Queen

When Victor Emmanuel received Luis's request for the hand of his daughter, he had instantly shown Maria Pia a picture of the Portuguese King and given her eight days to reflect upon the proposal. Knowing what was expected of her, Maria Pia had answered in the end, *"I will marry him, if it is the will of my father."*[1] This was, of course, the Italian King's intention, and on July 6, 1862 Victor Emmanuel responded to Luis's inquiry: *"The request that Your Majesty has just made, for the hand of my daughter has touched the heart of king and father... Before I replied I wanted to speak to my daughter who expresses entirely her assent and the desire to be able to make Your Majesty happy...By giving, Sire, my consent to this marriage, which renews our old bonds of family* [the House of Savoy had supplied Portugal with two previous Queens – Mafalda, the wife of Alfonso Henriques, the first King of Portugal, and Maria Francesca, who became the Queen of Portugal twice in the Seventeenth Century when she subsequently married two Braganza brothers, the Kings Alfonso IV and Pedro II], *I am at the same time making an act which will be accommodated with enthusiasm in Italy for the still very recent memory of the noble and affectionate hospitality given to my father by Portugal...Sire, the qualities of spirit and heart of my daughter as well as the sentiments which are high make me hope that in spite of her great youth she will be worthy of Your Majesty."*[2]

Word of Luis and Maria Pia's engagement spread rapidly throughout Europe to very mixed reactions. On July 23 Prince Oscar sent his heartfelt congratulations to the Portuguese King, though not without some advice concerning Maria Pia's youth. *"I have learned of the happy news of your engagement, I applaud your courage. You know my opinion on the subject, she is enchanting."* But in light of Maria Pia's tender years Oscar went on to caution Luis against having children right away. *"Only she is, according to my opinion, still a little young to be married. I think so because she has only fifteen years* [she was just shy of her fifteen birthday]. *With certainty she is well developed, but in any case, she still does not have the strength necessary for having children. This subject is too tiresome, dear Luis, of this I know some thing because of my own experience: My wife that Providence turned rich in children, became for that very same reason poor in health!"*[3]

It took the disgruntled Queen Victoria longer to respond to the news of the engagement. Angry that Luis had disregarded her advice by proposing to the Italian Princess, Victoria could only voice her disappointment when she had finally written to the King on August 2. *"Naturally the change so sudden...in your opinion astonishes me greatly. But since you have made your choice I have nothing more to say, except to wish that it will be alright and that you will be happy. What I regret is the extreme youth of Princess Maria Pia who...is hardly of an age to be useful to you.*

Let us always hope that she will possess all the qualities necessary for your wife and for a Queen."[4]

The youth in question wrote to her fiancé, herself, for the first time on August 10. Moved by the recent tragedies inflicted upon Luis similar to that her own family had endured, Maria Pia had staunchly declared, "*I am happy to assure you that the request you have made to the King, my father, has vividly touched me... Please believe that from my side I do not desire anything but to be agreeable to you, to gain your affection and to contribute to your return to happiness.*"[5]

As it turns out this would be easier said than done for the teenager. Although Maria Pia was sincere in her desire to restore Luis's happiness and would bravely face the challenges ahead of her, she perhaps did not always employ patience or understanding when dealing with obstacles, including at times her marriage.[6]

But for now Maria Pia's desire to restore Luis's happiness was her main purpose. Throughout their engagement she touched upon this subject again and again. "*You speak to me of your dear Mother; she is also mine... We will kneel and pray together to the Lord for her and your dear brothers. Dear Louis* [sic] *these must have been very painful moments for you, I have knowledge of these misfortunes, but now that I become family, I understand the immensity of all these losses and doubly feel them. It is to me a sweet duty to cheer you in your grief that I understand perfectly; I also, even so young, lost in 1855 my dear Mother, my Grandmother, and my Uncle Ferdinand, and all in two months. My beloved little brother Charles, whom I loved dearly had died two years before, only with three years of age.*"[7] And in yet another letter: "*I have hopes that I will be worthy of you... I pray to the Lord that he may make a benediction on the wedding and that he will make me be a good wife for you, to make you happy.*"[8]

For his part Luis tried to familiarize Maria Pia with his character. "*It is also necessary that I tell you a few of my tastes and qualities,*" Luis wrote, "*up to the point that I am able to know them myself. I am a big smoker, good enough hunter, passionate for music, and a mediocre dancer.*"[9] He was just as forthcoming about his rather troubling figure, which was inclined to stoutness. Of his picture Luis woefully explained its merit in giving Maria Pia an idea of "*my sad figure.*"[10]

Maria Pia's response was all Luis could have hoped for and more, as she quickly wrote in reassurance, "*It will be my pleasure to let you smoke, because I like the smell of the cigar. My father and brothers are going to be very happy about this, because they are used to smoking cigars.*"[11] Nor was Maria Pia overly bothered by the photograph that showed Luis's physical shortcomings as she believed compensation could be found in his character. "*I see printed in your face how much you are sweet and good,*" she kindly asserted. "*I take it* (his portrait) *from one room to another and I can't stop looking at it.*"[12]

Photographs of Maria Pia, on the other hand, proved that her reputation for beauty was well deserved. Luis was captivated with the thought of this attractive Princess, whose disposition appeared to be as equally pleasing since she so sweetly but oh so naively promised to "*do everything you want*"[13] as his bride. He eagerly awaited their union, writing increasingly passionate letters to his fiancée. *"I am impatient to see you. To be able to say I love you with my own lips my jewel. I suffer but my sufferings will end the moment I see you."*[14]

He would not have long to wait for the Conde da Carreira had finalized the marriage contract for the King with the proxy wedding quickly set for September 27, 1862 in Turin. But this was not soon enough for Luis as his ardor for Maria Pia only increased with each passing day.[15] *"I love you so much that sometimes I can't find the words to say it,"* Luis passionately declared just twelve days short of their nuptials. *"When I have you at my side directly, I will say it properly, reinforcing my words with a kiss to your beautiful face, my angel."*[16]

These feelings were fully reciprocated by Maria Pia. *"How happy we will be together, living for one another,"* she had written on September 11. *"The real happiness is to think that the day of my departure is approaching. The pain that I will endure at leaving my father and my brothers will be compensated by the hope of seeing you soon. United forever never to be separated again…What happiness to be able to embrace you for the first time…I will find in Lisbon a very good and kind husband!…I love you with all my heart."*[17]

The city of Turin was just as impatient for the marriage to take place. Unlike the previous marriage of their eldest Savoy Princess this upcoming union was greeted with great excitement within Italy, the high point no doubt that Maria Pia would become a queen. The diplomat's wife Madame Charles de Bunsen recalled the insistence that she attend the wedding festivities for *"this probably would be the last fete to take place at court till the marriage of the Prince of Piedmont* (Maria Pia's eldest brother Umberto)."[18] When Madame Bunsen attended a concert given the night before the wedding, she was struck by the change in the bride, who she had remembered as a rather plain child. She now found Maria Pia to be tall, though *"very slight, and with a most graceful bearing; she has a beautiful complexion, and a mass of red hair which does not look red at night. All this with her extreme youthfulness – she is only fifteen* (she was actually one month short of her fifteenth birthday) *– make her a very striking figure."*[19]

The private marriage ceremony itself took place in the Royal Palace of Turin on September 27. The Archbishop of Genoa officiated with the bride's cousin Prince Eugene of Savoy-Carignano, affectionately known as *Barba* within the Italian Royal Family, representing the absent bridegroom. Afterwards there was a public reception where the Turin municipality publicly serenaded the new Queen of Portugal. From the balcony of the Royal Palace little could be seen of the Savoys except for the *"pale face and high diamond crown of the young Queen as she turned from time to time. She looked very tired, but she never left her place, and was greeted with deafening applause each time that she stood and showed herself to the multitudes below."*[20] When the concert ended, Madame Bunsen was once again received by the Italian Royal Family. She noted the Queen's couronne fermee in diamonds, a regular high crown, very elegant in design, and interlaced with orange flowers, a present sent to her by her husband.[21] This crown may have been elegant, but it proved too heavy for Maria Pia, and that night ice had to be applied to her head for several hours.

However, as she stood receiving her guests with her head slightly bent from the weight of the crown, Maria Pia reminded Madame de Bunsen of the medieval Madonnas the old masters liked to paint.[22] Maria Pia presented a romantic image inspiring protection, with Madame Bunsen accordingly rhapsodizing, *"She was unlike any figure in everyday life, and one could not help feeling interested in one so young, on the eve of leaving all she had known and loved till now, to go to a strange land and an unknown bridegroom. The Portuguese allow no one to go with her of all her household but Mme. De Villamarina, who has brought her up."*[23]

Fragile though she appeared in appearance, Maria Pia's disposition was of a stronger nature. When she departed Turin for Genoa, from where she would embark for her journey to Portugal, the Queen took her leave from the sobbing Italian court with unshakeable dignity, calmly telling her younger cousin Princess Margherita of Genoa "ciao" as if she were only going on a carriage ride.[24]

On this leg of her journey, Maria Pia was accompanied by her eldest brother Umberto, who was to sail with his sister to Portugal to help her settle in, and her father who was to see her off. At the last possible moment Victor Emmanuel suffered from pangs of parental guilt, worrying that the conjugal reality of marriage would hurt his innocent young daughter. The King quickly penned a letter to be delivered to his new son-in-law, entreating Luis to be gentle with his child bride: *"My dear son, Your marriage with my daughter has just concluded; may the good Lord bless you both and for my part I bless you from the bottom of my heart and wish you every happiness. No wonder she pleases you. The poor child loves you very much and will do everything she can to be nice to you, and yet she is still so young and has so little experience of the world, I beg you to have compassion for her and show her... what to do... Your very affectionate father, Victor Emmanuel"*[25]

In Genoa on September 29, Maria Pia boarded the Portuguese ship *Bartolomeu Dias*, which departed in splendor having as its escort a squadron of the two Portuguese ships, the Estafania and Sagres, and the five Italian warships *Adelaide Marie*, the *Duke of Genoa, Italy, Garibaldi*, and the *Anthion*. Luis's great uncle the Marques de Loulé was in charge of conducting the young Queen to her new kingdom, a service for which he would be rendered a Duke. On board Loulé created an impromptu court, transforming two young sailors into pages for Maria Pia. During the course of their journey one of these inexperienced pages fell asleep while on guard duty at her door. When Maria Pia emerged from her cabin and discovered the young ten-year-old midshipman fast asleep, she prevented him from being awoken and with no one knowing of her intentions she returned to her cabin. When she reappeared, Maria Pia laid sweets and fruits upon the page's knees and then bent to tenderly kiss the boy's cheek. This could have merely been an example of Maria Pia's kind nature, or perhaps her actions were of a more personal significance. For this young midshipman would have been about the same age of her younger brother Charles Albert if he had lived.

The remainder of the journey passed without incident and Maria Pia sailed into her new capital on October 5, 1862. The ship anchored in front of the Belem Palace where Luis was awaiting his bride. Amidst waving flags and launching rockets, Luis boarded the corvette, where he would dine with Maria Pia. It was their first meeting and in their short time together Luis made a favorable impression upon Maria Pia, who found that his photographs had not done his physique justice. She would later confess, *"I liked him more than his picture."*[26] The following day on October 6 the marriage was once again ratified in the beautiful church of Sao Domingos, a most exquisite and effective piece of architecture, adorned with many religious designs in marble.[27]

While she would eventually become passionately devoted to Portugal, initially Maria Pia found her new home a disappointment. The old fashioned court was still in mourning and Maria Pia could not help but to compare it unfavorably to the brilliant society of her father's court in Turin. Nor could she speak Portuguese, and given her difficulties in learning languages it would take some time before she became fluent in the language of her adopted homeland. Her ladies-in-waiting were of no comfort as they had been chosen for their respectability not for their sense of humor. But the most disappointing aspect of all, agreeable first impressions aside, proved to be her husband.

The engagement between Luis and Maria Pia had been a surreal experience, with an emotionally bereft Luis falling in love with a woman he had never met. The young Maria Pia could not help but be flattered by Luis's tremendous need and she had responded in kind, convincing herself that she too was in love. Unfortunately, the dream fiancé turned husband paled in reality. Her ideal of manhood was the example set by her brothers Umberto and Amedeo: handsome, slim, and athletic, but alas nonintellectual. Luis could not have been more different. While not unattractive, Luis's troubling figure would become stouter and stouter each year. He could paint and sculpt, and played the violoncello well enough to win a compliment from Rossini. Literature was yet another of his devotions, and Luis enjoyed translating the works of Shakespeare into Portuguese.

Maria Pia was too proud to cry over her disillusionments, but according to tradition she did find an outlet for her resentment. Legend has it that one dismal, rainy day during that first winter Maria Pia clutched in her hand her heaviest ring and with the edge of its diamond carved into a window of the Ajuda Palace the words: *"Luis does not please me."*[28] However, it's extremely doubtful Maria Pia actually went this far as she did not criticize or complain about her husband in her correspondence at this stage of her life. Still adjusting herself to a grown man's actual physical desire was an entirely different thing than just reading about it in letters, and the disillusioned young Queen spent the majority of that winter preferably alone in her quarters embroidering, sketching or reading.

Nor can it be said that Maria Pia exactly pleased Luis. While Luis would become fond of his young bride, whom he affectionately called *Bichinha*, his wife, though intelligent, was in reality still a schoolgirl with an incomplete education.

Although the importance of a complete education had merely been used as an excuse for the Austrian Archduke to decline Luis's request for his teenaged daughter's hand, his words did carry certain relevance. A complete education on Maria Pia's part could have helped put the couple on more equal footing, providing them with a sound foundation to find common ground, though it must be noted that Maria Pia would admirably make strides in finishing her schooling on her own.

However, perhaps the most alarming aspect for the King was that his "angel" had the stereotypical fiery Italian temper. When something happened that she disliked Maria Pia would throw a glass with great force whether she was in private or at an informal occasion such as a party in the palace.[29] She would not say a word in the process, but a statement had certainly been made![30] At times Maria Pia could be quite merry, but she was also a bundle of nerves. She had maintained the nervous habit from her childhood of fiddling with her clothing, which now manifested itself into the tying of the ribbons of her skirts then unfastening them only to reattach them many times over. More frequently, however, Maria Pia revealed her nervousness by pulling and stressing the fingers of her gloves. As she aged the smell of perfume caused her to have migraines. Nor could Maria Pia bear loud noises. Once when the Queen was alone in a corridor of the Ajuda Palace a great gust of wind had swept through the passage blowing the windows open and then quickly shut again with a great bang. Terrified, Maria Pia had run away screaming to the alarm of a servant, who had immediately rushed to her aid. To this servant's astonishment the shivering Queen had explained, *"It was the wind that gave me a shock, cursed wind."*[31]

It says much for both their characters that Maria Pia and Luis were able to make their marriage work. While not the enduring love match they had both hoped to obtain during their engagement, their union would eventually evolve into one of understanding, friendship, a love born from companionship, and even passion as witnessed from their letters in the early years of their union, when Luis called Maria Pia *"my good little girl"* and *"love of my live."*[32] In one undated letter during a separation Luis had written longingly to his wife: *"Dear love,…I write you to say how much I think about you…How sad not to see you or hear your good voice say to me dear little husband. Maria I love you so much and you are good too. When I don't have you next to me I cannot find pleasure in anything. I look at this moment at your picture that gave me so much pleasure before knowing you and now only reminds me that we are apart…Goodbye dear love. Think about me as I think about you. Yours all Yours, Little Luis"*[33] Eventually, Maria Pia, herself, also wrote letters expressing her love for her husband and her desire to be with him.[34] *"I love you so much…that I can not be without you,"* she ardently declared during another separation.[35]

As the newlyweds settled into their marriage and grew closer to one another Luis wrote singing his wife's praises to Queen Victoria: *"My happiness is each time greater with my dear Marie, who has made me very happy. She is so good, so natural and…by no means boastful of her new position…She is never a moment…*

without being occupied and her favorite amusement is to go sometimes to the opera house which she greatly loves because of the music in which she takes an intelligent interest...I ask your pardon for writing to you at such length about Marie, but all my thoughts are of her."[36]

As evident in this correspondence and in the early letters between the couple themselves, it was clearly of no hardship for Luis to perform his obligations in the preservation of the Braganza monarchy, and despite his friend Oscar's advice to postpone the consummation of his marriage Luis had immediately seen to this duty with Maria Pia quickly becoming pregnant.

To escape the heat of Lisbon during the summer months, the heavily expectant Maria Pia had traveled north to the mountains of Sintra, and her letters to her absent husband show that by this time she had grown accustomed to Luis and desired to be by his side: "*It seems to me a century that I have not seen you, my love. Come quickly to your little one who loves you so much and who cannot be without you,*" she wrote on July 30, playfully attributing the symptoms of her morning sickness to her longing for his company. "*I have a little headache and feel nauseous, and I'm sure it is from the grief of not having you here my beloved...I love you so much...as you well know. I am so happy with you...my friend. Do you think of me?...I love you so much that I think about you constantly.*"[37]

In the fall she returned to Lisbon and on September 28, 1863 four days short of their first anniversary Maria Pia gave birth to their first child, a son. Maria Pia, however, broke years of rigorous court protocol at this event. Since time immemorial, Portuguese tradition dictated that eleven court physicians, the staff in the Queen's service, and that of the future Prince or Princess should witness a Royal birth.[38] But Maria Pia felt this custom was barbaric, and when her time came she allowed only her husband, the physician Magalhaes Coutinho, a pioneer in the use of chloroform, a midwife, and some of her ladies-in-waiting to be present.

This breaking with tradition not unnaturally caused some resentment within the court. One of Maria Pia's ladies-in-waiting, the Condessa Vila Real, was mortified that no one had remembered to call her to attend the birth,[39] while the noblewoman, the Condessa de Rio Maior, did not bother to conceal her outrage at her sovereigns' disregard for the accepted norm. This coupled with the Condessa's dislike for Luis, whom she found to be a poor replacement for his brother Pedro, caused her to profess only indifference at the birth of an heir to the throne.[40]

The general attitude at court, however, was one of great contentment. Lisbon society flocked to the Ajuda Palace, whose bell tower constantly rang out. Catherine wheels were lit and for three days the outside of the Palace was illuminated. Elsewhere many eagerly waited for news of the expectant arrival, and the announcement of the safe delivery of an heir to the King and Queen was immediately sent to anxious Portuguese diplomats at foreign courts. Significantly, the Portuguese Legation at Turin received their telegram in record time. The message forwarded to Italy's capital arrived exactly six hours and forty minutes after its dispatch.

When the Italian King learned of the birth, he was quite jubilant, but Victor Emmanuel also used the occasion to poke fun at himself. To his eldest daughter Victor wrote in self-mockery, *"Beloved Clo, poor Maria has also had a little one... Oh poor me, what an ugly man I have become! My daughters make little ones."*[A1]

In Portugal the birth of an heir to the throne was greeted by the populace not with amusement but with great joy and unmistakable relief for if Luis died without an heir his brother Augusto, who would always remain something of a mystery Prince to the people, would be King. The populace eagerly followed the customary ceremonies surrounding the birth, and there was much speculation as to what the prince would be named. Would he be Pedro after his uncle or perhaps Ferdinand or Victor after his respective grandfathers? Even still Carlos Alberto, the Portuguese version of Charles Albert, after Maria Pia's grandfather who had died in Portugal. The court and the remaining Braganzas themselves had wanted to name the hereditary prince in honor of Pedro, but Maria Pia was determined to have her son christened after her beloved little brother Charles, therefore introducing a new name into the line of Portuguese kings. When the baby was formally baptized on October 20 in the Sao Domingos church, with the Cardinal patriarch of Lisbon officiating, the Queen prevailed and the hereditary Prince was christened with the impressive list of names of Carlos Ferdinand Luis Marie Victor Michael Raphael Gabriel Gonzaque Xavier Frances d'Assisse Joseph Simon of Braganza, Savoy, Bourbon, Saxe-Coburg & Gotha, forever earning the animosity of her father-in-law Ferdinand, who would prove to be a dangerous enemy in the future.

Victor Emmanuel sent Maria Pia a magnificent jeweled bracelet for the baptism, and dispatched to Lisbon his son Amedeo, the Duke of Aosta, and Prince Eugene of Savoy-Carignan. Maria Pia was gratified to see one of her brothers again, but to her sorrow her sister Clotilde was unable to attend the event. Still the Queen designated her absent sister as her son's godmother, while Ferdinand stood as his grandson's godfather, which did little to soothe his rancor over Maria Pia's triumph.

Although little more than a child herself Maria Pia was from the very beginning a loving, devoted hands on mother. Shortly after her son's birth Maria Pia wrote to her former painting tutor, Virginia Panizzardi, describing the husky newborn in glowing terms: *"My little Charles* [sic] *is always good. Oh, it is a great fortune to be a mother. My little one is white and pink with the large blue eyes of his father, and he has blond hair. It seems that he has already six months instead of a few weeks. He is always, always with me!"*[A2] She proudly followed her infant's progress, carefully noting the date on Carlos's photographs, recording his height on her ribbons, and preserving locks of his hair. She made him gowns and until the age of one Carlos only wore booties knitted by his mother. The Queen was as always openly demonstrative with her affection, never sparing caresses, and she was often in the nursery reverently watching her child while he slept. Though always elegantly dressed – even at sixteen Maria Pia had impeccable taste in clothing – she would sit on the carpets of the palace with the voluminous dresses of the period spread out for the baby to play on.

While Maria Pia had no problems stepping into the role of mother, she was still having difficulties adjusting to other aspects of her life. The Royal couple lived in the most retired way and one official's wife could never recall hearing of any festivities. She did, however, note their majesties' financial woes, which was quite distressing to the Queen as alas Maria Pia, like so many other royals, had no true understanding of the concept of money, and she would prove to be the bane of her treasurers.

The Queen was also felt by the Portuguese Cortes to have spent too much time in her old homeland. Although she was coming to love her adopted country, Maria Pia still pined for her childhood home. Later the following year, while pregnant with her second child, the homesick Maria Pia had returned to Italy. It was quickly rumored that the Queen was leaving Portugal for good, and the Portuguese ministers pressured Luis to demand her return as it was thought unseemly for a Prince or Princess of Portugal to be born on foreign soil. In January of 1865 Luis wrote to his father-in-law requesting that he order Maria Pia to return to Portugal. Fortunately for Luis, Victor Emmanuel was understanding of his son-in-law's dilemma and although he would later become impatient with his daughter's homesickness for now he was sympathetic, arranging for his son Amedeo to accompany Maria Pia on her return. *"I expected it,"* the Italian King had responded to Luis's dispatch. *"My children leave for Lisbon at once. They have your provision."*[43] So that Luis would not feel threatened by his wife's continued affection for her homeland, Victor Emmanuel would later write in reassurance that it was Maria Pia's great love for Italy and her pride in her Savoy heritage that would fortify her in fulfilling her duties as Queen of Portugal.

Upon her homecoming Maria Pia wrote to her confidant Virginia that although homesick she was enjoying her life in Portugal. Luis was good to her and they had fun together. Dances were of a particular amusement, and they had thrown "two balls with two more planned, one of which will be in costume and masked" for carnival on February 15.[44] Determined to make the most of this event Maria Pia planned three changes of costume. Throughout the course of the evening the Queen was Mary Tudor, a Scottish noblewoman, and a domino. There was some grumbling as to the expenditure of the affair, but a Swedish diplomat caused true scandal by baring his entire leg from thigh to ankle for his costume, or one may say lack thereof.

In the later stages of her pregnancy Maria Pia resided at the Mafra Palace, where she was provided with all manner of distractions.[45] However, when the Queen gave birth to her second son on July 31, 1865, Maria Pia was again residing at the Ajuda Palace. The Queen had gone into labor a little after midnight, with the newspaper the *"Diario de Noticias"* reporting some days later: *"H. M. had an uncomplicated time and when the physicians of the Royal Chamber arrived the Royal baby was already lying in the cradle crying."*[46]

The infant was baptized on September 27 in the Ajuda Palace's Chapel. In honor of Portugal's first King the little Prince was christened Afonso Henriques

Napoleao Maria Luis Pedro d'Alcanara Carlos Humberto Amadeo Fernando Antonio Miguel Raphael Gabriel Gonzaga Xavier Francisco Ingacio, Duke of Oporto, with Napoleon III and the Dowager Empress Amelia, who shared the infant's birthday, standing as his godparents.

Robert Lytton, who had been appointed the First Secretary in the British Legation at Lisbon in May of 1865, witnessed the baptism finding the ceremony to be very curious, unlike anything he had ever seen.[47] He thought that, *"the music – of an operatic rather than ecclesiastical character – would have been good but for one woman who sang out of tune the whole time."*[48] Lytton did, however, have high praise for the Ajuda Palace's private chapel where the ceremony took place, highly appreciative of the *"comfortable Tribune arranged for the Corps Diplomatique like a spacious box at the theatre with easy chairs etc."*[49] He was not quite as complimentary towards the women attending the event, declaring that he could not find a single good looking one, with the exception of the Queen, who was looking her best: *"She has pretty shoulders and a dazzling skin."*[50] Of her newborn son, Lytton commented, *"The Queen's baby…looks like a little prince charming…* [He] *behaved very well on the whole, but occasionally cried lustily and shook his pretty fist at the old Cardinal who oiled, and sprinkled, and pinched, and blew over him in the most mysterious way."*[51]

Indeed, Maria Pia was in complete accord with Lytton's sentiments concerning her son, finding her little "Funco," a version of the Portuguese pronunciation of Afonso, to be so lovely that when he was only a few months old she commissioned an Italian sculptor of great renown to model the infant lying in a large shell of flawless Carrara marble.[52]

While Maria Pia was delighted with her second son, this birth adversely affected her well being. The Queen suffered from severe post partum depression with alternating moods of great excitement to periods of uncontrollable weeping. For a remedy doctors recommended exercise and the restless Maria Pia gladly began to attend military maneuvers. She could now be seen in the uniform of a colonel of the 5th Regiment galloping with her troops in the Park of the Ajuda Palace. The daring cavalier riders quickly became the Queen's favorite companions, and she was known to partake of their cigars while in their company. Surrounded by men reminiscent of her brothers, Maria Pia's spirits assumed a normalcy.

Unfortunately, just as she was beginning to heal the following year brought Maria Pia nothing but sorrow. It had begun promising enough with Maria Pia admitting to being content only a little fatigued, wishing to concentrate all of her energies on her growing family, instead of court entertainments. *"A few months ago I turned eighteen* (and) *already I have two children,"* she confided in bemusement to Virginia in early January. *"I feel tired. I need quiet here in Lisbon, and the less parties we have, the happier I'll be. My husband and children make me happy. Everything in my home is going well, so I am completely satisfied."*[53]

However, only days later, Maria Pia's ailing brother Oddone died at the tender age of nineteen. Oddone's sad, short life had been one of isolation. Due to his deformity Victor Emmanuel had always denied this son a public role, and in

1861 Oddone, weary of being ignored by his father, had gone to live in retirement at the Royal Palace in Genoa. There, Oddone, the most intelligent of the Savoy Princes, had dedicated himself to cultural pursuits, collecting pieces of art and archeological specimens. Oddone's relationship with his father remained strained, but his siblings still lavished loving attention upon their invalid brother. When rendered incapacitated due to his illness Umberto and Amedeo would carry their brother in their arms or push him about in his wheelchair. Maria Pia, however, knew that although Oddone adored his brothers and was grateful for their care it must have been difficult for him to witness their active lifestyles. *"The poor boy takes everything with great resignation,"* she had once reported to Luis, who liked to be kept informed of Oddone's well being, *"but I know he suffers seeing his brothers go everywhere while he stays at home."*[54]

Maria Pia worried terribly about Oddone's lot in life and she tried to plan distractions for him. She hoped to have Oddone stay with her in Lisbon, and she was once able to obtain permission from her father for a proposed visit. "I'm so happy that I cannot contain my joy," she eagerly wrote in anticipation to their mutual friend Virginia. *"I've asked and obtained permission from my father to have Oddone spend the winter with me."*[55] But this trip never materialized as ultimately the prince was deemed too ill to travel.

The end came in the early hours of January 22. Present at his deathbed were his brothers Umberto and Amedeo. Victor Emmanuel had also been summoned to his son's bedside, but he would not even cross the threshold of Oddone's chamber and upon realizing that the end was near he had quickly left. The King was driven away, according to the historian Glorney Bolton, not by heartlessness, but by a superstitious dread of death.[56] Still it is heartbreaking to know that Oddone could not even depend upon his father for support in his final hours. Thankfully, Oddone could at least rely on his brothers and he did not have to face death alone.

Yet once again the Savoy siblings had rallied around one another to find solace. To an old instructor of the late prince, Clotilde wrote of their collective sorrow: *"This loss is immense to us all, in every way...The good Lord and the sweet hope of the eternal happiness of our beloved deceased can alone console us. Oddone was so good, so charitable. He suffered so much!"*[57]

The following month the grieving Maria Pia learned of the birth of an illegitimate daughter to Virginia Roh and Victor Emmanuel, who without regard to the Queen's individuality had named the newborn Maria Pia. Her father's insensitivity would always be a source of great pain to Maria Pia.

That April she received even more disturbing news from Victor Emmanuel, who warned his daughter that battle with Austria was imminent. During the Austro-Prussian War, Victor Emmanuel sided with Prussia in the hopes of acquiring the Austrian dominated region of Venetia. Maria Pia was deeply disturbed by the thought of war and hoped it could be avoided, but she was also highly patriotic and if it came to actual combat the Queen then expressed the wish that she could be a man so she could join in the fight for her country! *"My God what a terrible thing war is! Oh the poor Italians,"* she wrote in dismay to Virginia. *"God willing this war can still be avoided. I pray constantly for the Italians and my family...* [But] *oh how I envy men because they can give their lives for the motherland! I would gladly give my life with joy for Italy."*[58]

Unfortunately, the Queen's prayers were not answered, and while Maria Pia, herself, was unable to take up arms in the hostilities, her father and surviving brothers all saw action, with Amedeo receiving a minor injury in the conflict. Though the Italian participation proved to have little effect in the long run, Bismarck's Prussia emerged triumphant and Venetia was returned to Italian sovereignty.

Elated for her homeland, Maria Pia also had good news on the home front to look forward to. The Queen was once again expecting. She had probably become pregnant in early March, but sadly on November 27, 1866 only seven months into her pregnancy Maria Pia went into premature labor and delivered a stillborn son, posthumously christened Miguel.

When Victor Emmanuel learned of the woeful occurrence, he wrote to his son-in-law on November 28 with a heavy heart. *"The news that you give to me causes me much pain, but I am satisfied knowing that at the moment things are going better...Maria had not been well for months."*[59]

Unfortunately, Maria Pia would continue to be unwell and it was soon discovered that the difficult birth rendered her unable to conceive again. At the tender age of nineteen, Maria Pia had had her last child. This was heartbreaking for the Queen as she adored children and as a mother with two healthy surviving sons she would always long for a daughter. *"It is a great pity not to have a little Princess in the palace,"*[60] Maria Pia once confessed in despair.

Maria Pia sought comfort from Clotilde, who often wrote to encourage her grieving and homesick sister. A typical letter written late in 1866 also gives insight into Clotilde's own rather unsatisfactory position: *"Tell me what you are doing. I hope you are no longer sad...It is necessary to rouse oneself (it is my method) and go forward. Certainly in this world all is not rosy...and since it isn't, you must take courage...In your position you have greater obligations, you can do much good to your country, your husband, your children for now and hereafter. You have a beautiful mission. Think of what Mama was, how she was loved by all. What an example she was for us, wasn't she? Do you read? Do you work? How do you arrange your day? A schedule is a great thing in order not to get bored, I assure you. Do you concern yourself with educational institutions? I try to make use of my time as much as possible."*[61]

In a relatively short time span Maria Pia had lost a beloved brother, endured war and the death of a child, and the devastating knowledge that there would never be the possibility of another. Each incident alone could break a person's spirit, and Maria Pia had the misfortune to endure all four of these blows one right after the other. Inwardly, she was fighting a losing battle with depression, but despite her low spirits she was still able at this time to represent her station suitably in public.

Lady Walburga Paget, the wife of the British Envoy to Portugal, who met the Queen for the first time at a New Year's reception the following year, was impressed with her composure. Maria Pia had startled the official's wife *"with her peculiar beauty. She was tall and stately, though very thin, but her shoulders were broad and she moved well. No smile ever flickered over her small pale face, which was overshadowed by a forest of reddish golden hair. Her turquoise-blue deep-set eyes gazed with a farouche expression, very like her father's, from under russet-colored brows. She wore a pale blue gown, absolutely simple except for a piece of priceless lace swathed around her shoulders. Chains of pearls and rubies were wreathed about her head, her neck and arms. It was with difficulty that she could be induced to speak to strangers perhaps from shyness, but she clung with passionate affection to everything Piedmontese and was very communicative to her father's envoy and his wife, though she was an English lady."*[62]

But the difficult suppression of her emotions eventually took their toll on Maria Pia's self possession, with her depression inevitably manifesting itself into physical complaints. The Queen's thinness and paleness that Lady Paget had earlier noted was now excessive. Court doctors finally advised Maria Pia to seek thermal treatment at a hot spring, and it was decided it would be best for Maria Pia to visit Clotilde for a time in France before going to Italy for the upcoming wedding of her brother Amedeo.

Luis wanted to be by her side, but Ferdinand, who never lost an opportunity to make trouble for Maria Pia, threw a wrench into their plans. Maliciously declaring he would not assume the regency, Ferdinand manipulated his son into staying behind in Portugal when he should have been supporting his wife. Unable to get on with either of his daughters-in-law, Maria Pia, just as Stephanie had before her, was discovering that while "Father" still enjoyed the privileges of royalty he was selfishly done with its duties.

When Maria Pia arrived in France with her eldest son Carlos, Clotilde and Plon-Plon were shocked by the change in her appearance, which gave testimony to her sufferings. After she suffered a fall while in their care, a concerned Plon-Plon consulted with doctors on Maria Pia's frail condition. A Portuguese doctor who had accompanied the Queen wrote to Luis with his conclusion. While his letter was somewhat vague on all of Maria Pia's health issues he did diagnose depression, recommending she needed patience and devotion, but above all that she needed her husband.[63]

In May of 1867 Maria Pia traveled to Italy for the wedding of her brother Amedeo, the Duke of Aosta, to a Piedmontese noblewoman, the Princess Maria Vittoria dal Pozzo della Cisterna. Victor Emmanuel had hoped for a grander match for Amedeo with perhaps a Bavarian or Saxon Princess, but as Amedeo was only the second son and not the heir to the throne the Italian King gave in to this child's desire to marry for love. Of all Victor Emmanuel's children Amedeo was the only one allowed to follow his heart, although sadly his union was not destined to be a particularly harmonious one as the Duke of Aosta was unprepared to give up his bachelor ways.

The wedding of Amedeo was purely a family affair, and the absence of Oddone was particularly felt amongst his siblings. Clotilde was grateful to find her surviving brothers well, but she could not say the same for her sister, finding no improvement in Maria Pia's state of health. Clotilde came to the conclusion that *"prayer was the sure remedy for a cure."*[64]

Maria Pia remained for some time in her homeland after the wedding of her brother, but she missed her youngest son and her husband. Although she very much wanted them to join her, Maria Pia was resigned to Luis's absence, realizing that his duties as King came first. *"But you have more patience than I do, my dear,"* she admitted painfully. *"I have suffered a lot but...tell me the truth and I will return, because as I am now more content it is my hope that my health can recover just as well there as here."*[65] On July 3, Luis finally arrived to escort his now more optimistic wife home.

That summer afforded another meeting for the Savoys when the scions of European royalty gathered for the annual International Exhibition held in Paris. All the Savoy siblings and their spouses were in attendance for the exhibition, and to the amusement of her Bonaparte brother-in-law it took six trolleys alone to transport the recovering Maria Pia's clothing for the event. This amounted to far more dresses than she could have possibly worn, but then the fashionable young Queen never repeated the same outfit twice.

Maria Pia was delighted to be in her sister's company again, which helped to contribute to a reprieve from her remaining melancholy. Both were still young women at twenty and twenty-four respectfully, and they became like children in their enthusiasm, examining everything from the latest fashions to the new miracle fuel called gasoline.[66] Although it must be noted that Clotidle's enthusiasm for the former was only for the benefit of her stylish sister, as she had never followed fashion. On one occasion Clotilde had even held up the index fingers of her two hands, then pushed them far apart, saying, *"Fashion and I are like this."*[67] Doubtlessly, the happiest moments for both sisters were when they were alone in Clotilde's private apartments where they could stay up late into the night talking.[68]

It was not until the spring of the following year that Maria Pia could see her siblings again this time in their homeland for the wedding of her eldest brother Umberto, the heir to the Italian throne, to their cousin Margherita, the Princess of Genoa. This was not Umberto's first engagement as he had been betrothed to the sixteen-year-old Archduchess Mathilde, the daughter of Archduke Albert of Austria, the very same Archduke who had claimed that his seventeen-year-old daughter had been too young to wed King Luis, the previous year. Umberto, however, had been quite dissatisfied with this engagement as he had wanted *"absolute freedom of action,"*[69] and if he had to marry an Austrian, then his heart had been set on the Princess of Este.[70] But she cordially hated both Umberto and his father for Italy's aggressions against Austria, and the Emperor Franz Josef refused to force her hand. Umberto bowed to the inevitable, consenting to the match his father had arranged, but tragedy would intervene on the Prince's behalf.[71]

One evening in 1867 Archduchess Mathilde was indulging in the *"forbidden pleasure"* of a cigarette when startled by her governess.[72] Mathilde tried to conceal the cigarette behind her back, but her dress caught on fire and she was quickly engulfed in flames. Mathilde died that night from her burns in *"atrocious spasms."*[73] Just what Umberto felt at his fiancée's death is unknown. Upon learning of his bereavement Umberto had written to his father, but the letter was *"entirely illegible."*[74] *"Thanks for your letter,"* Victor Emmanuel had replied. *"But I want you to know that we couldn't read it. If you have anything to say to me, send a telegram."*[75] Umberto would always be ashamed of his inadequate handwriting, and in his embarrassment at the difficulty it took him to produce a suitable signature he refused to sign documents in front of others.

Victor Emmanuel quickly found a replacement bride for his son in his own niece Margherita, which proved as equally unsatisfactory to the Crown Prince. The marriage of Umberto and Margherita was to be an exceptionally cold union, but Italy rejoiced in having a true Italian Princess for their future Queen. Great preparations were made in Turin, the former capital of the Savoys, where the marriage was to take place, and in Florence, the new capital of Italy, which was to receive the newlyweds. Three hundred thousand people gathered in Turin to witness the nuptials and among them were representatives from the leading Royal Families: Maria Pia, with her eldest son Carlos; the King of Saxony; Crown Prince Frederick of Prussia; Archduke Ludwig Victor, the younger brother of Emperor Franz Josef; Alfred, the Duke of Edinburgh, Queen Victoria's second son, and his future wife the Grand Duchess Marie of Russia, the daughter of Tsar Alexander II.

Unfortunately, not all of the invited guests were considered sufficiently royal enough by the scions of the European dynasties to view the nuptials. When Princess Ratazzi, a descendant of the Bonapartes, tried to take her place amongst the other Princesses and Queens, the offended Royal ladies had immediately moved to the other side. Only Maria Pia was kind enough to stand with her as it hurt the Queen's sensibilities to see this Princess, who though leading a somewhat scandalous lifestyle had personally done no harm to anyone present, so openly snubbed.

Maria Pia could well sympathize with the Princess as she too would experience the pain of being snubbed while on this visit. Immediately upon her arrival in Italy Maria Pia's first course of action had been to seek an audience with Pope Pius IX. It was the Queen's desire to introduce her godfather to her firstborn, but as she approached the Vatican a soldier on duty warned, *"No good is the wind for the Savoys."*[76] Her father's excommunication would cause many diplomatic difficulties for the Queen, but more importantly the fate of her father's soul weighed heavily upon her. Nothing would have pleased Maria Pia more than to help bring about a reconciliation between her father and the church, but unwilling to comprise the Pope ultimately refused to see the Portuguese Queen.

Maria Pia, however, was greeted with universal approval everywhere else in her homeland. The Italians were proud of this beautiful princess of Savoy and her appearances were applauded throughout Italy. With her grace and dignified countenance Maria Pia won the admiration of all those she came into contact with. Madame de Bunsen, who witnessed the royal procession to Florence, saw Maria Pia driving with Victor Emmanuel and recounted, *"She was lying back in the carriage looking very pretty and delicate, and leaving all the bowing business to her father. Her son, the pretty little Infant of Portugal, was on the front seat."*[77]

Maria Pia's delicacy was a continued cause of concern for her husband. *"Maria is still very ill. I don't know what to do,"* Luis had written in despair to his father-in-law. *"...The doctor who cares for her does all he can but the malady persists. Maria suffers and suffers a lot."*[78] Victor Emmanuel, himself, found his daughter's health much improved on this occasion, though he did admit she was suffering from fatigue. He kept his son-in-law well informed of Maria Pia's condition, but he quickly became exasperated with Luis' constant worrying, and the King finally complained to one official that in his telegrams Luis always made Maria Pia out to be at death's door.[79] However, Victor held his tongue when corresponding with Luis, instead writing to his son-in-law about what a pleasure it was to be able to embrace his grandson.

During their visit Victor Emmanuel did indeed become quite fond of this grandson who was proving to be a chip off the old block. While in Italy the precocious Carlos complained in the presence of one of the doctors to the Royal Court that the Italian chambermaids had heads like roosters! Well aware of the Savoy Princes' taste in women, the doctor had in amusement replied, *"Yes, sir, you have expectations for the future."*[80] Maria Pia, who overheard their exchange, however, was not amused and she had protested, *"You teach small ones thus?"*[81] This physician, however, remained astonishingly unconcerned at the royal censure and had merely riposted, *"Your Majesty doesn't want...us to educate the Prince?"*[82]

From Italy, Maria Pia and the newly educated Carlos despite her best efforts to the contrary embarked on a quick tour of Europe, visiting namely France, so she could see her sister again, and the German states, where she could partake of mineral baths. Her journey was a triumph, with an admiring Ludovic Halvey, a French author and playwright, declaring Maria Pia the *"Red Queen."*[83] Several weeks after their departure mother and son returned to the more placid court at Lisbon, which may have appeared somewhat dull to the queen after the extravagance of the Second Empire, but the calmness of Portugal, was about to be shattered by European politics. Fortunately, as her subsequent actions would show Maria Pia had at this time finally conquered any lingering depression, emerging as a spirited and energetic woman, ready to support and assist her husband in his difficulties just when he needed it the most.

Chapter IV

The Spanish Crown

In 1868 Queen Isabella of Spain was overthrown by revolutionaries and Spain's Prime Minister Marshal Prim was having difficulties filing the vacant throne that was more distinguished by its past glory than its current stability.[1] The deposed Queen's brother-in-law Antoine, the conspiring Duke of Montpensier, had had his eye on the crown for decades, but as the son of the former French King Louis Philippe, his candidacy was unacceptable to France's current Bonaparte sovereign, Napoleon III. To his chagrin the Emperor could not offer an alternative candidate, but he would not have to worry about the Orleans Prince for long. Montpensier took himself out of the running when in a duel he killed his wife and Isabella's cousin Enrique, the Duke of Seville, also the brother of Isabella's consort Francisco. Montpensier was banned from Spain for a year, but from his exile in Portugal he continued with his intrigues against the other candidates, including the Braganzas, for the crown.

Both Luis and his father were considered for the throne, but it was Ferdinand who was the forerunner within the Spanish Cortes. Although Ferdinand had no desire to leave his comfortable retirement or his mistress, Montpensier, it is alleged, took the precaution to point out to the papal nuncio in Lisbon that Ferdinand's relations with this lady were notorious.[2] Ferdinand, however, was more than prepared to marry Elise, and with the support of his sons the ex-King finally espoused the former opera singer on June 10, 1869. On the same day Ferdinand's cousin, Ernest, the Duke of Saxe-Coburg & Gotha, obliging created the bride the Countess of Edla.

Ferdinand's other relations were not as obliging. Of his children only Augusto, who made his home with his father, fully approved. Luis's reaction can best be described as lukewarm. He had previously entertained the idea of having his father legalize his relationship with his mistress to prevent undue gossip, and he had believed conferring a title upon Elise would make the morganatic union less scandalous. But when Luis had approached the Bishop of Viseu, the president of the ministry, with his idea of granting Elise the title of the Countess of Sintra, all the King received for his trouble was a burst of laughter from the astounded Bishop. When the Bishop had sobered, he informed Luis of his brother-in-law's answer to the dilemma: *"I have, however, one solution that seems best. The Prince of Saxony says that if he is asked to grant any title to a singer that it would be the safety of the honor of a convent!"*[3]

When Ferdinand finally wed Elise, Luis was present at the ceremony and afterwards dined with the couple at the Neccisadades Palace. It would be Luis's sisters that would suffer the most from their father's remarriage as Ferdinand had allowed his relationship with his daughters to grow distant.

Perhaps the only good result from Ferdinand's remarriage in regards to his children was that it helped to reconcile Luis and Antonia, who put aside their past differences in their united disapproval of their father's actions. The once close brother and sister relationship had become strained shortly after Luis had been rendered King. Antonia had been devastated by the simultaneous death of her brothers, particularly that of her gifted eldest brother Pedro, and she had tried to transfer the qualities of the esteemed Pedro upon Luis.[4] Luis had more than his fair share of admirable characteristics, but even he could not fill the revered Pedro's shoes, and Antonia made the situation worse in her letters by unwisely comparing him to Pedro. It must have been difficult for Luis to live in his brother's shadow, and in his bitterness, coupled with his tendency to be a lazy correspondent, he did not always respond to Antonia's letters. Antonia, however, genuinely loved Luis, and she realized her mistake over time. Though he generally ignored her letters, Antonia still treated Luis as a confidant,[5] stubbornly writing to him despite the *"coldness that you have for me that costs me tears."*[6] It was not until Ferdinand wed the Countess of Edla, however, that Luis's attitude towards Antonia softened, and he now invited her to return to Portugal despite *"Papa being married."*[7]

Maria Pia was as equally disapproving of this union, and had not been present at the marriage ceremony. Luis had tried to smooth matters over by sending his father a letter and sweets on behalf of his wife, and in return Ferdinand had tried to appease Maria Pia by telegraphing and inquiring after her health, but this was no where enough to mollify the Queen. Her response implied that his actions had caused her to become even weaker and more nervous.[8]

Much of Maria Pia's disgust with her father-in-law's remarriage can probably be attributed to the unequal unions she was forced to endure within her own family: the House of Savoy was rife with morganatic marriages. Her cousin Eugene was married to Turin's most popular actress, Felicita Crosio, and her aunt of Genoa had taken as her second spouse an obscure lieutenant, Marquis Niccolo Rapallo.[9] But the most difficult of the Savoy morganatic unions for Maria Pia to endure was that of her father who had finally remarried his own long time mistress Rosa Vercellona in the same year as Ferdinand wed Elise.

Victor's affair with Rosa had always been a source of embarrassment for his royal children, but when he chose to legalize their union Victor Emmanuel did his utmost to remain in the good graces of his eldest daughter Clotilde, the only one of his children that he truly cared for the good opinion of. To this cherished daughter the Italian King wrote a self-serving letter full of white lies in order to justify his behavior:

"I have worked up the courage and I am writing to you. You will think that I have waited too long, but to tell you the truth I was too frightened by the first part of your letter, in which you gave your miserable old papa an old-fashioned tongue-lashing. But in the second part you said that my Kekina forgives me and that she still loves me, which gives me the courage to undertake this labor, trusting myself to

your good will and, in knowing that, I will speak of everything. Listen, dear Clotilde, I have suffered much in my life because of that affair, but I believe I have paid for whatever harm I have caused, and now I would like to have a little peace. Put yourself in my shoes and imagine yourself in the stormy life I lead. I believe there no longer is anything for which to reproach myself and I feel that what I have done is not such a terrible thing...In this world I have loved only your sainted mother and then this woman, with whom a terrible destiny and a great love on both our parts has united me. I sought, we sought, both of us, from the very beginning, many times, to separate from another, but strange circumstances always reunited us in spite of ourselves... Now I must tell you still another thing which will seem strange to you, but that's the way it is: La Rosina, guided by sentiments of the highest delicacy, has never spoken to me of marriage...Now, dear Clotilde, I have opened my heart and I assure you it has taken great pains. Do not think badly of me and have a little pity for your poor old papa...I have suffered much in my life; I have had many family misfortunes, have passed many years in war. I lost my father in exile; my head was ruined by too much serious thinking...I wish to be able to die in tranquility. I need therefore to be united with that person who for seventeen years was my inseparable companion in all my pain and in all my labors for the fatherland, my companion in all my long sufferings. Excuse me if I have exhausted you, my dear daughter. Write me something good, something to cheer me. I need that. Farewell, love and kisses...Your miserable father, Victor, known as the unfortunate..."[10]

It would take the tangled affair of the Spanish Crown to temporarily distract Maria Pia's displeasure from her father and father-in-law's actions. Around the time of Ferdinand's remarriage his son-in-law, Prince Leopold of Hohenzollern-Sigmaringen, was suggested for the Spanish Throne. Maria Pia had it was said in her displeasure at Ferdinand's actions sought a cure for her nerves in Baden, where Leopold's mother Josephine's relations reigned. Although Maria Pia did her utmost to conceal her involvement in government activity, she was a known advocate for Portuguese and Italian interests.[11] Thus, it was now rumored she was in Baden to take measure of the idea of Leopold and Antonia as Spain's sovereigns which could greatly work to Portugal's advantage, and to lend her support to her in-laws faced with this difficult decision.[12]

Despite having traveled to Baden incognito, Maria Pia's presence in Germany attracted worldwide attention. Napoleon III, who found the thought of a German Prince as the King of Spain even more offensive than the prospect of Montpensier, became quite suspicious of the Queen's motives for being in Germany, and soon malicious rumors began to be spread in Lisbon by the French minister to Portugal. The capital pulsated with the gossip that the Queen was leaving Portugal permanently, but in the vilest rumor of all it was asserted that Maria Pia's illness was really insanity.

While Maria Pia found the idea of Leopold and Antonia as Spain's sovereigns far preferable to that of Ferdinand and Elise, she perversely went out of her way to avoid meeting with certain family members of the Royal House of Baden. Her imperious behavior caused offense, and although Antonia offered excuses for Maria Pia's comportment the Princess was made to suffer the consequences of the Queen's actions with her in-laws. To her brother Antonia elaborated upon her difficulties: *"I come to you today to speak on a matter difficult for me but I find that it is my duty because all talk about...how the Queen behaves in Germany...the Queen has treated the sister of my Mother-in-law badly; she was made to wait 5 hours before she was received...a better impression it is said would be if the invalid did not receive at all...I myself am made nearly ill in this matter."*[13] As Princess Marie of Baden had married a mere English duke it is not surprising given Maria Pia's recent upset at the unequal unions within her immediate family that she went out of her way to avoid meeting with the lady in question. The last thing the Queen wanted to do at this juncture was engage with a participant of a morganatic marriage.

It would seem that Maria Pia's presence in Baden caused undo worry for all parties concerned as in this instance neither Leopold or Antonia were enthusiastic at the prospect of becoming Spain's sovereigns. Leopold was hesitant to undertake the task as he had for an example his brother Karl, who having recently obtained the Romanian throne was having such difficulties in his position that he often wrote home of his determination to abdicate. Leopold declined his offer of an even more unstable crown, but the Prince's refusal was not absolute. Although his father Karl Anton realized it was costly to the family coffers to supply princes for impoverished countries, he made it clear that Leopold would overcome his apprehensions if King Wilhelm believed the acceptance of the Spanish Crown was in the best interests of Prussia.[14]

Fortunately for Leopold, the King saw little benefit in the proposal for Prussia, and in addition Wilhelm was extremely protective of Antonia, whom he greatly admired. He refused to intervene on the grounds that it was none of his business, and to his Chancellor Bismarck, who actually had ulterior motives concerning the Spanish throne, the King reported: *"The Hereditary Prince cannot make up his mind to renounce his position as a German, Prussian and Hohenzollern for so utterly insecure an existence. I, too, must confess that I should regard it as highly undesirable to see the disappearance of the name and family from Prussian and Germany...The Hereditary Princess has again expressed herself with the utmost decision to the effect she would regard it as impossible to enter upon a station of life which would necessarily bring her into the most lamentable conflict with near relatives, especially if the Iberian question were to crop up again, perhaps even seeking, precisely on her account, the union of the Spanish and Portuguese crowns which would be made possible only by the expulsion of her father and brothers...My view of the question being what it is I do not feel in a position to give the Hereditary Prince the required command."*[15]

As Maria Pia returned to Portugal from Germany so did Marshal Prim's attention. He had as an ally General Saldanha, a hero from Portugal's civil war, who now dreamed of uniting the Iberian Peninsula as had King Phillip II of Spain, but this time under the control of Lisbon. He proposed that Luis should reign in Madrid, with his second son Afonso as his heir, leaving Ferdinand as Regent in Portugal for Carlos. Luis retreated in face of the speculation to the Royal Palace at Mafra, but he did issue a statement to his Prime Minister Loule disavowing any intention of undertaking the Spanish throne. *"I was born a Portuguese,"* he proudly asserted, *"and a Portuguese I will die."*[16]

Frustrated by Luis's lack of ambition and eventually feeling that Loulé had insulted his honor, the General organized a palace revolution. At dawn on May 19, 1870 Saldanha surrounded the Ajuda Palace and attacked the palace guard, demanding the dismissal of Loulé's ministry and proposing himself as an alternative. Luis met with Saldanha in private, acquiescing to his demands. It was not a surprising move on Luis's part as the King disliked any form of conflict, and besides Saldanha had previously dominated his mother's reign often overturning her ministries in what he saw for her own good. But Maria and Ferdinand had always forgiven Saldanha, indeed, they would even invite the Marshall to sit by their fireside and tell them their faults![17] He clearly expected the same treatment from Maria Pia, and confidently requested to meet with the her so that he could pay his respects and kiss her hand. The Marshall, however, had greatly underestimated his new Queen.

Unfortunately, Maria Pia had slept through the revolt. When the Queen was finally informed of Luis's acceptance of Saldanha's demands, Maria Pia became enraged at her husband's inability to be a firm King, and her volatile temper was further provoked when she was told of the Marshall's desire to pay her homage. Maria Pia consented to meet with him, but as all parties involved were soon to discover it was only to give Saldanha a piece of her mind. According to legend, the infuriated Queen scathingly told the Marshall, *"If I were King I would have you shot tomorrow in a public square. Now you can go. I have told you what I think of your behavior."*[18]

By her own account of the events, Maria Pia merely stated she would have had Saldanha arrested. In a sixteen plus page letter to her father, the Queen elaborated upon the incredible event, admitting that when she had learned of this act of "disgrace" against the Constitution and King, she had become terribly angry with that *"old man,"* who had the audacity to claim he had acted to save Luis, the children, and her, and a thousand other absurdities. The Queen further confided that while the indignation with Saldanha was immense in Portugal, to her astonishment she was surrounded by an incredible pacifism. She named no names, but clearly Maria Pia was dismayed by Luis's refusal to handle the situation. While remaining diplomatic in describing her husband's reaction to the uprising, she did believe in giving credit where credit was due and for once was complimentary of her father-in-law, who had rushed to the Ajuda Palace to offer his support.

An even stronger ally in Maria Pia's corner against the *"despotism and foolishness of the duke"* was Oldoini, the Italian diplomat at the Portuguese court. Publicly condemning Saldanha's armed action, Oldoini then went on to extol the exemplary behavior of the Queen. As punishment Saldanha spitefully refused to receive the Italian minister officially, which eventually provoked the departure of Oldoini. With contempt Maria Pia explained that Saldanha believed Oldoini was responsible for her opposition. *"Incredibly, men here think I can't form opinions of my own,"* she had exclaimed. Maria Pia couldn't resist adding, *"the Beast."*

Maria Pia worried the Duke might try to recall Oldoini, but only because he wished to harm him and probably also herself. However, when everything was calmer and Saldanha no longer in power, she wanted Oldoini to return because he was a good man and had the courage to tell the truth.

The Queen then proceeded to inform her father that she liked being privy to all political questions so that she may know the truth and help as she had done the past winter. (Whether she had helped her father or husband in this instance is unclear.) Maria Pia added that she was discreetly networking behind the scenes meeting many people (politicians) and they were beginning to know her.

Finally, she declared the King must pay attention and stay firm because if he was unable, she would assume the regency rather than allow the command to remain in the hands of *"that old duke."* Maria Pia's final thoughts show she was looking to the future. Their neighbor Spain was trying to obtain a new King, but if one was not found then the nation could become a republic, while Saldanha's current coup was setting a dangerous precedent in their own country during these radical times. He had easily overturned the ministry, could he have not just as easily overthrown the monarchy? Revolutionary fever must be averted and she ended with assuring her father that under her watch the Iberian Peninsula would not become a republic.[19]

In the end Maria Pia didn't have to assume the regency as under her influence Luis wrote to Queen Victoria requesting that Marshall Saldanha represent Portugal at the Court of St. James's in England. It was a move recognized by all as an honorable banishment. Queen Victoria complied with Luis's request, but she was appalled at how Luis had handled the whole situation. *"Poor Luis of Portugal showed neither strength of character or courage on the occasion,"* bemoaned the Queen to her eldest daughter. *"He absolutely stopped all the faithful troops who had been sent for and told them not to come – as he wished no disturbance lest it should wake the Queen!!* (Probably out of fear at being scratched and beaten by her - which has often been the case.) *And he told Saldanha to do what he liked!! How deplorable!"*[20] Victoria's reference to Maria Pia in her letter merely demonstrates her prejudice against an equally strong willed Queen more than any truth of the matter. While she had a fierce temper and was known to throw things in frustration, Maria Pia was certainly not abusive, and she would never have physically hurt her husband or anyone else for that matter, including the provoking Saldanha, who she had not wished to inflict bodily harm upon but only incarceration as her letter attests.

Due to Maria Pia, Saldanha no longer had any influence over Luis, but the Marshall still held considerable sway with Ferdinand. Before his departure Saldanha did his utmost to convince Ferdinand to accept the Spanish Throne, and the former King began to draw up his terms for taking the crown. But on July 2, 1870 it would seem that the search for a king was over when Ferdinand's son-in-law Leopold announced his acceptance of the crown.

Leopold had proved to be no match for the determined Bismarck, who believed the prospect of a German Prince on the Spanish throne could provoke a French attack that *"politically...would be very beneficial to our situation."*[21] Having failed to cajole the Prussian King into giving his blessing for the project, Bismarck had taken to working behind his sovereign's back. On June 19, 1870 the Chancellor's men were able to extract a letter from Leopold – although it was composed by his father – asking for Wilhelm's permission to accept the Spanish throne. Wilhelm reluctantly gave his consent to the even more reluctant would-be monarch, who asserted, *"But I am only accepting because everyone tells me it is the interest of the* [German] *States. I have not the ambition and I do not want to."*[22]

Needless to say Napoleon III didn't want him to either, and the French began making speeches threatening war on July 6. To her eldest daughter, the Crown Princess of Prussia, Queen Victoria wrote in dismay, *"We are much startled by the news of Leopold of Hohenzollern's election as King of Spain, and a telegram from Paris saying that France will resist this and hopes we will also, which is quite preposterous but alarming."*[23] She went on to advise her daughter, *"This unfortunate affair of Leopold H. may set Europe ablaze. If only he would retire...it would be a blessing, though the conduct of France is most...shameful."*[24]

Leopold did renounce the crown to the horror of Bismarck, giving France a great diplomatic victory. But all was not lost for the Chancellor who hoped to provoke the French into declaring war. When Napoleon III demanded assurance from Wilhelm that he would never authorize a renewal of the candidacy, the Prussian King rebuffed the ultimatum and entrusted Bismarck with his reply. It was a situation that Bismarck exploited in the fullest, editing Wilhelm's reply into a humiliating defiance of France. Bismarck's wish was fulfilled when France declared war on July 19 just days after receiving the dispatch.

From Paris, Maria Pia's brother-in-law Plon-Plon upbraided his cousin for mishandling the crisis. He believed that Leopold, who was openly mocked by the Spaniards for his perceived eagerness to gain a crown, had stood no chance of staying permanently on the throne.[25] *"We should have let it happen,"* the Prince often said, *"The Hohenzollern would have fallen on his own, and his fall would have been a formidable check to Bismarck's policy."*[26] He believed rightly that war with Prussian would be the end for the Bonapartes. Turning in disgust from the fanatical cries of the warmongers in the Parisian streets, Plon-Plon asked, *"Do you hear them, the imbeciles? Oh, you'll come back from Berlin, but without having entered it, and we, the Bonapartes, we can pack our trunks."*[27]

While Prussia and France were locked in battle, Prim was reviewing Ferdinand's candidacy, but he also had a new promising candidate in Maria Pia's brother Amedeo, who had the support of Great Britain. Amedeo, however, like the other candidates was also hesitant to undertake the political strife in Spain, and he confessed to his father a *"secret repulsion"* to leave Italy.[28] Although Amedeo had his doubts, Maria Pia eagerly endorsed his candidacy. The prospect of having one of her siblings in closer proximity on the Iberian Peninsula undoubtedly allowed Maria Pia to overlook her brother's misgivings. But the possibility her father-in-law could ruin this opportunity particularly rankled the Queen, and she would never forgive Ferdinand for the review of the throne. In her endorsement of her brother's candidacy, Maria Pia voiced her opinion of the improbability of Ferdinand and his morganatic wife as Spain's sovereigns. *"The Spanish would never accept Ensler for Queen,"* Maria Pia explained to the Portuguese Minister Andrade Corvo in Madrid. *"And what of the weak character of Ferdinand who has not the age for such an undertaking, there is my brother: he is the King of Spain."*[29] Her wily father, however, for the time being refused to commit to the prospect as he awaited the outcome of the war.

As Plon-Plon had predicted Prussia was decisively beating the French, and discontent within the Second Empire was widespread with factions in Paris already clamoring for revolt. Worried for his daughter's safety, an anxious Victor Emmanuel wrote to Clotilde on August 22 beseeching her to flee Paris. But Clotilde's conscience would not allow her to abandon her adopted country in its time of need. Having taken the precaution of sending her children out of harm's way to Plon-Plon's Pragins estate in Sweitzerland, Clotilde defended her decision to remain behind, asserting that her siblings including her sister Maria Pia would do the same in a similar situation:

"I assure you that it is not the moment for me to leave. I realized that it is your affection for me which makes you urge my departure; but be convinced, dear Papa, that it is not necessary. Moreover, my departure would have the worst and most deplorable effect…It is my duty to remain as long as I can…The good of my husband, of my children, of my country demands that I remain here; and if I may add, the honor of my name and even of your honor, dear Papa, and the honor of my native country…nothing will make me neglect my duty, and I would be negligent if I departed at this time…I shall not commit any imprudence, for I realize it would be foolish to do anything imprudent; so be at peace. My children are safe and this is enough for me. If I leave now, perhaps neither my husband nor my children will ever be able to re-enter France. This is not just a notion or an illusion which I have but the truth. Reflect and think over this, dear Papa, and I am convinced you will agree that I am right. You would not leave; my brothers would not leave; Maria would not leave. I am not a Princess of the House of Savoy for nothing! Do you remember what is said of princes who leave their country? To leave when one's country is in danger is to incur dishonor and disgrace forever."[30]

On September 2, at the Battle of Sedan, Napoleon III was captured. The Emperor had no choice but to admit defeat and surrender to King Wilhelm. When the news reached Paris, riots broke out and shortly thereafter the Third Republic of France was enthusiastically proclaimed. Finally, the time had come for Clotilde to leave, but her departure was conducted with her usual calm and dignity. While a heavily veiled Empress Eugenie fled by hackney cab to the house of her American dentist, who was to hide her for the night before smuggling her to England, Clotilde insisted on riding in her usual carriage decorated with the royal emblems.[31] When cautioned to close the windows least she be recognized, the Princess refused, admonishing, *"Savoy and fear have never encountered each other."*[32] Clotilde was indeed recognized as she rode through the rabble in the streets, but not a voice was raised against this revered Princess; the national guard even presented arms as her carriage drove by.[33]

Before reuniting with her husband and children at Pragins, Clotilde spent a few days in Italy with her father and brothers, but the Princess would not remain in her old homeland for long. The pious Clotilde could not bear to witness the imminent seizure of Rome by the Italian government. Now that French troops were no longer protecting the Pope there was nothing to stop Victor Emmanuel from taking possession of Rome and thus finally uniting all of Italy. On September 20 the Holy City fell to Victor Emmanuel's troops, and Pope Pius, who had voluntarily made himself a prisoner in the Vatican, would be confined within its limits, as would his successors, for the remainder of his life. The Pope's only venue for revenge against the King was to issue yet another excommunication, an action that was a devastating blow to both of Victor Emmanuel's devout daughters.

Rome was made the capital of Italy the following year, and the Pope's former residence, the Quirinal Palace, was designated the new home of the royal court. Victor Emmanuel, however, was never comfortable occupying this Palace, and he once confessed to the Queen of Holland, *"I would love to see the Pope leave Rome, because I can't look out the window of the Quirinal without seeing the Vatican, and it seems to me that Pius IX and I are both prisoners."*[34] Consequently, the King spent as little time as possible in his capital, staying in Rome only when required by his official duties.

Victor's seizure of Rome had angered the other Catholic courts, and with a republic declared in France and the possibility of one in Spain if a King was not found, Victor felt his own crown threatened. To safeguard his throne Victor believed it was in his own best interests to have his son rule in Spain. Out of filial duty Amedeo bowed to his father's wishes and accepted the Spanish Crown, though with the condition *"if the vote of the Cortes proves to me that it is the will of the Spanish nation."*[35] In the ensuing ballot Amedeo had hoped to achieve at least 291 votes, but he had to settle for a hundred less. It was not an auspicious beginning.

Luis, too, had a pessimistic view of Amedeo as Spain's sovereign as he had little confidence in his unenthusiastic brother-in-law's ability to stabilize the troubled nation. *"I am extremely doubtful that Amedeo can keep himself there,"* Luis confided to Queen Victoria.[36] Understandably, however, Maria Pia was thrilled to have her brother seated upon a throne, though her high hopes for Amedeo's rule would never be realized.

Maria Pia stayed in constant contact with her sister-in-law and Dragonetti, her brother's man of confidence, to offer her support, but the Savoys were not well received in Spain.[37] The Queen Maria Vittoria, who began life as a mere noblewoman, was contemptuously referred to as *"La Cisterna,"* while the simplistic loving Amedeo, who disliked pomp and ceremony, was considered uneducated and lacking in culture. According to his unappreciative subjects when the King once drove by the house where Cervantes, the Sixteenth Century novelist, had lived and his aide had pointed out the structure as a point of interest, Amedeo had retorted, *"Well, if he is so famous, even though he has not come to see me yet, I'll pay him a visit soon."*[38]

After a tumultuous reign of less than three years, which had included an assassination attempt, Amedeo came to the conclusion that he had no choice but to renounce the crown as *"he had learned that he had no other supporters than they who were monarchist and partisan of his dynasty only while he gave them power and who turned against him the moment he changed his cabinet."*[39] Within the Spanish cortes Amedeo formally abdicated on February 17, 1873, announcing, *"I can do nothing in the face of indifference of some, the eradicable enmity others, and the impotence of the few who are truly faithful to me."*[40]

Initially, Amedeo decided to remain on the Iberian Peninsula by staying in Portugal. This would allow his wife, who had just recently given birth to their third son Luigi and who was also suffering from tuberculosis to sufficiently recover her strength. This would also enable Amedeo to avoid Victor Emmanuel, who believed that his son had acted too hastily.

On February 18 at 6 a.m. the former monarchs and their children left the Royal Palace for the train station. Maria Vittoria was so weak she had to be carried. Their journey would not be a comfortable one for their compartment in the train was without heat or dining facilities and Amedeo was reduced to buying his wife sausage soup at a station canteen.[41] Thankfully, the trip was of a short duration. The following day they arrived in Lisbon where the remorseful Maria Pia and Luis were awaiting them. Amedeo and Maria Vittoria were treated with every honor by the Portuguese sovereigns and given residence at the Belem Palace. There, surrounded by her husband and children and solicitous care of her in-laws, Maria Vittoria slowly regained some of her equilibrium.

In Italy Victor Emmanuel had had time to rethink his son's actions and now he looked upon Amedeo's abdication with favor. Soon he telegraphed, *"Better informed. I approve your conduct."*[42] He went on to add the Italian ship the Roma was at their disposal. On March 2, 1873 Amedeo and his family returned to Italy, where it soon became apparent that the trials Maria Vittoria had endured had aggravated her tuberculosis. In vain Amedeo moved his family twice in hopes that a better climate would improve his wife's condition, but to no avail. On November 8, 1876 at 7 o'clock in the morning the former Queen of Spain drew her last agonizing breath.

Maria Pia, herself, never fully recovered from the blow of her brother's abdication. Amedeo would always be the rightful King of Spain to his sister; however, after his withdrawal the Spanish had quickly reinstated their original reigning family. In 1874 Isabella's son assumed the throne as Alfonso XII, but he was barely tolerated by his neighboring sovereign's Queen. Years later, when forced to receive Alfonso and his second wife Maria Christina while on a state visit, Maria Pia did not bother to conceal her anger from her servants. As she stormed through the Palace to the ballroom where she was to receive the visiting monarchs, Maria Pia was visibly annoyed. But when her entrance was announced, the Queen became the consummate hostess, as she wouldn't allow her negative emotions to cause diplomatic difficulties for her husband. Maria Christina was won over by Maria Pia's graceful manners, and eventually the two Queens were on friendly terms, but Maria Pia never warmed to the Spanish King. It would be to Maria Pia's extreme satisfaction that, while on a return visit, her eldest son Carlos, renowned for his marksmanship, easily beat Alfonso in a shooting match. And with that she had to be content that the Savoys' honor had been avenged.

Chapter V

Daily Life

Maria Pia's daily life revolved principally around her children, the many charitable works to which she gave her special attention, and her official duties as Queen.[1] While Maria Pia found fulfillment in all of these areas, the most enjoyable role was that of mother. Practically a youth herself, Maria Pia would cast aside all formalities and romp with her children. One visiting dignitary recalled that when her sons leaned lovingly against her, the Queen looked more like their sister than their mother. However, despite her playfulness and youth Maria Pia could be a strict disciplinarian with her sons when their bad behavior required reproof, though whilst not sparing punishment, she did not permit excess.[2] A playmate of the Princes recalled that even when the boys were at their most trying Maria Pia could never be what one could call a scold.

In amusement the family's servants would relate tales of their Princes' misbehavior. With no less than two years separating them, the brothers were the best of friends, but there were the inevitable squabbles of all siblings. On one such occasion when Afonso displeased his elder brother by refusing to do something he wanted, Carlos had exclaimed, *"When I am King, I shall have you arrested!"*[3] To which Afonso retorted, *"When you are King, I shall be president."*[4] In another nursery quarrel Carlos scornfully kicked over a toy bridge constructed by his brother, who from an early age was fascinated by engineering. Afonso reacted immediately, whereupon there was a mutual punching of heads.[5] After being forcibly separated, an action that caused Carlos some additional pain as Afonso came away with clumps of his brother's hair, and inquires made, Carlos was duly punished which he accepted since no other course of action was open to him, but in lieu of tendering an apology to Afonso Carlos instead stuck out his tongue.[6]

When Luis learned of the incident, he tried to restore peace between his two sons. In an interview with the boys the King acknowledged that Carlos had behaved badly, but he found Afonso's physical attack upon his brother to be inappropriate, even ugly behavior. He required that Afonso apologize to Carlos, but this irritated the younger prince anew. When Afonso protested that he had the right to defend his belongings, Luis had his son confined to his room, where he was to reflect upon his actions. After recalling with what turns out to be wistful thinking a repentant Afonso, Luis found the little Prince remained steadfast in his denial of any wrongdoing. Of this son's refusal to give away when he believed that he was in the right Luis would later comment in admiration mingled with some apprehension, *"This child has character, but praise to God who conserves with him when he will be a man!"*[7]

Of the two brothers Afonso was definitely the most naughty. During one summer at the Queluz Palace, Afonso was confined to his room for some infraction, but the Prince had his ways of eluding vigilance.[8] When a servant went to take Afonso his lunch, he found the Prince's quarters empty. In the ensuing search Afonso was found sunning himself in the windows of a corridor, but when they went to retrieve the truant, Afonso upon feeling himself seized latched onto a chair and shouted like the most terrible of revolutionists: *"Hurrah for the Republic."*[9] For days afterwards the temporarily subdued Afonso resigned himself to his confinement, while Luis good-naturedly endured the ribbing he received for having a democratic Prince for a son. In truth Luis was never overly perturbed by his sons' mischievous ways, finding the *"antics that Prince Carlos and Prince Afonso got up to in the Palace amusing."*[10]

The Princes' earliest years were spent playing in their apartments or in the Ajuda Palace's Botanical Gardens, where the King *"liked to watch the children at play running happily, under the tender gaze of the nursemaids."*[11] Their toys consisted of the usual offerings of the era such as stuffed animals, miniature soldiers, rubber balls, jump ropes, etc., but the Princes also possessed the latest amusements technology offered. When the Countess of Daupias gave the first pair of known roller skates in Portugal to the Queen in 1873, Maria Pia had quickly procured tiny replicas for her sons.[12] To the astonishment of their servants and courtiers the Queen and her sons could now be found skating down the corridors of the Ajuda Palace shouting at the surprised spectators to *"Make way!"*[13]

Along with ensuring that her children's daily play life was rewarding, Maria Pia made certain that Carlos and Afonso would retain happy memories of the holidays. For Carnival masked balls were thrown for the Princes, to which Maria Pia invited the children of the aristocracy. Thomaz de Mello Breyner, who became a good friend of the Princes, recalled the first rather traumatic children's Carnival he attended at the age of six in 1871, made bearable only by the Queen's kindness:

"The Princes appeared both dressed as mazzanielos that is to say Neapolitan fishermen…In a corner of a window I recall seeing a young aristocrat wearing a sailor's costume and having a tantrum. His name was and still is, Fernando de Brederode and he eventually became a minister of the republic…Dressed as Mephistopheles was a young foreign boy, son of a diplomat, perchance Spanish. I do not recall his name, but I do recall that he was a real devil of whom the others were afraid and who provoked protests from the little ones when he tore the cambric skirts and broke the magic wand of the poor innocent fairy who wept so profusely!…Also there were not a few pierrots as it was a cheap costume…As a pierrot therefore went I to the parties with the costume of so obvious cloth made by a modest seamstress in my neighborhood… As in nearly all children there is a little bit of innate malevolence, I, as a fairly well-off young boy, was scoffed at by the rich young boys. One of them even tore my jacket and all mocked me because I did not smell of eau de Cologne. At that moment, the Queen took me by the hand, dried my tears with her own kerchief, [and] took me to the private apartments, where a maid arranged the suit. Afterward she drenched me with the best of perfumes. Never will I forget the pomp of hair of this good woman or

the purple velvet of her dress."[14]

At Christmas the Braganzas celebrated with the Germanic traditions introduced by Ferdinand. After attending midnight mass on Christmas Eve there would be a Christmas tree party in which the Princes received their Christmas presents. Christmas day was dedicated to the distribution of presents to the children of the nobility.

Thomaz de Mello Breyner, who begun attending this event in 1872 maintained fonder memories of these childhood parties:

"The children taken by the parents gathered together in the great waiting room which adjoins the room known as the halberdiers. I can hear the impatient hullabaloo of the little ones and also hear the exclamation of everyone when the Viscount of Mossamedes with an amiable face opened both doors to the Council of State room, wherein was the whole Royal Family. In the middle one could see an enormous illuminated fir tree and full of presents. A wave of children furiously invaded the room and such was the wonderment of everyone that in the first minutes they were silent only later to start shouting once again with renewed force. Order restored with difficulty, the distribution of the presents was begun. On one such occasion I had a hussar uniform and on another a box of games of which I still have the remains and already more than half a century has gone by. Aside from the large present each little guest went home loaded with sweets, chocolates and tubes of candy. The party ended in a dinner, or a supper, in the marble room presided over by the King's two sons. The table had at its center a fountain of running water. Many uniformed servants would serve. The families leaning against the walls were enchanted with the happiness of the respective youngsters. The Queen was never still, always going to the guests of the children to see if they were happy."[15]

But the lives of Princes cannot be all fun and games. There were responsibilities due to their positions and particular concern was given to their schooling to prepare them for their future roles. Their formal education began in 1870 and Luis and Maria Pia were in perfect accord concerning their expectations of their sons' teachers. Luis instructed his sons' tutors to *"forget that they are Princes; treat them as you would any other student,"* while Maria Pia would not permit the teachers to give the Princes' hands the kiss of respect.[16]

The Queen diligently followed her children's education, still maintaining her sons under her own supervision. Indeed, Maria Pia had even been her boys' very first instructor as she herself had taught them how to read in French. Now, as they matured she enjoyed furthering her own education alongside the princes. *"I continue my studies as you know,"* Maria Pia would inform her husband, *"but in truth I find the astronomy of the Princes very difficult…because of the mathematics, but it's lovely and that pleases me very much. O'Neill gives me other courses in science, and they are very interesting. Oh! How I would like to have a memory for retaining everything."*[17]

Her eldest son Carlos would possess such a memory. Showing his Coburg heritage, Carlos proved to be a disciplined student, being especially interested in science and the arts. Dedicated to his studies, Carlos liked to keep his mother updated on his progress. Dating from his earliest lessons, Carlos once reported: *"My darling Mamma, I am very pleased with the lesson of today because my teacher is satisfied with me for the way in which I have learned the lessons."*[18]

Maria Pia's second son Afonso, resembling his mother's male relations, cared little for reading or the artistic inclinations of his brother, and occasionally avoided his lessons by hiding on the Ajuda Palace's roof. He was not, however, without a kind of shrewdness, and had once stunned a teacher with his wit. *"One day the engineer Augusto Jose da Cunha…was explaining to his somewhat inattentive pupil that part of arithmetic relative to the prime numbers becoming a little taken aback when the Infante asked him: 'So do the numbers also have cousins?'"*[19] It was *"a clever play on the Portuguese plural of prime, 'primos,' for 'cousins'."*[20] Ultimately, however, Afonso never applied himself to his studies, instead preferring exercises of strength or dexterity.[21] Thus, the only school subjects Afonso excelled at was those involving physical activity such as gymnastics, fencing, and horseback riding.

Not surprisingly given his resemblance to his Savoy uncles, Afonso developed the reputation of being Maria Pia's favorite. One dissenter, however, from this tradition was the Princess Ratazzi, who believed Carlos was his mother's favorite but that as the heir he was less available to Maria Pia than his brother was. Regardless of whether Maria Pia had a favorite she appreciated and believed in celebrating both her sons' strong points as is evident in her confidences to her friends. The Queen's letters show her pride in her eldest as Maria Pia expounded upon all his signs of intelligence, while she admired her youngest courage and daring.

Maria Pia would have a chance to prove her devotion to both her sons in October of 1873, when on the third of that month she and the Princes were walking along the shore at Cascais, a seafront town just west of Lisbon. They were exploring the rocky shoreline at Mexilhoeiro Beach when a huge wave swept Prince Carlos and Prince Afonso into the sea. An exceptionally strong swimmer, herself, Maria Pia had without hesitation or thought of the danger to her own person launched herself into the waves to save her sons. It would be the lighthouse keeper of Mexilhoeiro, Antonio d'Almeida Neves, however, who prevented the catastrophe of irreversible measures to the Braganza dynasty, when he was able to drag all three to shore before they could drown. When the drenched trio had safely returned to their royal residence, Maria Pia wrote to Luis of the dramatic events:

"…As we were walking a huge wave caught us – the children, the man and then me…Nico [a pet name of Maria Pia's for Carlos] fell in, and we could barely see his head. The man threw himself in after Nico and admirably saved him. At practically the same time Alfonse [sic] fell in and I could barely see him. I threw myself in after him and took him with my left arm. I swam under water with my right arm for some time. No longer knowing where I was, I found myself hung up on a rock, where the man who had brought Nico to dry land came to help me pull myself and Alfonse [sic]

out of the water. The waves caught us again, but we were able to get to dry land... Finally we all came back to the house, where I dried the children off and put them to bed...I'm writing all of this to you because you might have heard about it this evening, and the story could have been told incorrectly."[22]

When Luis learned of the event, it was he who for once was in a temper as he believed Maria Pia had exposed their sons to unnecessary danger. In a letter to his father-in-law Luis vented his frustration with his headstrong wife:

"Dear Father, I prefer to...write you instead of telegraphing, to tell you all the details of the incident in Cascais....Marie [sic] was walking on the boulders on the side of the sea with the two children, I myself was in Lisbon where I had been called to business affairs, when a very steep wave spirited away the two children...Marie and a man from the neighboring lighthouse threw themselves into the water to retrieve the children...I classify this like a miracle that they escaped unharmed. It was an inexplicable carelessness of Marie to go on a walk in bad weather...After that I...tried to keep all my patience. It cost me to keep it...But you will always find me devoted with a loyal heart." Your affectionate and devoted son Louis [sic] "[23]

When Luis was in a calmer state of mind, he could acknowledge the courage of his wife along with the heroic deeds of rescuer. Generously, he rewarded them both with medals. In addition Luis gave the lighthouse keeper a lifetime pension, while he published a letter expressing his gratitude for Maria Pia's valiant efforts:
s

"My excellent Princess and Lady, Maria Pia, Queen of Portugal, my very loved and wanted wife...To your Majesty I am publishing this certification on the above love, respect, and gratitude, that I have for the person of Your Majesty for your courage in the tests of this day concerning your great dedication to save the lives of the Hereditary Prince and Infant Afonso, our August and Wanted Children, who having been...besieged at Mexilhoeiro ran risk of drowning...As King I confer to Your Majesty for this excellent service, and the continuance of My and the Kingdom's happiness, offer Your Majesty the medal of gold granted for merit, philanthropy, and generosity."[24]

Despite the near tragedy at Cascais this town remained a favorite retreat for Luis and Maria Pia, which lead to the development of the area. In Cascais the Royal Family was highly visible as they would daily walk or drive through the streets of the city. For entertainment Luis indulged in fishing or attended music halls. Music was highly appreciated by both the King and Queen, both of whom were quite adapt on the musical instruments of their choice. While Luis's skill with the violoncello is the more lauded today, Maria Pia proved quite proficient on the piano, as according to her music teacher, Miss Cart, Maria Pia's technique on the piano was correct, and she possessed a small, but in tune singing voice.[25] Still, while in Cascais Maria Pia's preferred activity was to walk on the beach with her sons, though undoubtedly she was now far more cautious of the sea.

Queluz and Sintra, cities northwest of the capital, were also summer refuges for the Royal couple. While Luis delighted in Queluz and the Queluz Palace, inspired in part by Versailles, the Queen admired the beauty of Sintra. She was not alone in her admiration, for poets have lauded the beauty of Sintra for centuries. Discovering Sintra on their grand tours, the adventurers Lord Bryon, Robert Southey, and William Beckford were all unanimous in their praise for this region of Portugal. *"The village of Sintra is perhaps in every respect the most delightful of Europe,"* proclaimed Lord Byron of this district since it contained *"beauties of every description, natural and artificial. Palaces and gardens rising in the midst of rocks, cataracts and precipices; convents on stupendous heights, a distant view of the sea and the Tagus...it unites in itself all the wildness of the western highlands with the verdure of the south of France."*[26] Writing of his sojourn in Sintra, Southey declared, *"Sintra is the most blessed spot in the habitable globe."*[27] Beckford, the wealthiest of the trio, was so impressed with Sintra he had a palace built there. *"The scenery is truly Elysian and exactly such as poets assign for the resorts of happy spirits,"* Beckford wrote enthusiastically of the landscape surrounding his intended home.[28] Maria Pia herself would ask every stranger presented to her, *"Have you been at Sintra?"*[29] And if the answer was no then she would exclaim, *"Ah, then you have not seen Portugal!"*[30]

While in Sintra the Royal Family resided in the Palacio Nacional de Sintra, a beautiful structure consisting of a mixture of Moorish, Gothic and Manueline (*"Portugal's own distinct gothic style incorporating plants, sea creatures, and a wide array of beasts"* devised in the reign of King Manuel I[31]) architecture dating from the Sixteenth Century. This Palace had a colorful, but sad history involving an ancestor of Maria Pia. It was here in the late 1600's that the former King Afonso VI, who was mentally ill, was kept a prisoner for twelve years until his death in 1683, while his brother Pedro assumed the throne and his brother's wife Queen Maria Francesca, formerly a Princess of Savoy. In his room, little more than a cell, the caged Afonso had paced incessantly wearing away a path still visible in the tile floor today.

Maria Pia created far happier memories at Sintra for her family and subjects. In the courtyard of the Palace the Queen held fried fish concerts once or twice a week for the populace.[32] Great platters of small fried fish were offered to the public, while the function was accompanied by music from the Royal Band.[33] From the balconies and windows of the Palace the Royal Family and court enjoyed watching the proceedings.

The Royal Family spent autumns and winters between the Royal Palaces at Mafra and Vila Viçosa, where Luis could indulge in hunting. Maria Pia rarely accompanied her husband on his hunting trips, but when she did she always carried a rifle given to her by her brother Amedeo, while he was still the King of Spain. Usually, however, Maria Pia occupied her winter months with horseback riding or archery with her ladies-in-waiting.

The principal leisure activity at the Alfeite Palace was also hunting, but because this Palace was near the sea it was also used as a place for convalescence.[34] Maria Pia stayed here for some time in February of 1875 with Prince Carlos when he was suffering from whooping cough. Throughout his recuperation Maria Pia was preoccupied with the well being of both her sons and with the health of Luis who appears to have also contracted a cold during this time. Letters that Maria Pia wrote to her husband from this period at Alfeite are full of updates on Carlos's recovery, concern over Luis's condition, and maternal advice on how to deal with Afonso. *"I am happy with the health of Afonso,"* she counseled in one letter, *"...but poor boy...everyone to him is old or sad, I believe that men in general don't know how to amuse a child.* [With her father setting the precedent it's not surprising Maria Pia held this view.] *Make sure that he is well amused, so that he is not made to feel sad...I hope that you have only a cold but say to me truthfully if you want me to come to take care of you...Nico is well, he coughs but does not vomit...and the cough is weaker, he is very content here except when he thinks of those that are absent."*[35]

The Royal Couple's main residence would be the Ajuda Palace, though in the beginning of their marriage Luis, who was accustomed to the Neccesidades Palace, had expressed the desire they return to his childhood home. However, his father Ferdinand, who had wanted his freedom to conduct his relationship with Elise, had been vehemently opposed to this idea, and he persuaded Luis that they would be happier maintaining separate dwellings. *"He knows well I am his friend,"* Ferdinand diplomatically assured his entourage, *"and how much pleasure I always have seeing him.* [But]*...his dwelling here would hinder greatly...*[my] *freedom and independence, which all have the right to."*[36]

The decision to remain in the Ajuda Palace, which had always been her preference, pleased Maria Pia immensely as she had no desire to share a home with her father-in-law as she too wanted complete freedom of action, and she was not about to allow Ferdinand to infringe in any way upon her independence. She immediately began to impart her forceful personality onto the Ajuda Palace, occupying herself with the decoration of the Palace with the exception of her private apartments, consisting of a bedchamber, a dressing room, two wardrobes, and an eventual bathroom, which had been decorated before her arrival to Portugal by Luis, who had paid careful attention to their decoration and had a direct hand in selecting furnishings and fabrics to ensure that his wife was welcomed to Portugal with every comfort.[37]

In the beginning of her endeavors Maria Pia had the full support of her husband, who *"wanted the Portuguese Royal House to resume the magnificence and splendor of past times which had made them unique and admired by all other courts."*[38] Luis would discover soon enough that he had married a woman whose taste in luxury would exceed all his expectations. In a very short time, Maria Pia transformed the remaining rooms of the Palace *"into an example of the good taste and comfort of the era. With her artistic ability she succeeded in creating a palace equal to the other royal residences throughout Europe, particularly those of Italy. This preoccupation with the reorganizing the Portuguese Royal Palaces was to become for Maria Pia a lifelong obsession, with the accumulation of innumerable pieces of furniture, silver, china, glass, jewelry and other ornaments, not only of Portuguese origin but also imported from abroad."*[39]

One collection that she took to an extreme was that of Saxe porcelain, mainly acquired by benefit of her sister-in-law Maria Anna. Maria Pia dedicated an entire room situated off her dressing room to this form of decoration. Hung in pink silk, her favorite color, this chamber contained *"festoons of delicate saxe flowers run around its walls with cornices of the same. The fireplace, fender, handles of the brushes and fire irons, footstools, writing table and its appointments, bookcases, and even the covers of the books themselves were made of saxe."*[40] The only other collection of this genre that can compare to the Queen's is that of King Ludwig II of Bavaria, housed in his palace Linderhof, in Germany.

A far less intimidating room in the Ajuda Palace was the Blue Room, a salon that functioned as a retreat from the formal court etiquette. According to Thomaz de Mello Breyner, this family drawing room contained *"a large round table displaying magazines, illustrations, newspapers, and Laferme cigarette cases. The Prince* [Afonso] *and I helped ourselves from these cigarettes to smoke secretly in the corridors and courtyards. A bench also carried magnifying glasses to better view engravings, and there was no shortage of silver, ivory and tortoise paperknives with which to cut papers...Evenings were spent playing cards or chess, performing plays, reading, or simply conversing beside the open fire on cold winter nights. On such occasions, the rigid rules of etiquette, observed in drawing room ceremonial, could be waived. In this room, the royal family and their closest circle would enjoy moments of leisure and relaxation, and included lively evenings attended by actors, singers and magicians invited to the palace to perform."*[41]

The daughter-in-law of the disapproving Condessa de Rio Maior, the Marquesa de Rio Maior, who became a lady-in-waiting to Maria Pia in 1886, fondly recalled the many happy hours she spent in this family drawing room. *"In the days of great rain, it was the custom to be in the Blue Room...At 11 o'clock in general, the queen arose herself, the king left with her; they gave each other a kiss on the forehead, and departed for their respective chambers."*[42]

Separated from the Blue Room by an antechamber were Luis's private apartments, divided into a bedchamber, dressing room, study, and bathroom all surmounted by a false ceiling of canvas on the orders of the King.[43] In his private quarters Luis spent much of his spare time in his study, where he devotedly translated the works of Shakespeare into Portuguese. As early as 1878, Luis had written to Queen Victoria of his efforts in making available in Portugal *"Shakespearian literature which is completely unknown here."*[44] As Luis would sit at his desk translating the plays of *"one of the greatest geniuses"*[45] the King would always be smoking a cigar, covering his desktop with ashes, which was hardly noticed among the confused mass of papers, newspapers, books, and pamphlets, his servants being expressly forbidden to touch his work space.[46]

Smoking cigars had also become a lifelong habit for Maria Pia. According to one architect of the Ajuda Palace she smoked constantly like a man, shooting the tips of her cigars carelessly wherever she happened to be. When awaiting his orders while walking behind his Queen, this architect had learned to tread carefully for fear of catching on fire! However, unlike Luis who did not mind a messy desk covered in ashes, Maria Pia had for more exacting standards, and she expected the remainder of the Palace to be immaculately maintained. Frequently, when Maria Pia happened to be in a corridor of the Palace and transpired by a door, she would glance into the room to see the placement of the chairs, but before she could be at her ease Maria Pia would repeatedly return to the same door to ensure that all the chairs were in their proper place. Whenever she left the Ajuda Palace for another residence for whatever amount of time, Maria Pia sent ahead carriages of furniture and clothes, porcelains and crystals, and once for a stay at Mafra even a piano.[47] And she required that everything be in its proper place before her arrival. Unfortunately, the Queen did not always perceive the difficulties her servants faced in carrying out her demands. In preparations for one of her travels a servant of the Ajuda Palace recalled her departing order, *"And do not come back without everything being ready."*[48]

Years later Thomaz de Mello Breyner, who had not experienced the difficulties of the servants in carrying out their tasks, but who enjoyed the outcome of their work, would fondly reminisce over the great preparations made for Maria Pia's journeys to the varying Royal palaces:

"In those times the royal family did not travel with the same facility as they would come to do later on. There were no trains, or automobiles, or, above all, the simple life, almost bourgeois, of the last two reigns [Carlos and Manuel's]. The royal journeys were announced some three and four days beforehand and with great fanfare. First would come carts of all kinds and sizes, oxen carts loaded with trunks and furniture. Even salon stoves and braziers would appear. It was with all this that the Queen managed to transform the enormous inhospitable mansions of King Joao V into comfortable, elegant and beautiful salons. Then came the carriage and charabancs with the personnel composed of personal servants, chambermaids, cooks, silverware butlers, trunk boys, pantry servants and the royal pantry and lastly at the last minute the apothecary cart with the boxes of the flasks and jars, accompanied by the chief pharmacist, an assistant and two servants. All this for 3 or 4 days and sometimes for one only!"[49]

Just as Maria Pia worked tirelessly in ensuring that the Portuguese Royal Palaces remained on par with those of Europe, she would also take extreme measures to present herself suitably as Queen. Despite her shyness with strangers, Maria Pia was capable of displaying the pride and vanity of her position in life: that of a Princess of the age old House of Savoy and Queen of Portugal.[50] Ever conscious of her royal dignity, Maria Pia never appeared in public in anything but the most regal of attire. Nor did she ever repeat a gown; after she wore a dress it was donated the following day to the National Theatre. To maintain this grandeur Maria Pia could personally spend whole mornings and afternoons in her wardrobe organizing her ensembles. But this is not to say she was a slave to fashion. The Queen did not always conform to trends instead she showed her independence by pursuing her own ideas of fashion. Maria Pia had abandoned the crinoline long before it went out of style, with the pronouncement: *"A crinoline is a dress inappropriate for a lady."*[51] Instead she preferred to model her gowns after historic engravings. In her later years the Queen would show a preference for rose-colored gowns in varying shapes.

But clothing alone could not always cultivate the stylized image Maria Pia wished to present to the public, and other measures had to be taken. One day she had a Te Deum in the Lisbon Cathedral postponed by half an hour in order that the sunlight would fall through the stained-glass windows at the right angle to catch her red hair at the moment she entered the sanctuary.[52] Maria Pia's efforts would not go unrewarded; her grandeur would aspire awe in her contemporaries, with one appreciate Frenchwoman proclaiming, *"elegant, extravagantly dressed, and always haughty and distant in her manner, Queen Maria Pia figured in the eyes of* (the) *populace...as the characteristic Queen of the Fairy Stories – The Queen depicted as the incarnation of pride, always seated on a golden throne, with a golden scepter in hand."*[53]

While this behavior would lead Maria Pia to being characterized as standoffish, the Queen had adroitly judged her situation, realizing that over familiarity with one's subjects could breed contempt for the institution of monarchy. Maria Pia clearly viewed *"royalty as stage"*[54] in which public appearances demanded a star performance, and with her flair for the dramatic and attention to detail Maria Pia assured herself the staring role not only in Portugal but also upon the world stage at large for years to come. A teen beauty the Queen of Portugal was on par with the other leading royal beauties of her day, the Empresses Elisabeth of Austria and French Empress Eugenie. Unfortunately, Maria Pia's good looks would fade, in large part due to the illnesses she endured, before theirs. However, it is unquerstionable that of the three consorts, Maria Pia would eclipse the others by always maintaining the reputation as the best dressed royal consort of her time.

Most, however, forgave Maria Pia for her aloofness, as in direct contact she was warm and personable, just as they forgave the Queen's whimsies and spendthrift ways as Maria Pia was as charitable as she was prodigal, earning herself the title 'Angel of Mercy'. The Queen's generosity would inspire in her subjects love and fidelity, and today she is remembered for her constant work to help the poor.

One of her many acts of philanthropy occurred during the winter of 1876, which had produced mass flooding leaving many families in misery. Maria Pia immediately organized a commission to distribute donations to those in need. For her initiative the French Society of L'encouragement au Bien conferred to Her Majesty their great medal of honor in their session of May 27, 1877.[55]

Within this same year the region of Cerra was afflicted with draughts, causing widespread hunger among its inhabitants. To feed those suffering from this latest disaster, Maria Pia arranged to have portions of the funds designated to the victims of the flooding that could be spared to go towards the abatement of the current catastrophe.

For soldiers who were victims of tropical illnesses Maria Pia established the hospital the Sanatorium D. Luis I in Lisbon, the first of its kind in the country.[56] Frequently, the Queen sent candies and flowers to the patients, and often visited the asylum *"serving the soldiers supper and livening them up,"*[57] having put them at their ease with her delicate attitude and enchanting gestures.[58]

The Marquesa de Rio Maior, who often accompanied the Queen on her charity rounds to hospitals, vividly recalled the enthralling affect Maria Pia had upon the patients. When Maria Pia had ceased to talk to one patient moving on to another, the former recipient of her attentions would go from animated to repressed, with eyes as *"flat as water."*[59] The two women witnessed many horrors throughout their good deeds and the Marquesa surmised that few could have guessed of the painful oppression of emotions behind the mask of this correct sovereign.

This oppression, however, did eventually take its toll on Maria Pia and she could not always prevent a breakdown of her nerves coming to the fore. The Marquesa de Rio Maior recalled an incident, perhaps because of its rarity, when Maria Pia's nerves got in the way of her charity work. When on the way to visit the poor of Rilhafoles the Queen was overcome by the more eccentric part of her personality. The Marquesa knew Maria Pia was having an attack of nerves when she stressed the fingers of her gloves, but she would be astounded when Maria Pia, in what the Marquesa could only describe as a fit of madness, had suddenly exclaimed, *"Of two years of my life, I remember nothing!"*[60] Frightened, the Marquesa believed that it was in the best interest of the overwhelmed Queen to halt their visit, and the distraught Maria Pia had yielded to her lady-in-waiting's judgment. Unfortunately, word got out and it was said that the Queen did not visit the poor of Rilhafoles because she had become crazy from the cold, the incident having occurred in January.

This, however, was an isolated occurrence as Maria Pia rarely allowed her eccentricities to disrupt her charitable acts, and throughout her life Maria Pia was dedicated to helping those in need. One significant example of her generous nature occurred twenty-four years after her arrival in Portugal. When the Queen was told in March of 1888 that a great fire in the Baquet Theatre in Oporto had killed many people, she dressed in mourning and despite the heavy rain that night she immediately left Lisbon for Oporto. On arriving at her destination Maria Pia walked through the dirty streets and dark alleys of the city without fear, to join her tears with the unfortunate. To all those she encountered, Maria Pia gave words of comfort and distributed money. The grateful inhabitants of Oporto wanted to award Maria Pia a medal, but she refused their gesture insisting that her generosity in this instance was to repay the hospitality that Oporto had shown her grandfather.[61] Nonetheless, there in Oporto the Queen was acclaimed *"The Angel of Charity"* and *"Mother of the Poor,"* but they were titles she had conquered long ago with her benevolence.[62]

But even these many acts of generosity could not silence her few critics, mainly the Republican Party, which first appeared in 1870. At this time, however, the Republicans were merely an annoyance instead of a danger, and Maria Pia blithely ignored what little criticism she received. Any who actually dared to censure her were met with the regal retort, "*Those that want Queens should pay.*"[63]

Others that Maria Pia found suitable to ignore were her father-in-law and his wife. She had not forgotten Ferdinand's involvement in the Spanish throne, and their relationship had not been improved by his remarriage. Her father-in-law's wife was merely that person on whom Maria Pia would always turn her back, and the court gleefully followed her lead. While Ferdinand as the King's father could not be excluded from court festivities, the Countess was not issued invitations. Therefore, Ferdinand made a point of only attending official ceremonies with the condition that his wife was included. But the gatherings she did attend could not have been comfortable for the Countess. In his book on the Coburgs, the author Edmund B. D'Auvergne describes the typical reaction to Elise's presence at receptions: "*On the occasion of some festival the Countess found herself waiting in some ante-chamber of the Palace, with a crowd of diplomats, functionaries, and courtiers. When the doors were thrown open, no one offered an arm to King Ferdinand's wife. Seeing this, the Spanish Ambassador politely offered his escort, and led the lady into the hall. Every seat was occupied, according to instructions issued overnight. The Portuguese snobs stuck fast to their chairs and grinned. The Ambassador motioned to his wife, who at once surrendered her seat to the Countess; whereupon, to make the insult still more marked, a number of courtiers sprang to their feet, offering their places to her Spanish Excellency.*"[64]

Unlike the previous incident with Princess Ratazzi, it clearly did not hurt Maria Pia's sensibilities to see the Countess snubbed, as the Queen believed Elise to have an inherently bad character, being an opportunist of the worst kind.

There was a distinct animosity between Maria Pia and Elise, and the relationship between the court of Ajuda and that of Ferdinand's was hostile and tense, with Luis torn between the two. On one hand he had Maria Pia who extorted him to "*use your power as King to tell the lady she cannot be the center of attention.*"[65] On the other Luis had his father who bombarded his son with bitter letters complaining about the lack of protocol concerning his wife and with the jealous guarding of his own position. Ferdinand would fire off on particularly heated letter when Maria Pia gave her brother Amedeo, during his stay in Portugal after his abdication, the seat of honor at the table. A deeply offended Ferdinand believed he alone had the sole right to this position, asserting "*Amedeo is not superior, he is not a king.*"[66] Ferdinand tried to console himself with the thought that Luis had played no role in the matter as he chided his son, "*I would like to think the Queen alone had this idea.*"[67] Ferdinand went on to add that he could not trust himself to speak with Maria Pia on the subject as he would only end up saying things that one could not say to a lady.

A sorely tried Luis would try to maintain peace, but neither party was willing to give an inch. When Luis once sought to please his father by making a toast to the Countess of Edla, Maria Pia made it clear that if he carried through with his intention she would break the glass.[68]

For her part the Countess spoke disparagingly of Maria Pia to any one who would listen. She was always criticizing the Queen to Ferdinand's friends, but she made the mistake of thinking that his daughter Antonia would join in with her bashing of Maria Pia. When on a visit with her husband to Hohenzollern-Sigmaringen, Elise openly attacked Maria Pia's character. Antonia, however, was disgusted at Elise's actions, and afterwards she expressed to her brother Luis her complete sympathy for Maria Pia with what she had to endure when dealing with the Countess. *"She does all she can to discredit Maria,"* Antonia wrote in abhorrence. *"I will never forget the scene that I had with her…when I said that Maria had pleased me…and she said that the Queen speaks accordingly to the people she speaks to and I told her it would not be polite to talk about my sister so I called Father so we could talk about something else."*[69]

Eventually, Ferdinand and Elise were forced to retire from court life settling into Ferdinand's Pena Palace in Sintra. Maria Pia did not consider Ferdinand or Elise to be a suitable influence and would have preferred for them to have little contact with her children, but for the benefit of her sons she wisely chose not to cut off relations between Ferdinand and his grandsons. Frequently, Ferdinand visited the Ajuda Palace to see Carlos and Afonso and at other times it was the princes who visited their grandfather at the Pena Palace.

Unfortunately, their other grandfather Victor Emmanuel, whose contact with his Braganza grandchildren was limited due to the geographic distance between them, never really got to know these grandsons, though Maria Pia liked to keep her father informed of their development. Knowing Victor Emmanuel cared little for education derived from books, she mainly wrote to him about her "treasures" physical accomplishments, such as in a letter from 1875, where she praised their advances in practice with weapons, riding horses, and performing gymnastics.[70] However, at times Maria Pia like any proud mother could not resist from bragging about her eldest son's intelligence. In one of her last letters to her father in April of 1877 Maria Pia proudly extolled Carlos's virtues, declaring, *"he was endowed with a clear intelligence and was quickly becoming a man, as he was almost her height."*[71] Sadly, Victor Emmanuel would not have a chance to see Carlos become a man as he did not have much longer for this world.

Chapter VI

A Death in Rome

When the fifty-seven-year old Victor Emmanuel caught a cold on New Year's day of 1878, no one suspected, let alone the robust King himself, that he would be dead in little more than a week.[1] On the fourth day of the New Year Victor, not able to shake the general feeling of illness, summoned the royal specialists, who all came to the conclusion that the King was suffering from pneumonia.[2] To treat his affliction doctors prescribed quinine *"to prevent complications from the chronic malaria Victor had contracted in the marshy south lands while fighting for his country's independence. They applied freshwater leeches to his flesh in order that the 'bad' blood might be sucked away, and, in spite of the king's forbiddings, they also opened the veins in his arm, expecting that the letting of blood would facilitate his arduous breathing."*[3]

However, any remedy the doctors employed, including pure oxygen – a luxury at the time – was not a cure for his malady, and the King began to fade. It was Lorenzo Bruno, the court physician from Turin, who worked up the courage to inform Victor of his impending death, when he asked His Majesty whether he would care to receive the comforts of religion.[4] Notwithstanding his usual superstitious dread of death, Victor Emmanuel took the news with unexpected calmness. *"Then my illness must be quite serious,"* replied the astonished King;[5] up until that moment he had believed he would recover.[6] Now, he bravely made preparations for his death, with a readiness to receive Holy Sacraments. *"All right, let's have it,"* Victor Emmanuel declared. *"I feel no remorse; nor do I have anything to repent. Whatever I have done, it has been in the service of my country, never with any intention of offending religion or its leader."*[7]

But the Holy See was not prepared to let bygones be bygones. Parish priests, fearing the wrath of the Vatican, were afraid that they would be called upon to perform the Last Rites, and in a caucus came to the conclusion that Last Rites could only be administered if the King formally apologized for taking church lands, preferably in written form so that they could show it to their superiors.[8]

Despite the forestalling tactics of Father Pietro Desiderj, the parish priest of the Quirinal Palace, Victor Emmanuel's chaplain, Father Valerio Anzino, was finally able to obtain the sacraments, with his assurance that the King repented for any wrong done to the Pope, although Victor Emmanuel's anti-clerical ministers would later categorically deny that His Majesty made any declaration that repudiated his glorious life as the Italian King.[9]

Father Anzino administered the last rites at noon on January 9. After the priest's departure, an aide helped Victor Emmanuel to a chaise lounge. There, flanked by two of his sons, the Crown Prince Umberto and his illegitimate son by

Rosina, Count Emmanuel Albert Mirafori, the King drew his last tortured breath at half past two in the afternoon.

There began an immediate fight over the body. The municipality of Turin wanted Victor Emmanuel to be buried at Superga, the traditional resting place of the Savoys, which had been the King's desire as well, but his ministers were determined that he would be laid to rest in the capital to assure the Savoy's claim to Rome, with his bones serving as an eternal cornerstone to the new state.[10] Turin staged a riot, but the royal troops were sent in to crush it, and the matter was brought to a close.[11] Sadly, it was as Victor had always said; he was a prisoner of Rome.

But the Vatican was just as determined that the King would not be buried in the sacred ground that had until so recently been property of the Papal States, with the Pope refusing the use of any of his basilicas as a tomb for the King's remains. Again it is thanks to Victor Emmanuel's chaplain, Father Anzino, that a compromise was finally reached. Due to Anzino's skillful negotiations the Pope reluctantly agreed to the use of the Pantheon, which he deemed appropriate as long before it had become a Christian church the Pantheon was a temple for worshipping Rome's secular rulers, dedicated to Augusta and Agrippa in 27 B.C.[12]

The King's remains lay in state in the chapel of the Quirinal Palace for a full week after his death. Despite the belief that the embalmers had perfected a new process that would preserve the conservation of the body for a very long time, the embalmment was a failure leading to an unusually early onset of decomposition.[13] The body was so enormously swollen and disfigured by the unsuccessful embalmment that his catafalque was raised almost to the ceiling of the chapel to render the remains difficult to view. This attempt at concealment, however, proved to be in vain as one Englishwoman, whose sight was improved by the aid of opera glasses, was able to get a good glimpse of the remains. But Matilda Lucas would not like what she saw, complaining that the face did not look human, instead resembling that of a mastiff or a bulldog.[14]

Italians numbering over 150,000 gathered in Rome for the funeral. They had not been blind to their sovereign's faults, but they were genuinely moved by his death. His subjects were in perfect accord with Victor Emmanuel's eulogy in the *New York Times*: "*Victor Emmanuel was a man in whom Italy had the greatest trust. The nation was not unaware of his private errors and did not attribute to him the genius of his great ministers. His prestige did not stem from an exaggeration of his qualities. It was based on the secure knowledge that at all costs he would be faithful to Italy.*"[15]

The diplomat's wife Lady Paget best describes the effect the King had upon his people. "*Everybody knows the fascination the 'Re Galantuomo' exercised over those who approached him…His genial address, his generosity, kindheartedness and mother wit won all hearts. What did it matter that his private life was not without reproach, or that in conversation he often drew the long bow, or paid without asking the debts of anybody who approached him in the right way? He had all the qualities and defects dear to the Latin heart.*"[16]

European royalty was gathering in the capital, too. Maria Pia was an especially early arrival. Upon learning of her father's serious illness, Maria Pia had immediately began making preparations to travel with her eldest son for Italy, and this included making arrangements to ensure the care of her husband and youngest son who were staying behind in Portugal. The day before she embarked Maria Pia called Thomaz de Mello Breyner's father to the Palace *"asking him during Her absence to always be with the King"* and to bring his son *"with him to keep the Infante Afonso company."*[17]

Maria Pia arrived too late to attend her father's deathbed, but she would be present for the funeral. Still, the pious Queen could not bring herself to sleep under the roof of the Palace that had been seized from the Pope, so she stayed at the Portuguese Embassy.

On January 17 at 10 o'clock in the morning the funeral procession from the Quirinal Palace to the Pantheon began. It was an impressive sight, which the populace had ample opportunity to witness as the process took about four hours to arrive at its destination. Eight horses draped in black and led by Victor Emmanuel's first aide-de-camp mounted on horseback, drew the royal hearse. Walking in the procession was Victor's son Amedeo, his grandson Carlos who was dressed in the uniform of a Hussar, Archduke Rainer of Austria, the German Crown Prince, and Queen Victoria's representative Lord Roden, who as an unmarried lord-in-waiting was a slap in the face to the Italian Royal Family. Also notably absent from the procession were cardinals and bishops, as the Pope had forbidden any clergy beyond simple priests to take part. But these insults could not detract from the dignity of the funeral rites, and perhaps the most affecting sight of the procession was that of the dead King's old war horse. The sturdy gray Arab was nearly thirty, but still a beautiful animal. His saddle was sadly empty, but the flags of the many wars in which the monarch and his charger had fought stiffened in the wind.[18] It was not until dusk that the funeral services were complete, and Victor Emmanuel was finally laid to rest.

That long day had been a trying, emotionally draining one for Victor's heir Umberto. In the mortuary chapel during the repetitive receiving of condolences Umberto had become faint, and it was Maria Pia who led and supported her brother through those official visits.[19]

She would continue to lend her support to her brother and remained in Italy to see Umberto sworn in as King. On January 19 Umberto took his solemn oath of office at the Bernini Palace, which housed Italy's Chamber of Deputies. Upon his return to the Quirinal, Umberto and his wife Margherita came out onto a balcony to greet their subjects, who were especially delighted when the new King and Queen held up their only child, the little Crown Prince Victor Emmanuel. When they reentered the Palace, the people enthusiastically called them out once more, and this time Maria Pia joined them.[20]

Just as her brother was entering a new phase in his life, Maria Pia's sister Clotilde was forging a new path for herself. The exile against Plon-Plon in France had been lifted, and he had returned to Paris, where he openly paraded his new mistress. In the past Plon-Plon had never bothered to conceal his affairs, but now he had abandoned Clotilde completely at his Prangin's estate, and to make matters worse he had removed their two sons for her care. Clotilde's vast supply of tolerance had finally run out and she wrote to her father shortly before his death to inform him of her sorry plight, but he was too coarse fibered to understand it, or perhaps in a stalling tactic simply pretended not to.[21] *"Can't get a clear idea of your position,"* he had replied. *"Don't worry. Everything will come out all right."*[22] Victor Emmanuel died before Clotilde could finalize her plans to return to Italy with her daughter Laetitia, but the new King welcomed his sister back to her native land and put the Moncalieri Castle, the Italian Princess's childhood home, at her disposal.[23]

Maria Pia, herself, had remained in Italy to support her brother's ascendance to the throne, but her intended departure for Portugal was delayed by the death of her godfather. The ailing Pope Pius outlived his old adversary by only one month, dying on February 7. The Queen was not able to return to Portugal until the 14 of February. Five days later Cardinal Pecci was elected to the papal throne as Leo XIII, and he would continue the stance of hostility towards the Savoys, including the Queen of Portugal.

Years later when visiting Rome with her sons to kneel at the tomb of her father, Pope Leo XIII refused an audience with Maria Pia and the Portuguese Princes. As the rebuffed Braganzas began their departure for Naples, Carlos's devoted Lieutenant Colonel Cesali, who could not bear to see his sovereign insulted in such a manner, cried out publicly, *"Long live the Queen of Portugal! Long live the House of Savoy!"*[24] A crowd of onlookers enthusiastically embraced the cry and spontaneously began to sing the Portuguese anthem, turning an intended insult into an outpouring of homage for their former Princess of Savoy.

Upon her return to Portugal immediately following Victor Emmanuel's death, Maria Pia sought a way to honor her father's memory. Although in all fairness it must be pointed out that while Maria Pia had loved her father it can not be said that she had particularly liked him and these feeling were mutual. The two were perhaps too much alike to get along with one another properly as both had mercurial natures, prone to bouts of depression, but possessing a quick temper.

It was his adult daughter's fiery temper, which ironically she had inherited from him that Victor so disliked. Though it must be noted they differed in one very important aspect when handling their rages; while Maria Pia was content to take out her anger on inanimate objects such as glasses, Victor Emmanuel personally pummeled the objects of his wrath, which once even resulted in his beating a man to death.

Clearly, Victor had no room to criticize his daughter's temper, but criticize her he did. He once cruelly remarked that Luis was the only man willing to put up with Maria Pia, and was always displeased when his homesick daughter had tried to visit Italy. Maria Pia was naturally hurt by her father's harsh attitude towards her, and due to much of his behavior in his private life she could not think of Victor

Emmanuel as a good man.

She would never have closure and years after his death Maria Pia still felt the wounds caused by this unsatisfactory relationship. *"Know that my father was very, very bad,"* the Queen would bitterly confide to her confidant the Marquesa de Rio Maior.[25] Commenting on one of his reactions to a sojourn of hers to Italy, Maria Pia had disclosed, *"Know what he said thus when he saw me? What the devil did you come here for?"*[26]

Nonetheless, she regretted Victor's passing and this correct sovereign was determined to carry out her duty to her father's memory. Due to her affiliation with the Royal Association of Day Care Centers, which she had founded in 1875, the Queen ordered the construction of the Victor Emmanuel Day Care Center in Lisbon, a somewhat ironic gesture given how little Victor Emmanuel had been involved in his own legitimate offspring's' childhoods. The finished institution had the capacity to care for 50 children between the ages of thirty days to three years, and was endowed by the Queen with clothing, furniture and money to cover other expenses.

The following year Maria Pia, herself, would become deathly ill. In April of 1879 Maria Pia developed pleurisy. On April 12, newspapers finally alerted the public of the sad news of their Queen's poor condition. People of all social status, in raised numbers, gathered anxiously outside the Ajuda Palace in search of information on the state of the royal patient.[27] When the news of her gradual improvement was disclosed, to the general satisfaction of the Portuguese, the churches rang with Te-Deums and a concert of rejoicing took place in the theater of S. Carlos, where the hymn entitled Maria Pia, composed by Guillermo Daddi, was sung.

Maria Pia had conquered her serious illness, but other members of the House of Braganza would not be so fortunate. Her father-in-law and sister-in-law were soon to succumb to their varying diseases.

Chapter VII

The Death of Ferdinand

After his remarriage Ferdinand had been forced to retire from court life, and he had bitterly retreated with his wife to his Pena Palace in Sintra. But aside from his bitterness over his wife's ostracism, Ferdinand in many aspects still led a rewarding life with the woman he loved. The couple traveled extensively, and Ferdinand became a great collector during his journeys. When abroad he ransacked shops, procuring antiques and curiosities – he took a particular delight in books, pamphlets, and other publications (many rumored to be pornographic) that had been banned or censored by governments[1] – to enrich his home, which eventually became known as one of the most interesting houses in Europe.[2]

Such was his collections' reputations that Ferdinand was often approached to display his pieces abroad. In 1881 Queen Victoria's youngest son Prince Leopold, who chaired a planning committee to exhibit Spanish and Portuguese art at the South Kensington Museum, asked the former regent to lend some of his items for the display.[3] But Ferdinand was so attached to his possessions that he could not bear to part with any of his pieces even briefly, and ultimately he declined the request. *"I feel it would be very painful to me to part even for a short time with some of those old things, I am accustomed to see every day around me."*[4]

At home in Portugal,s Ferdinand was far more generous in sharing his works of art. He and wife enjoyed receiving distinguished visitors and after suitable introductions were made Ferdinand would personally escort his guests through his galleries and gardens, his pet parrot faithfully following him about like a dog all the while.[5] After the tour, they would find tea and tea cakes, prepared by the Countess of Edla, waiting for them. These tea cakes were enough to convince the visiting Mrs. Grant, wife of the former president Ulysses S. Grant of the United States of America, that her countrywoman, whatever her past misdeeds, must be of a character fundamentally virtuous.[6]

Ferdinand and the Countess of Edla lived happily in this manner for about fourteen years until it was discovered that Ferdinand was suffering from cancer, when a sore on his face developed into a disfiguring malignancy. He sought the opinion of Europe's best doctors, but they merely verified what the leading Portuguese physicians of the day had already diagnosed.

It was Luis who would confirm Ferdinand's condition to his brother-in-law Leopold. *"I have called to Lisbon Dr. Bilbroth of Vienna...Sadly his highly skilled opinion...confirms the diagnoses of the Portuguese doctors...My father is attacked of a tumorous* [sic] *cancer...The disease progresses with a distressing quickness for us and we fear...a fatal end. Fortunately...my poor father ignores his state...he* [goes] *on the same...and takes part in all with a cheerfulness, which distresses my heart when I must do the same for him never in doubt of anything."*[7]

Although Ferdinand continued with his usual activities, he was preparing for his death. Ferdinand drew up a controversial will in which he left virtually all his possessions, including the Pena Palace, which he and his first wife the Queen had begun building in 1844, to his morganatic wife. Finally, he requested that Luis permit Elise to continue to live in her apartments in the Necessidades Palace. However, before this scandal was made public, the Royal Family would be taken aback by the unexpected death of the elder of the Braganza Princesses, Maria Anna.

On May 11, 1859 Maria Anna had wed Prince George of Saxony against her elder brother King Pedro's better judgment. *"Maria seems satisfied with her luck,"* Pedro had confessed to Queen Victoria upon their engagement, *"which satisfies me more than my future brother-in-law, who in my opinion is not kind."*[8]

Queen Victoria, however, thought highly of the prince, finding George to be *"pleasant, gemutlich* [sic], *accomplished – passionately fond of music"*[9] and very fond of children *"only excessively absent, like his father."*[10] She appreciated his correct manner and believed that the haughty reserve so many found off-putting was a result of his absent mindedness. Victoria was very much in favor of a marriage between George and Maria Anna as it would relate *"our family to the royal Saxon line – she is clever – unbigoted – amiable, strong, and healthy and may do a great deal of good – in every way."*[11]

Despite Queen Victoria's recommendation, Pedro still remained wary of the Saxon Prince later complaining, *"He is cold, unpleasant, haughty, and sarcastic to all those whom he thinks it is inappropriate to show benevolence... Whether or not he is a dangerous man, he is at least a theatrical misanthrope."*[12]

Maria Anna's departure from the close-knit family was a difficult one. *"She is happy and loves him,"* Queen Stephanie believed, however, she noted the princess, *"can not think or speak of the time she leaves the family without crying."*[13] Pedro would take the parting just as hard, writing to his confidant Prince Albert, *"Our dear Maria, the pearl of our family circle, who will soon leave us."*[14]

As it turns out Pedro's concerns for his sister's future would prove valid. George did not live up to Maria Anna's youthful expectations and he was often away on military duties. Accustoming herself to Saxony would prove difficult too. The Saxons would not permit Maria Anna to speak Portuguese, a mandate the Princess found extremely painful as she confessed to her sister that she feared she would forget altogether the language of their homeland. But the Saxons would soon discover that whatever language Maria Anna used she was very outspoken as she believed in telling the strict truth. *"I must speak. It is my duty,"* was her mantra.[15] Whether the Saxons liked it or not they knew exactly where they stood with her.

Maria Anna's sister Antonia, who joined her shortly in the German States, found the country just as unwelcoming. Although Antonia had found happiness with her German Prince, she complained that his countrymen were cold with her from the very beginning, criticizing her for either being too merry or too sad so that she had to learn to hide her emotions. The two Princesses remained in close contact with one another, but what comfort Maria Anna could provide was not enough for her younger sister, who found Germany so uncongenial that she contemplated leaving the country permanently. Ultimately, however, Antonia decided against such an action, as separation from the husband and children she loved would be her *"death."*[16]

While Maria Anna did not even have the solace of a contented marriage like Antonia enjoyed, she still does not seem to have been as adversely affected by the hardships she endured as was her more temperamental younger sister. Instead Maria Anna dedicated her considerable energy to her artistic endeavors, embroidering masterfully and painting with passion,[17] and to her ever increasing nursery: Mathilde, Frederick August, Maria Josepha, Johan George, Maximilian, and Albert. Unfortunately, her first two children, daughters Maria Johanna and Elisabeth Albertine, did not survive infancy. Maria Anna's eldest son succeeded in 1904 as King Frederick August III of Saxony, while her daughter Maria Josepha was married to Archduke Otto of Austria and they were the parents of Emperor Karl.

It was her devotion to her children that would cost Maria Anna her life. In 1884 her youngest son Albert contracted typhoid. Maria Anna nursed him devotedly, contracting the same disease. She died of typhoid on February 5, 1884 at the age of forty-one. Sadly, it was just a few weeks before her silver wedding anniversary. Her husband George would never remarry.

Luis made it a point to visit his sister's widower and their offspring, but was to be upset by the strained and distant relationship between George and his children. From his stay in Saxony, Luis wrote to Maria Pia of his concerns: *"They are the same as always, always very good but glacial, it is their habit. Matilde is a person of much judgment and the head of the family. Marie Josepha is very gentle, but still a child. George was very moved when I first saw him; but then he was as always."*

When trying to comfort her husband, Maria Pia approached the subject philosophically. *"I can see you were well received by George and that the children are remarkably cold towards their father. You known them better, but that is the common character of the Germans."* She went on to add her admiration for Maria Anna's eldest daughter Matilde as Maria Pia believed Matilde would step into the role of a mother for her younger siblings just as her elder sister Clotilde had done for her years ago. Maria Pia hoped Matilde's presence in the lives of her siblings would alleviate some of Luis's worries. *"Matilde has such knowledge to find forces within herself,"* Maria Pia commended, *"I think she is very brave to stay with the others."*[18]

Maria Anna's premature death had come as a shock to the Braganzas and to add to their sorrow was the knowledge that Ferdinand, despite his still active lifestyle, was soon to follow. Ferdinand had continued his interest in the arts, though he had to have a grille placed in front of his box at the opera, so that he might still attend without others being able to view his disfigurement.[19] It was during an interval of the opera The Huguenotes on December 12, 1884 that Ferdinand fell, bashing his face violently against a wall. He could not recover his equilibrium and quickly sank into a coma. Ferdinand died surrounded by his family, royal as well as morganatic, on December 15, 1884. The former regent was sixty-nine-years old.

In spite of the heavy rain on the day of his funeral, one hundred thousand of his former subjects followed his funeral procession. Ferdinand would eventually be interned in the Royal Pantheon, a mausoleum situated in the former refectory of the Patriarchal Church of St Vicente da Fora that he himself had commissioned for the Royal House of Braganza. Ferdinand's remains were laid to rest beside that of his royal wife Maria and the remains of their seven dead children.

The mourning period for the former regent, however, would be clouded by resentment when the contents of Ferdinand's will were revealed, causing the press to open a campaign of criticism without precedence in Portugal.[20] There was shock that Ferdinand hadn't left any bequests to his charitable institutions, but moreover at the impersonal, ungrateful way in which he referred to his Royal Family compared to the loving words he had reserved for Elise,[21] his *"much loved wife."*[22] However, it was the thought of the Countess inhabiting the Palace where Maria da Gloria had educated her children and where the revered Pedro with his sainted wife Stephanie had died so tragically that truly enraged the nation.

While Luis mourned his father's passing, he acknowledged that Ferdinand's dying request had tarnished his reputation with the people. When writing to Queen Victoria to thank her for her support during the devastating aftermath of the former regent's death, Luis admitted that Ferdinand's good name was now tainted: *"My Dear Aunt, Your good letters on this sad occasion have been a true balm for my cruelly tested heart. Poor dear father…He was a great heart, too great perhaps! What I [must] next tell you dear Aunt, [is] that unfortunate marriage and above all his will, have made a very bad impression. You can believe how much all this grieves me because it all pains me to see the name of my poor father tainted."*[23]

The Royal Family was also naturally upset by Ferdinand's will, but the King was torn between what he considered his duty in carrying out his father's wishes and with his own growing distrust of Elise. Luis sought the opinion of his sister Antonia, who did not hesitate to elaborate on her mistrust of the Countess and to condemn the behavior of their brother Augusto, who inseparable from his stepmother, had become her champion:

"My good and dear brother! …I can't tell you the homesickness that I have for You all, over all you my only Friend in Lisbon, no one else understands me; Augusto is in such a way under the charm of the Countess that he is not able to think… If I can give you advice in this case and that is to allow her to remain this winter in the Necessidades but afterwards don't allow yourself to be guided by your excellent heart, it is necessary when one has children to think of them, there are not many palaces in Portugal and when your children marry, believe in what I say to you, no princess will want to live in the same house that the Countess inhabits and I can say to you that if I come to Lisbon I will never visit the Countess; all the regards that I've had for her have been of course only because of our Father."[24]

Subsequent letters between brother and sister reveal their uncertainty on how to dispense with their father's belongings, but a determination that Elise would not profit unduly for his death:

"My good and dear brother of the heart! I'm very grateful to you for your two kind letters so full of details even though they were so sad, I am not astonished, it is like I wrote in my last letter that that woman would show her true character after the death of our dear Father…I will tell you what we'll do, leave everything in the hands of the judges, I will not leave to her a single button that belongs to us so reject all the propositions that she'll perhaps ask

through Brother Augusto. It would be very bad on the part of Augusto if he protects the Countess, he must go in accordance with the family and his duty, sadly Augusto has little judgment and like all these people is very stubborn... Do not allow her in any palace where the revered memory of our good Mother lives, this woman poisons everything that she touches. From a letter of a person well informed I know that Edla weeks before the death of poor Father, began filling boxes with valuable things from the Necessidades."[25]

Antonia particularly worried over the fate of their mother's jewelry, which the Countess had always blatantly wore when visiting her stepdaughter in Hohenzollern-Sigmaringen. But the Princess was as equally determined not to possess *"anything worn by that woman."*[26] *"God knows what it cost me and what I suffered...being made to see things that belonged to mother on her,"*[27] she would lament.

Still, the family began to scramble to recoup whatever they could of the Braganza treasures. Ferdinand's former secretary Grobbles gave the Royal Family his assurance of loyalty and he began to catalog the pieces in the Necessidades Palace. The Braganzas, however, were rather suspicious of him as he had been inseparable from Ferdinand and his wife, and Antonia believed he played a *"double game."*[28] Nevertheless, she consulted his work and wrote to Maria Pia with her preferences to the pieces of her father's collections. *"He* [Grobbles] *made a list of the objects in my father's collections... the objects in silver, I desire to reserve very few, having in account that Carlos must like to be with them; pots of china, enamels and clocks I much prefer, many I still remember from childhood...They have said that the Countess of Edla is very sick, of what I do not know and if this is true what will happen to all the objects of our father's collections if she dies?* [This worry would prove groundless as the Countess would outlive virtually all the principle parties concerned, dying quietly in 1929 at the age of ninety-three]...*It is very sad that her relations would have everything later, as well as my mother's jewels. It is all very sad and shameful."*[29]

Eventually, the thought of what Prince George of Saxony and his eldest daughter would do with their restored share of the Braganza treasures also distressed Antonia. *"What to me would be a terrible pity is to see everything that Papa collected with so much love to be sold by auction. But I don't know what to do, since George only thinks of money as you know and the love and piety for things of our dear Father he certainly doesn't have; I don't know what he did with poor Maria* (Anna's) *things; Matilde has already given one of my servants a broach that was Mother's, that hurt me since I find it incomprehensible.*"[30]

Amongst the remaining Braganzas it was quickly decided that Carlos would receive the vast majority of Ferdinand's possessions, at least those of the most historical and artistic value, although the Countess did get away with quite a few Braganza treasures.[31] It would not, however, be until the reign of Carlos that a solution concerning the ownership of the Pena and Neccesidades Palaces was finalized when the government formally purchased the estates on November 25, 1889.

Queen Maria Pia of Portugal
(1847-1911)

Maria Pia was a "child bride" sent to a foreign land to further the interests of her dynasty.

Maria Pia, even in her early years, was always quite fashionably dressed.

Maria Pia's beauty was usually enhanced by the fashionable dresses she chose.

Maria Pia soon after her arrival in Lisbon.

Maria Pia, Queen of Portugal.

King Luis and Queen Maria Pia of Portugal in the mid-1860s.

King Umberto I of Italy.

King Victor Emanuel II of Italy.

Prince Amadeo, Duke of Aosta,
aka King Amadeo I of Spain.

Prince Oddone of Savoy, Duke of Monferrato.

Queen Maria II of Portugal, "Maria da Gloria," succeeded to the throne at an early age.

King Ferdinand of Portugal, a Prince of Saxe-Coburg & Gotha, was Maria II's second husband.

From the left: Queen Stephanie and King Pedro V, Infante Augusto, Infante Ferdinand, Infanta Antonia, King Ferdinand, Infanta Maria Anna, Infante Joao and future King Luis.

King Pedro V of Portugal.
(1837-1861)

Infante Joao of Portugal.
(1842-1861)

Infante Ferdinand of Portugal.
(1846-1861)

Infante Augusto of Portugal.
(1847-1889)

King Luis of Portugal.

Infante Luis of Portugal in the mid-1850s.

Infante Luis chose the navy as the branch of the armed forces in which to serve. Had events not catapulted him to the throne, he would surely have become a notable sailor.

Luis, after succeeding to the throne, was fond of attending costume balls. Maria Pia also thoroughly enjoyed doing so as well. In this rare image we can see the King dressed in medieval costume for the Carnival Ball in 1865.

Infanta Maria Anna of Portugal, who in 1859 married the future King George of Saxony.

King George of Saxony. (1832-1904)

Infanta Antonia of Portugal, who in 1861 married Prince Leopold of Hohenzollern.

Prince Leopold of Hohenzollern. (1835-1905)

When Maria Pia joined the Braganzas, not even a year had passed since the death of many of its members. Her arrival was welcomed by not only King Luis, but also by King Ferdinand and Infante Augusto.

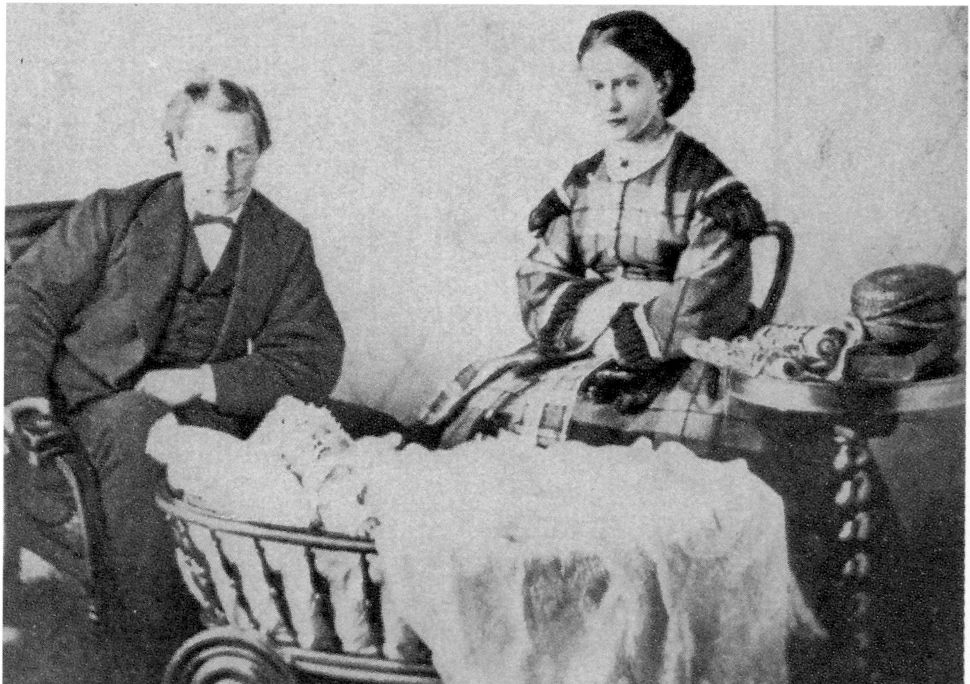

The birth of a son in 1863 not only secured the succession, but it also made Maria Pia a mother at the age of sixteen. Here she is with her husband Luis, baby son Carlos.

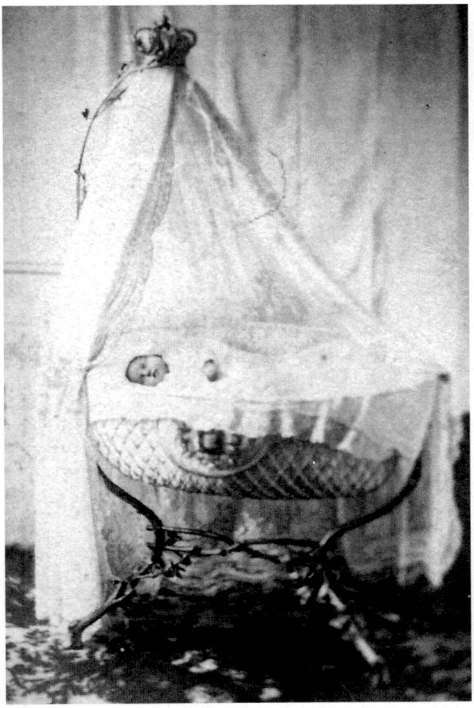

A rare carte de visite of Infante Carlos of Portugal resting in the royal crib.

Infante Carlos of Portugal, c. 1864.

Queen Maria Pia during her second pregnancy.

The heir, Carlos, Duke of Braganza, and his brother Infante Afonso, c. 1867.

King Luis, Queen Maria Pia and the Duke of Braganza, with her sister Princess Maria Clotilde Bonaparte and her son Prince Victor, who years later became the head of the House of Napoleon.

King Umberto I of Italy.

Queen Margherita and her only son, the future King Victor Emanuel III of Italy.

The Portuguese Royal Family visiting their Italian cousins in the early 1880s. Standing from left: Queen Maria Pia, Infante Afonso, Queen Margherita and the Duke of Braganza. Seated are King Umberto I and his son Victor Emanuel.

A rare image of Carlos, Duke of Braganza, in his childhood.

The Duke of Braganza in the late 1870s.

The Portuguese Royal Family in the mid-1880s. From left: King Luis, the Duke of Braganza, Queen Maria Pia and Infante Afonso, Duke of Oporto.

King Luis of Portugal.
(1838-1889)

Queen Maria Pia.

King Luis toward the end of his life.

The Duke of Braganza and Princess Amelia of Orléans, eldest daughter of the Count of Paris, the royal claimant to the French throne.

Queen Maria Pia and her beloved grandson, Crown Prince Luis Felipe c. 1889.

Queen Amelia with her sons, Luis Felipe and baby Manuel, c. 1890.

Queen Maria Pia and her son Infante Afonso at the time when she traveled around Europe hoping to find her son a suitable bride. Her efforts, unfortunately, were unsuccessful.

Queen Amelia of Portugal.
(1865-1951)

In 1887, Carlos and Amelia with their firstborn son, Luis Felipe.

Infante Manuel was born a few months after the death of King Luis. He was Postugal's last king.

The difficult times that plagued his reign made King Carlos feel frustrated with Portugal's seemly never ending string of weak governments. In the end, the King's decision to support a dictatorship was chiefly responsible for the evnts that led to his assassination in February 1908.

Queen Maria Pia.

Queen Amelia.

For decades, the Portuguese Royal Family retained strong connections with their Royal English cousins. In this group image we can see, standing in back from left: Princess Victoria, Queen Amelia, the Duchess of Fife. Seated, in the same order: King Carlos and Queen Alexandra.

From the left: Queen Alexandra of Great Britain with Queen Amelia and Queen Maria Pia of Portugal. King Edward VII was quite fond of his Portuguese cousins.

The Dukes of Connaught visited Portugal in 1905. In this image, taken at Cintra, from the left are: Princess Patricia and her mother the Duchess of Connaught, Queen Maria Pia and Princess Margaret.

Queen Amelia wearing some of her exquisite jewels, many inherited from her mother.

King Carlos became quite corpulent as the year's passed and this raised many concerns.

In 1907, King Edward VII hosted a large gathering of royals at Windsor Castle. Standing from left: The Duke of Connaught, Queen Maud and Crown Prince Olav of Norway, Kaiser Wilhelm II, the Princess of Wales, Princess Patricia of Connaught, the Prince of Wales, King Alfonso XIII of Spain, Kaiserin Augusta Victoria, Prince Arthur of Connaught, Queen Alexandra, Grand Duke Vladimir Alexandrovich of Russia, Queen Victoria Eugenia of Spain, the Duchess of Connaught and Princess Victoria of Great Britain. Seated: King Edward VII, Infanta Isabel of Spain, Princess Henry of Battenberg, Grand Duchess Marie Pavlovna of Russia, Queen Amelia of Portugal, and the Duchess of Aosta.

Prince Albert and Queen Victoria.

Princess Victoria, The Princess Royal, later Empress Frederick, mother of Kaiser Wilhelm II.

Grand Duke Ludwig IV and Grand Duchess Alice of Hesse and by Rhine.

King Edward VII and Queen Alexandra of Great Britain and Ireland.

Crown Prince Luis Felipe.

Infante Manuel.

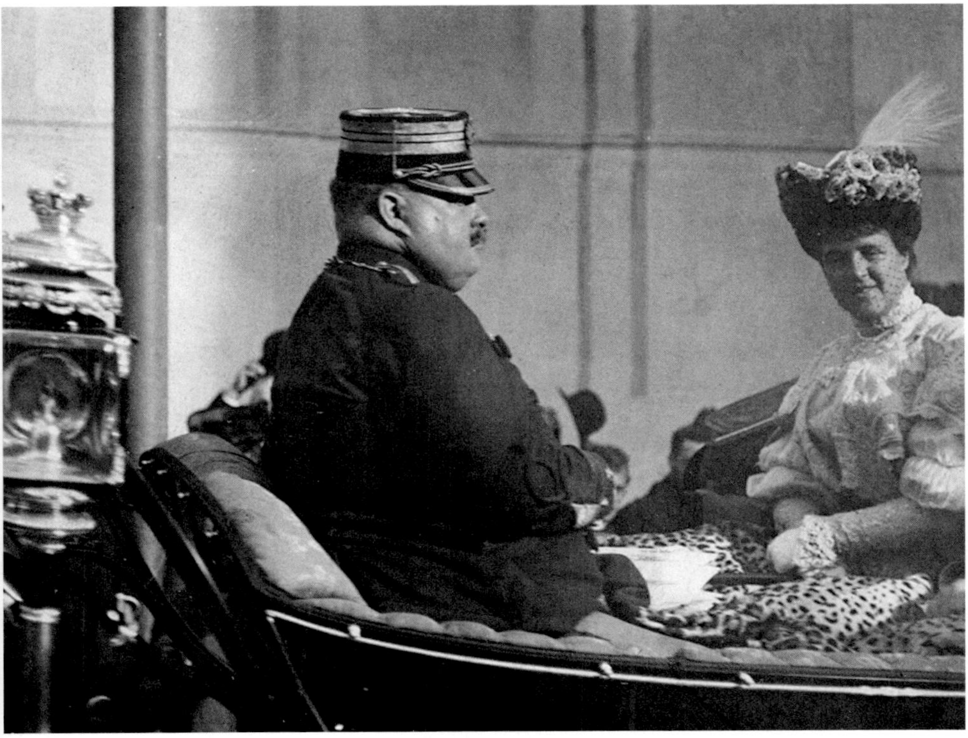

King Carlos and Queen Amelia riding an open carriage in Lisbon.

Crown Prince Luis Felipe, King Carlos, Infante Manuel and Queen Amelia.

Queen Amelia in hunting gear.

King Carlos was an expert shot and hunting happened to be one of his favorite pastimes. In fact, on the day he was assassinated the Royal Family were returning to Lisbon after spending time at their estate in Vila Viçosa, where the King indulged in his favorite sport.

CHRISTÃOS, ORAE
PELA ALMA DE S. M. F.
EL-REI D. CARLOS I
E PELA ALMA DE S. A. R.
O PRINCIPE D. LUIS FILIPE

Requiem æternam dona eis, Domine,
et lux perpetua luceat eis

MATOU-OS O ODIO AO PRINCIPIO DE AUTORIDADE
Á ORDEM SOCIAL E Á RELIGIÃO.
O SANGUE DE QUEM TANTO AMOU O SEU POVO
CLAMA AO CÉU SÒMENTE
PIEDADE E BENÇÃOS PARA PORTUGAL.

OM AUCTORISAÇÃO DO ORDINARIO

A memorial card to the regicide's victims. In spite of the difficult times, the country was in shock and mourned deeply.

Death card for King Carlos and Crown Prince Luis Felipe, assassinated on February 1, 1908.

On February 1, 1908, the Royal Family returned to Lisbon after a vacation at Vila Viçosa. Awaiting the arrival of Carlos, Amelia and Luis Felipe, were Manuel, Afonso and members of the government. Minutes after seating in the carriage that would drive them to the Royal Palace, tragedy struck. Carlos and Luis Felipe were assassinated; Manuel was wounded in the arm; Amelia was unscathed.

The Dowager Duchess of Aosta and her son the Count of Salemi.

Queen Mother Margherita of Italy.

From left: Princess Maria Clotilde Bonaparte, Queen Maria Pia of Portugal and Queen Mother Margherita of Italy. Maria Pia and her sister Maria Clotilde died in 1911. Margherita survived until 1926.

Infante Afonso, Duke of Oporto (Porto).

King Manuel and Queen Augusta Victoria. They married at Sigmaringen in 1913. Augusta Victoria, born a Princess of Hohenzollern, was the granddaughter of the former Infanta Antonia of Portugal, one of the sisters of King Luis. Antonia lived long enough to witness this alliance.

Queen Amellia in the 1930s.

Queen Amelia was very close to her siblings, particularly her sisters Helene (Duchess of Aosta) and Isabelle (Duchess of Guise), In this photo from the early 1930s, we can see her spending time with her sister Isabelle and her family. From left: the Count and Countess of Paris, the Duchess of Guise (Isabelle), Queen Amelia and the Duke of Guise, claimnt to the French throne.

Infante Duarte Nuno and Infanta Maria Francisca, Duke and Duchess of Braganza.

The Dukes of Braganza with their sons: Duarte, Miguel and Henrique.

Queen Amelia in old age.

Chapter VIII

The Marriage of Carlos

At the time of Ferdinand's death Carlos, the Duke of Braganza, was twenty-two, and he had matured into a true Coburg, possessing much of his father and grandfather's artistic talents. The Hereditary Prince excelled in sculpture and painting, specializing in watercolors which often won prizes when exhibited. Carlos was also a skilled linguist, fluent in seven languages including English, which although he did not enjoy speaking, he did like to assist his father with his translations of Shakespeare into Portuguese. On a less positive note, Carlos like his father and grandfather explored all areas of the arts, showing an especial interest it its female components, and soon the court became concerned at the rumors resulting from the prince's affairs.

In typical Victorian fashion it was decided that marriage would settle Carlos down, and when searching for an appropriate bride for his son Luis looked no further than his Coburg relations. Despite his own dashed hopes when seeking a union with the daughter of Queen Victoria due to the difference of religion, Luis was now determined that his son would marry one of this Queen's granddaughters. In late 1884 Luis made inquires towards this monarch's second Prussian granddaughter, Princess Victoria, who more often than not was called "Moretta" to distinguish her from the numerous Victorias within the family. The German Chancellor Bismarck embraced the idea as he wanted to put to an end to her controversial attachment to Prince Alexander of Bulgaria, a democratically elected sovereign who had begun life in a far less auspicious position as a morganatic prince of Battenberg. The Chancellor feared this German Prince would offend their Russian neighbor by appearing to be too much under the influence of Great Britain, by virtue of a marriage to Queen Victoria's granddaughter. However, Bismarck's formidable adversary the Crown Princess was just as determined, indeed if not obsessed, that her daughter would marry the handsome Bulgarian ruler. She refused to give any consideration to the proposed Portuguese match using the difference of religion as an excuse, but it was left to Antonia to inform her brother of the Crown Princess's unequivocal no.

When reporting this setback, Antonia expressed her relief that the plan fell through, asserting that Moretta was *"more Protestant than you can possibly imagine; she wouldn't make your son happy."*[1] Antonia wisely tried steering her brother's thoughts towards Europe's numerous Catholic princesses, and she even speculated on an union between Carlos and Princess Maria Josepha of Saxony, the youngest daughter of their sister Maria Anna. Ultimately, however, Antonia decided against this idea as she believed that the relationship of first cousins was *"too close"*[2] and besides the Saxon Royal Family was *"not very sane!"*[3] In the end Antonia recommended that Luis turn his attention to the deposed House of Orleans. The *"Paris girl* [Princess Amelia the eldest daughter of Louis Phillipe, the Comte de Paris, head of the exiled house] *is truly very gallant and educated, and I don't see any consequences* [if the bride] *were to be an Orleans."*[4]

But it would be about a year before Luis would act upon his sister's suggestion. It was not until 1885 when the Countess Fernand de la Ferronnays visited Lisbon and extolled the virtues of Princess Amelia of Orleans to Maria Pia that the Portuguese Royal Family was spurned into action. Unlike her husband, Maria Pia was not one to dither and she made sure that the Countess sent a picture of the potential bride to Carlos. He obviously liked what he saw for the Prince immediately planned a tour of Europe in order to secure a wife, with his first projected stop in France. By January of 1886 Carlos was installed in the Hotel Bristol in Paris.

The proposed bride Amelia, in a happy coincidence, shared the same birthday as Carlos, though she was two-years younger being twenty years of age. Amelia had been born in exile at Twickenham, England, however, at the age of five she and her family were allowed to return to their homeland of France after the Bonapartes had been expelled. A decree had restored his former domains to the Comte, and Amelia's father had chosen the Chateau d'Eu as his family's main residence.[5] There he lived as a private individual, concentrating his energy on his children's schooling. Consequently, Amelia had matured into a well-educated young woman, although her intelligence was perhaps upon a first meeting overshadowed by her Amazonian proportions. While not considered a classical beauty due to her height, Amelia was comely enough, and the princess had already received her fair share of attention from powerful suitors.

Grand Duke Nicholas Mikhailovich of Russia had been completely smitten with the statuesque Princess after just two encounters. Theirs had been a meeting of the minds, as they enthusiastically discussed everything from politics to literature, but the Russian Grand Duke was just as attracted to the Princess physically. When writing to his mother of a possible union, Nicholas rhapsodized on Amelia's physique, which he found *"beautiful and large of stature, beautiful eyes, but not very pretty - all the while a beautiful person."*[6] His mother, however, sent a scorching and negative reply to the prospect of his marriage with a Catholic princess.[7] An obedient son Nicholas ceased to pursue the project and contritely apologized, *"I was very sad to have to abandon the idea...This grieves me very much. It is that* [I] *imagined that I had climbed to the top with Amelia."*[8] Sadly, this Grand Duke never married, but his loss would be Portugal's gain.

However, while the Braganzas clearly saw the potential of a union with the Orleans Royal Family, Amelia's father the Comte was not initially enthusiastic with the idea. His preferred candidate for his eldest daughter was the Heir to the Austrian Empire, Franz Ferdinand, but the Habsburgs had continually thwarted the Comte's matchmaking attempts. Now, instead of meeting with Carlos himself the apathetic Comte dispatched a trusted servant to the hotel to look the Duke of

Braganza over, with careful attention paid to his height. It was said that Carlos was short and if there should be too much of a disproportion between him and Amelia then there would be no meeting between the two.[9] If the delegate was not favorably impressed with Carlos then he was to regrettably make excuses as the family had already made travel arrangements for Cannes.

Despite having to wait for Carlos two hours later than their appointed time, the Comte's representative was duly impressed with the Prince, who thankfully passed the height requirement, and he was extended an invitation to Chantilly.

When Carlos arrived at Chantilly, he would not find those in attendance as easy to impress. The Marquis de Beauvoir, who witnessed the proceedings, left his impressions and initially he did not have a favorable opinion of Carlos. He disliked Carlos' appearance, scoffing at *"his large pink and white face, his fair curly hair and beardless chin."*[10] Beauvoir's harsh attitude towards Carlos was perhaps the result of the continuing disappointment of the Comte and his entourage at having failed to capture the Austrian heir for Amelia. Eventually, the Marquis would come to grudgingly admire Carlos's intelligence and energy, but he remained convinced that the Prince was not the ideal match for Amelia as he believed Carlos was too immature for marriage. *"In my opinion his great defect is that he is much too young to be with a serious young woman, who needs as a companion a true man, on whose arm she could rest with confidence, not a child she would have to educate, correct, and mold."*[11]

But it would be up to the couple in question to decide their future. That first afternoon the two had walked together in the gardens of Chantilly and it was seen to that they were seated next to one another at supper. Carlos was enraptured by the Princess, finding her more delightful than anything he had yet to see in France, and he told her so at dinner. Amelia found the prince equally attractive and was glad to have pleased Carlos, though she felt she made him shy.[12]

Carlos's enthusiasm for Amelia showed in his quick telegrams home where he declared one couldn't find an *"individual more adorable than this princess."*[13] He had found his bride. There was no need to further his travels, and Carlos wanted the matter settled immediately. The next morning Carlos sent the Marques de Seisal, who had accompanied him on his journey, to telegraph his parents of his intentions. On February 6 Andrade Corvo, now Portugal's minister to France, delivered to the Comte de Paris the letters of Luis and Maria Pia where they formally asked for Amelia's hand for their son.[14]

With her father's permission Amelia joyfully accepted Carlos's marriage proposal, confiding to her friends she was *"full of happiness at knowing herself loved."*[15] Though she found the Duke of Braganza to be *"more and more after my own heart,"*[16] Amelia was not unaware of the difficulties and sacrifices that lay ahead of her as the future Queen of Portugal. *"As I see a life full of great duties beginning for me,"* the princess wrote, *"I pray God to inspire and bless me."*[17]

During their short engagement, however, there would not be much time for worries as the couple was preoccupied with getting to know one another better.

"The more I know of him, the more certain I am that ours will be a happy life,"[18] a blissful Amelia concluded. The couple would be further distracted from any anxieties by the magnificent festivities thrown to celebrate the engagement, the most brilliant of which occurred on February 20 at the residence of the Duchess of Chartres. Unfortunately, this celebration would have disastrous results for the Orleans family as the eagerness in which foreign powers attended the festivities disturbed the French government.[19]

On April 6 Carlos returned to Portugal to help supervise the wedding preparations, but he left the majority of the details to his parents, who were minutely involved in the wedding preparations. As always money was an issue for Their Majesties. The cortes had voted to supply only a limited amount of funds to cover the wedding preparations, but it was necessary to reline the rooms of the Necessidades Palace, which would be used to accommodate many of the attending high ranking guests, and several rooms of the Ajuda Palace, particularly the Throne Room. While Maria Pia with her typical disregard for money, happily poured over stunning fabric samples, Luis compared measurements and costs, making rapid calculations, until he finally declared there wouldn't be enough money to cover both Palaces.[20] *"How can this be?"* a distressed Maria Pia had repeatedly asked.[21] Luis, consulting his figures again and again, could only reply, *"The budget won't allow it."*[22] It was the Marquesa de Rio Maior who came up with a solution to their dilemma when she suggested they turn the silks that were lining the Throne Room of the Ajuda Palace to their reverse side, thus enabling Maria Pia and Luis to concentrate the majority of their resources on the Necessidades Palace.

Soon it became indispensable for Maria Pia and Luis, accompanied by the Marquesa de Rio Maior and the Count of Zicalho, to go to the Necessidades Palace.[23] It would be a highly emotional experience for Luis as he would be entering his dead siblings' quarters for the first time since their tragic deaths. When Luis ordered Pedro's rooms opened, the party, with the exception of Maria Pia – as she had never known the dead King – was overwhelmed with grief. They found by Pedro's bed a picture of Stephanie and a jar containing the decaying remains of the last flowers he had given his wife. It was Luis who took on the difficult task of clearing out his brother's secretary. Inside he would discover several labeled bundles: the first letters of the Queen, the first drawings of Maria Anna, Antonia, etc. The Marquesa, who had been a childhood playmate of the royal siblings, could no longer suppress her grief upon this discovery and she burst into tears. When she had sufficiently regained her composure, she noticed that the Count of Zicalho, who had been a close friend of the Pedro, was also furtively wiping away tears.

From Pedro's quarters the subdued party entered that of his wife's. It was here that Maria Pia finally voiced her concerns at the thought of any lingering germs. *"How can I in good conscience let someone lie here where the Queen died?"*[24] a nervous Maria Pia had questioned the Marquesa. Her fears would be settled when the Marquesa assured Maria Pia that she would order everything to be disinfected and waxed.

Everyday leading up to the wedding the King and Queen visited the Palace to oversee the progress. It was during this time the Marquesa would be amazed by the extraordinary memory of the Queen. Maria Pia wanted the mismatched utensils and chairs of Neccisidades Palace to be returned to the other Palaces in order to complete sets, and she was absolutely certain without any consultation where they needed to go. One of Maria Pia orders, for example, was: *"This chair will go to join with its match in Mafra, and still one of the same furnishes the Queluz."*[25] When the Marquesa compared Maria Pia's orders with a list supplied by the storekeeper of the Palace she would find that all of Maria Pia's conclusions were correct!

Maria Pia was, needless to say, on top of all the arrangements. Under her control the wedding was to be a Royal pageant in perfect accord to her subjects' taste. Unfortunately, it was not necessarily that of her more bourgeois future daughter-in-law, who like most young royal brides of her time period had no input into her own wedding.

It was arranged for Carlos to meet Amelia, accompanied by her family and entourage, at Pampilhosa from where he would escort them into Lisbon. *"In ten days from now, my dear Amelia, we will be reunited,"* Carlos wrote when informing his fiancé of the arrangements. *"I will await you at Pampilhosa, and until [we reach] Lisbon we will find time to talk and I will be able to then say once again how much I love you."*[26]

On May 19 Carlos and Amelia were reunited at 9 o'clock in the morning at the train station in Pampilhosa. From Pampilhosa it was about a five-hour ride to Lisbon, where Maria Pia and Luis were awaiting their son's fiancé at the Santa Apolonia Train Station, which had been elaborately decorated with the banners and the coat of arms of the Houses of Braganza, Savoy, and Orleans. When Amelia disembarked on this festive platform, she immediately went to kiss her future mother-in-law's hand as was the customary protocol, but Maria Pia would not allow this, instead affectionately embracing her son's fiancée. However, despite this show of informality Amelia clearly found the poise and grandeur of the Queen intimidating. Later when alluding to her first impression of her mother-in-law, Amelia would comment that Maria Pia was *"distinguished with her aspect a little imperious…no woman has a more royal and imposing air."*[27] This did not bode well for their future relationship.

The wedding of Carlos and Amelia was on May 22 at three o'clock in the afternoon. Syrian horses with plumed heads transported the wedding guests in lacquered coaches more sumptuous than any others in the world to the Sao Domingos Church.[28] From the first coach descended Carlos and Luis dressed traditionally in the uniforms of a major and general, respectively, from the regiment of the Lanceiros. Maria Pia was with them, but as usual she displayed her own sense of fashion. With her love for historic design, Maria Pia had turned to the famed couturier Worth, who having studied historical paintings extensively for inspiration, could be relied upon to produce an accurate historic costume.[29] For this event Worth was inspired to create a gown of blue velvet for the Queen from the painting *The Triumph of Marie de Medici* by Rubens, but instead of an exact replica, he substituted the fleur-de-lis upon the mantel of the original dress with white silk pomegranates. Their shared sense for the theatric was rewarded when waiting to enter the church a ray of sunlight fell upon Maria Pia's train of peacock-blue embroidered with the white pomegranates making it sparkle as if strewn with jewels.[30]

Maria Pia's perfectionism over her attire was in marked contrast to that of the mother of the bride. On the morning of the nuptials the Marquesa de Rio Maior was at the Necessidades Palace with the other wedding guests, all of whom were appropriately adorned in court dress, when she spotted the Comtesse de Paris smoking a cigarette and still clothed in her normal attire of a flannel skirt that barely reached her ankles and a man's coat. The only concession she had made for the wedding preparations was that *"a magnificent diadem of precious stone"* set incorrigibly upon her head.[31] Embarrassed to be caught in such a state by the Marquesa, the Comtesse had exclaimed, *"Oh, my lady! Pay no attention to all this!... It will be soon enough for the train* [and] *a dress of etiquette, all these things that I am too small for!"*[32] Though she paid little attention to her toilette, the Comtesse, true to her word, had arrived to the church dressed in a striking gown of red velvet.

The radiant bride escorted by her father was the last to arrive. Amelia wore a simple but stunning white high collared satin dress with a long embroidered veil, which was a gift from her friends in France. In her hands she carried a book decorated with the entwining arms of the Houses of Braganza and Orleans.

Cardinal Patriarch Jose Sebastiao Netto presided over the nuptials and when the final marriage ceremony was performed the ringing of two bells and a twenty-one fire cannon salute announced to the populace of Lisbon that there was a new Duchess of Braganza.[33] The newlyweds then departed the church under a rain of roses for their official residence the Belem Palace.

That evening the wedding party dined at the Ajuda Palace where Amelia received her wedding gifts from her husband and his family. Afterwards there was a ball that lasted until the wee hours of the following morning. Maria Pia danced with her guests until dawn, while Luis happily performed in the orchestra.

The celebratory festivities continued for days after the wedding. On the night directly following the wedding the entire party had attended a gala held at the Sao Carlos Theater. In the first row of the theater sat the three most prominent royal ladies; Maria Pia, Amelia, and her mother. The Comtesse, however, despite being dressed in a magnificent gown, obviously felt insecure at the image she projected next to that of the elegant Maria Pia and her pretty, fresh daughter. Before the break she confided her feelings of inadequacy to the Marquesa de Rio Maior: *"Ah Marquesa! That act of humility,"* bemoaned the Comtesse with her usual complaint. *"Between the Queen, so majestic and so beautiful, my daughter so young and so lovely,* [and] *me with this physique; I've always wanted to have a pretty figure!"*[34] The Comtesse would have to find comfort in her habitual cigarette.

Her husband would be preoccupied with graver matters. Royalist demonstrations had broken out in France to the dismay of the Republic, and the Comte and his family's future remained uncertain in their homeland. The Marquesa related in her memoirs the conversation she had with the Comte over the tense political situation. *"I know well my duty and my responsibilities,"* the Comte had sadly explained. *"I am prepared for all sacrifices. But...a movement in my favor... kindles discord that seriously damages France...The demonstration they are making now in Paris, for the farewell of my Daughter, alarm in such a way those men, who have briefly returned from exile; they will leave soon while they can still pass through France to look a little at what is ours."*[35]

The Orleans had quickly departed for France, but they would find that their presence was not welcome. In their absence the French government had formed a new law of exile against all former houses that had ruled over France. On June 22, 1886 the Orleans family was once against sent into exile. Ironically, it was exactly one month to the day after the marriage of Amelia and Carlos.

Were it not for the situation in France the newlyweds' happiness would have been complete. "You tell me you are glad to know I am away from all this sadness," Amelia had confided to her good friend, the Duchess de Luynes, immediately following the expulsion of her family from France. *"But, dearest, you don't know what I suffer at feeling myself so far away, at thinking while I was happy here my father was going into exile – that everyone, relations and friends, were with him and had at least the comfort of seeing how their enthusiasm and sympathy softened his grief. Do you forget that I was French and have still the right to love France passionately, and that I, too, know what exile means, all the pain and bitterness contained in that word? I think no one feels it more than I. Don't suppose that I have forgotten my early years, the profound impression the very name of my country made upon me when, as a child, I was told about it; and think what a grief it has been to me not to be with my parents in the midst of their sorrow...You know me so well that you will understand how I must suffer and yet try to keep up appearances, and it does me good to write to you just as I should talk. Without my husband, who was almost as sad as I, I don't know how I should have got through the last few days. I should be so happy if only these frightful politics had not come to throw us here into anxiety and mourning."*[36]

While adjusting to her marriage and new country, Amelia could not help but be preoccupied with her family's fate. To her confidant the Duchess of Braganza wrote, *"You ask me if I am happy, yes, dearest, I am exceedingly happy, and I wish you, who love me, could read the joy that fills my heart. I get on very well in my new life; my husband's parents are most affectionate to me; high and low continue showing me the same sympathy. In fact, but for the anxiety about France, I should be perfectly happy."*[37]

Amelia had her sorrows and as she was soon to discover the family she had married into had sorrows of their own.

Chapter IX

The Turbulent Eighties

A month after his son's marriage in August of 1886 Luis traveled to Great Britain where Queen Victoria left a detailed account of his visit: *"He was most affectionate & friendly, embracing me warmly, & kissing & pressing my hand. He is quite the same good kind Louis, whom dearest Albert used to chaff & laugh at, & has remained quite unchanged, excepting that he has grown very fat, & like his mother, but he has not lost his hair, nor has it become gray. He had tears in his eyes, when he came & thought of the frequent visits he paid us, – 2 or 3 with his dear Brother, & several alone. It made us both feel sad. We took him into the Drawing room & stayed there a little while talking. He was here last in 65, – 20 years ago!...Louis talked a great deal to me, confidentially & affectionately, of his troubles & difficulties."*[1]

Indeed the 1880s would prove to be a difficult period for Luis and the other Braganzas as strains were beginning to show in their relationships, particularly in that of Luis and Maria Pia.

While Luis had great affection for his wife, particularly in the first decade of their union, he had always been a discretely unfaithful husband. Within a year of his marriage Luis was writing to his good friend Prince Oscar of his continuing enjoyment of women. The Swedish Prince had enthusiastically responded, *"I'd like very much to come see you in Lisbon...You know that I haven't become blind despite marriage, I feel totally willing to admire the beautiful Portuguese."*[2]

Luis would become quite angry on this friend's behalf when newspapers in 1865 gleefully reported on Oscar's own amorous episode with a woman who seems to have tried to benefit financially from the affair. *"Devil of a newspaper column...no one can slip up without them knowing...like what happened to you in Paris with that actress of dramatic follies who...tortured the pure life of an honest man."*[3] Luis clearly adhered to the belief prevalent of the men of his era that extramarital affairs in no way compromised a man's integrity.

By 1867 the sophisticated Empress Eugenie, herself married to a philanderer, recognized Luis's persistent love for women. In a coquettish letter she playfully scolded the King and even invited him into her confidence. But the Empress' letter also reveals her condescending attitude towards Maria Pia's saintly sister Clotilde, who shunned the affectations assumed by Parisian society, including her Bonaparte in-laws: *"I will wait for our next interview to tell you all my thoughts, that is I have complete confidence in* (you in) *regards to matters of state, but the remaining portion... I will wait for the exhibition for being a good occasion for you to see Paris, likewise the Queen and then we will speak amicably of these things without scaring Clotilde too much."*[4]

Not all of Luis's dalliances were lighthearted. When in his thirties Luis wrote his own secret will in which he made no mention of his wife, but left bequests for one of his mistresses, the artist Marina Mota, and their illegitimate son Pedro Pretti. While it is clear Marina Mota and this son were special to Luis, the date of the conception of this will is also of particular significance. Composed on October 18, 1869, this testament was drawn up during a particularly difficult period in Maria Pia's life. The Queen had finally emerged from her bouts of depression, only to be confronted by the morganatic marriages of her father and father-in-law. While Luis's goodness, according to the Minister Julio de Vilhena, was revealed at every step in his relations with the Queen as in his affection and love for his wife he had a kind of compassion for this sensitive and nervous woman, the King was at times frustrated and impatient with her melancholy.[5] A key characteristic of depression is withdrawal from one's surroundings, and the embittered Luis clearly at some point felt emotionally abandoned by his wife. Perhaps this testament was written with the intention to punish Maria Pia, as it appears over time Luis changed his mind and never followed through with having the will witnessed which would have legalized the document.

It was, however, in the 1880s that the King, using the pseudonym of Dr. Travers, accompanied by his friend and personal secretary Dr. Magalhaes Coutinho, openly searched horse races, bullfights, and theaters for ladies with whom to conduct affairs.[6]

Maria Pia had knowledge of her husband's liaisons, which although she considered *"a little crazy,"*[7] would benevolently refer to as *"out of doors amusements."*[8] She tried to turn a blind eye to her husband's indiscretions for this was a tradition she had been raised in, with her father often boasting, *"Know...that all the princes of the House of Savoy are rouges. But remember, all our princesses are virtuous."*[9] This stance, however, would become increasingly difficult for Maria Pia to maintain when Luis ceased to be discreet and began the most publicized of his affairs with the twenty-year-old blonde actress Rosa Damasceno, who ironically bore a slight resemblance to the Queen. Luis was so besotted he once even snuck Rosa into the palace. Maria Pia showed her awareness of the situation by shoving her lace handkerchief into the locked keyhole of the room where the paramour of the King was received.[10] On another occasion Luis asked his wife to select jewels that he later offered his ladylove, cruelly taking Maria Pia to the theater to see the effect of these same jewels upon the younger woman.

Maria Pia tried to repress the pain that Luis's unfaithfulness caused her, but it was a losing battle, and she once again began to suffer from attacks of melancholy. It was during this period that the Marquesa de Rio Maior recalled her Queen's often-depressed plea to distract her. However, in the ensuing amusement Maria Pia's eccentric streak would occasionally emerge and she *"would apparently without reason, suddenly start in chorus."*[11]

In lighter moments the two women would walk together and Maria Pia would relate *"interesting details of her life."*[12] It was thus little by little and indirectly that the Marquesa was learning to love and admire the extraordinary courage that the Queen showed in the face of adversity as well as deploring the grand misfortune Maria Pia endured.[13]

The one bright spot in the 1880s for Maria Pia was the birth of her first grandchild. On May 21, 1887 Amelia delivered a son, the Prince of Beira, christened Luis Filipe in honor of both of his grandfathers. For the moment of his birth *"little Luis,"* as he was affectionately known within the family, held a special place in Maria Pia's heart. She loved nothing more than to take the infant for a stroll in the morning through Lisbon's streets, always returning him to the Belem Palace at 12 o'clock in time for his feeding. It was on one of their many outings together that the populace staged such a manifestation of homage that this usually correct sovereign for once let her mask slip in public. As the Queen raised her tiny grandson for all to see Maria Pia made no effort to conceal the tears of happiness that poured down her face.

She was likewise delighted when Luis Filipe was left in her care. Shortly after his birth Carlos and Amelia, as Luis and Maria Pia's representatives, went to London to attend the celebrations to commensurate the fifty-year reign of Queen Victoria. Their visit would also allow Amelia to see her family, who had once again chosen England as their home in exile. Assured of the tender care Luis Filipe would receive under Maria Pia's protection, Carlos was comfortable with his and his wife's decision to leave their son behind. *"We are happy we sent little Luis to Ajuda, where he will be completely under your guard,"* Carlos summarily, but satisfactorily wrote from abroad. *"My mother knows well, without my saying of new, how much I am rested and confident when She* [sic] *answers for my son."*[14]

Still the separation from their small son was difficult for the new parents, particularly his mother. *"You understand what it cost me,"* Amelia wrote Maria Pia contritely from London, *"and how much I lament being so far from you."*[15] Soon, however, Amelia and Carlos had good news to impart as they would shortly confirm that Amelia was again pregnant. While assuring his mother that Amelia was under the care of the best doctors in England, Carlos continued to write of their gratitude for the loving attention Maria Pia bestowed upon their firstborn. *"You can not imagine the pleasure we feel for knowing…that you tend our little son with the same affection that you dedicated to your sons."*[16]

Although Maria Pia was pleased with this turn of events, Luis was increasingly frustrated by his family's behavior. He was particularly critical of his daughter-in-law's decision to leave her baby behind. Luis wrote to his sister of his concerns and of other woes, primarily pertaining to his family's spending habits. Antonia did her best to comfort the King, offering an explanation for Amelia's behavior: *"Amelia…I think she spends too much…It is alright to spend when you need to…but I am certain if Amelia has many children, Maria will be jealous…but she* [Amelia] *has the figure for it…I would never have left my children alone…but you must remember that Amelia is French and that in France they leave their children alone. They are more careless of children than the Portuguese and pay people to care for their children...It would be better if she would raise the other children herself."*[17]

In her letter Antonia made reference to Maria Pia becoming jealous if Amelia produced many children and her prediction in all fairness has a valid point. Unfortunately, the role allocated to women in the Nineteenth Century was to marry and bear many children, hopefully males. A woman's self worth was tied to fulfilling her duties as wife and mother and if she failed to become a mother then the blame was laid squarely on her shoulders never on the male partner. While Maria Pia had successfully produced two boys, her third pregnancy had resulted in a stillbirth rendering her incapable of bearing further children. If Maria Pia subscribed to this Nineteenth Century mindset that she had failed in fulfilling her duty by her inability to bear more children it may have indeed proven painful for the still youthful Queen to watch her daughter-in-law produce the large family that she had been unable to. But it is also important to note that Maria Pia's potential for jealousy was only Antonia's opinion and the princess could have been projecting her own feelings of inadequacy onto her sister-in-law as due to ill health the Princess, herself, had been unable to have further children after the birth of her own third son.

Regardless of whether Maria Pia had the potential for jealously, with her adoration of children, Maria Pia relished her newfound role as grandmother, and with her longing for a daughter unfulfilled she doubtlessly hoped one day to have a granddaughter to love and spoil. She eagerly anticipated the arrival of her second grandchild.

In October of 1887 the Duke and Duchess of Braganza returned to Portugal, where at the wish of Amelia they settled into Vila Viçosa to await the birth of their second child. Unfortunately, only tragedy awaited them there. Somehow the cradle where of the seven month old Luis Filipe slept caught on fire, and according to tradition it was Amelia who saved her son from the flames. However, the correspondence between Maria Pia and Luis tell a very different story.

Initially, all seemed well. Luis Filipe had sustained some burns from the accident, but his recuperation went smoothly. Throughout that November Amelia regularly sent Luis Filipe's concerned grandmother updates on his recovery. "*The scabs of his burns are beginning to fall!* [off], *he is...more cheerful and sleeps admirably.*"[18] She was also quick to assure her mother-in-law that "little Luis" was consuming the chicken soup Maria Pia endorsed as the Queen firmly believed chicken broth was essential for the maintenance of health. Maria Pia, herself, would partake of this substance everyday.

But the anxious Queen would not be content until she could examine her grandson herself. She quickly set off for Vila Viçosa and from her first night there Maria Pia wrote her husband a detailed account of the frightening incident: *"Amelia and all the others were having dinner when they heard a wet nurse scream fire. Turning they saw her run in her nightgown with the child in her arms, down the hall...where they caught up with her trying to flee with the boy into the street, fearing it seems that the fire might spread throughout the whole palace; she was mad with terror. Then everyone ran to the child's bedroom and Carlos and the other men…were able to extinguish the fire in a few hours."*[19] Of the heroic woman who saved their grandson, Maria Pia wrote in Portuguese that she was not *"embarrassed"* at being seen in only her nightclothes and that this confidence was *"priceless."*[20]

Unfortunately, Maria Pia did not specifically identify the wet nurse and her name is lost to history. Nor does it appear this courageous woman received a monetary reward for her brave act like the lighthouse keeper had in similar circumstances.

Maria Pia had barely returned to Lisbon when days later she once again received tragic news from Vila Viçosa. On December 14 while only in her sixth month of pregnancy, Amelia went into premature labor, resulting in the breech birth of a daughter, Maria Ana, who sadly lived for only two hours. Fortunately, the exhausted Amelia was able to hold her daughter briefly, before Maria Ana's cries grew so faint that the attending physician realized the child would not survive. As a last resort he took the infant into another room, where he dipped her into water and rubbed her frail limbs to stimulate circulation, but to no avail.

It was Maria Pia who took charge in the devastating aftermath, as the traumatized Amelia was now suffering from a fever and the doctor believed it was in her best interest to withhold the news of her daughter's death for the time being. After spending some time with her agitated daughter-in-law, the Queen insisted on viewing her deceased granddaughter, who she poignantly described to her husband as *"very small, but perfect and beautiful, with well defined features."*[21] Maria Pia then registered the birth and made preparations to accompany the remains to Lisbon for burial. Taking into account that Luis was now suffering from ill health, she wrote to her husband in brief detail of the funeral arrangements and determinedly decreed it was *"…best that you don't even think about this and that you speak no more of this – this is what I desire."*[22]

There was also perhaps an element of self preservation in Maria Pia's decree to her husband, as talk between the two of them concerning their granddaughter's death would doubtlessly bring up painful memories of the stillbirth of their own son. Yet throughout this difficult period the Queen, whatever her inner turmoil, remained stoic, a tower of strength that her suffering family could lean upon.

Amelia, in particular, was in need of consolation, and desperate for answers as to why she went into premature labor. To explain the loss of their granddaughter Maria Pia proposed to Luis that if he approved they should maintain that what happened was the result of shock due to the fire, which seemed true enough as the distraught Amelia asked her mother-in-law repeatedly about whether this could have been the cause.[23] If it comforted Amelia to believe this then Maria Pia would support it.

Thus, the theory that the shock over the potentially fatal accident her son had been involved in as the cause of Amelia going into premature labor was begun by Maria Pia.[24] But the Queen, who believed in giving credit where credit was due, did not ever suggest that it was her daughter-in-law who saved *"little Luis."* French historians, however, particularly Lucien Corpechot and Laurence Catinot-Crost, in their attempt to glorify their subject, embellished upon the dramatic events, casting Amelia in the sole role of heroine, while ignoring the facts. So for more than a hundred years this version of events has been the accepted norm, with the poor wet nurse never receiving the accolades she deserves.

Once back in Lisbon Maria Pia kept in constant contact with her son, offering her support and expressing concern over her daughter-in-law's physical and mental well being as she had finally been informed of Maria Ana's death. A grateful Carlos would telegraph, *"My Dear Mother shows herself as always so good and affectionate with us. Amelia continues the best as possible (considering the circumstances)."*[25] In his name and that of his wife Carlos quickly invited his mother to return to Vila Viscosa: *"We have so much love for you that when you leave from here it seems to us that the house becomes empty."*[26] And finally when relating how Amelia was dealing with the trauma of losing their daughter, Carlos revealed, *"It is proper that Amelia speaks to me of the death of the little one…the shock will lessen. Anyhow she is very sad."*[27]

At the beginning of the following year Amelia finally felt well enough to write to Maria Pia herself. *"I am very sad my dear Mother,"* she acknowledged, *"and in this sadness you have been so good to me."*[28] That January Maria Pia's sister-in-law Queen Margherita of Italy also wrote to her friend Princess Ludwig Ferdinand of Bavaria concerning the tragedy the Braganzas had endured. *"My niece Amelie* [sic] *is now somewhat better. What must not the poor woman have gone through; my sister-in-law wrote to me quite in despair about the health of the poor girl; she loves her daughter-in-law tenderly, and tells me she is very much beloved in Portugal."*[29]

While Margherita's heart was in the right place, her sentiments were unfortunately an exaggeration. The relationship between Maria Pia and Amelia at this time could hardly be called loving, nor was Amelia particularly popular in Portugal, which was in itself the root of the problem between the two women. In the very beginning of their relationship Maria Pia had hopes of forming a close bond with her daughter-in-law, and had written optimistically to Luis: *"The marriage goes well, and I believe that Amelia is…very good for him* (Carlos)*…She is listening to me and is very intelligent and I believe she likes me."*[30] Amelia, however, despite claiming she was *"very glad to know"*[31] Maria Pia did not care for her mother-in-law. She disapproved of her Maria Pia's extravagance, but overall she was jealous of the Queen's great popularity with the Portuguese, who had not wholeheartedly embraced their new Duchess of Braganza.

Antonia, who had visited Portugal for the christening of *"little Luis,"* had gotten to know the two women sufficiently well,[32] and having witnessed how they interacted with one another had foreseen the difficulties that lay ahead. To her brother Antonia had confided her *"fear that* [Maria Pia] *won't get on well with Amelia who is…also short tempered; two strong headed* [women] *never get on well together."*[33] Antonia's fears had proved all too true.

Within a mere four months of the death of Maria Ana there erupted a civil war between the courts of the Belem and Ajuda Palaces. Amelia was intensely competitive with her authoritative mother-in-law, who was a stickler for protocol, and Carlos, anxious to establish an identity separate from his parents, sided with his wife. In April of 1888 Carlos was heard to make bitter complaints against his mother.[34] Maria Pia, according to her son, seemed determined to steal all the philanthropic ideas and incentives of Amelia, desiring to keep for herself the monopoly on charity.[35] The previous month was when the great fire in Oporto had occurred, and Maria Pia's relief efforts had won such acclaim. At his wife's side, Carlos was frustrated by their inability to participate and they were jealous of Maria Pia's appeal with their subjects. But even if Maria Pia so desired to take all the credit for the Braganzas' philanthropic endeavors this would have been difficult to accomplish as Amelia always deliberately planted news of her charitable activities in the press.

Luis voiced his displeasure at his family's squabbles to the one Braganza he could always rely on, his loyal sister Antonia. "*Poor Brother what a pity to ask me… what I have to say on your annoyances,*" the Princess consoled. "[I don't mind] *it is a pity that Carlos does not work well with his Mother but in my opinion that is not really easy, and for Amelia quite unpleasant.*"[36]

As Antonia's letter was also demonstrating, she, too, was turning against Maria Pia. As her brother's confidant Antonia was well aware that the couple was having difficulties. She particularly resented the worry that Maria Pia's extravagance caused the King, and would occasionally send Luis money to help cover Maria Pia's expenses. When Maria Pia's brother Amedeo had remarried in January of 1888 (his second wife was their own niece, Princess Laetitia Bonaparte, the only daughter of their sister Clotilde), the Queen had spent extravagantly on her toilette for the wedding in Vienna. "*She must have had lovely dresses for the marriage in Turin,*" Antonia had dryly commented on Maria Pia's purchases, "*according to the descriptions of the magazines they had to be the prettiest; and the most expensive.*"[37]

Maria Pia had for some time shown an all-consuming need to possess the best for herself and her family. This latest shopping spree could have been in compensation for her unhappiness at her deteriorating relationships with her husband and eldest son or perhaps simply her desire to present herself suitably as Queen.[38] But if it was in compensation for her melancholy Maria Pia had found another source of comfort to the dismay of her family. She had finally taken a lover of her own.

Chapter X

Breaking Point

Ever since her arrival in Portugal the young and beautiful Queen had attracted the attention of the opposite sex, but the inexperienced teen had always been uncomfortable when confronted with their passion. Malicious courtiers, however, delighted in relating all the titillating details.

By 1864 Senhor Catalania, an aid to the Italian minister in Lisbon, had become infatuated with the Queen, and in his enamored state he began stalking her. He spied on Maria Pia through his binoculars while they were at the San Carlos Theater and shadowed her movements whenever possible. While at the Sintra Palace his lovelorn gazes could no longer be ignored and Luis had finally had enough. With Victor Emanuel's approval the obsessed Catalania was dismissed and given twenty-four hours to vacate Portugal.

Catalania was not alone in his fascination for Maria Pia. Poets found their stunning new Queen to be an inspiring muse. *"I have for her an ardent passion,"* admitted the poet Fernandes Costa.[1] Another bard who developed a grand passion for Maria Pia was Luis de Campos. When she was in attendance at the San Carlos Theater, he could never take his eyes off her. If the Queen was not in attendance then de Campos would search desperately throughout other theaters in the district in pursuit of her. The Royal Family was well aware of Campos' fixation and used the situation to tease Maria Pia. During intervals at the theater, Ferdinand had never failed to ask his daughter-in-law, *"Maria have you visited the poet?"*[2] His son Augusto always mimicked, *"Maria have you visited L. de C.?"*[3] While Augusto was simply imitating his father, there was always a malicious undertone to Ferdinand's taunting as he enjoyed the Queen's discomfort.

When there weren't any salacious incidents such as these episodes to exploit, tale-bearers had to create scandals where there were none, and soon malicious court gossip linked her name to numerous other males. Two supposed lovers attributed to Maria Pia were the Portuguese Minister Fontes Pereira de Melo and the Conde de Vale de Reis, as both men were devoted to their Queen; this devotion would be spitefully misconstrued by the troublemakers. Maria Pia and Fontes Pereia worked well together, and though no poet she had inspired de Melo to put pen to paper, composing a sonnet dedicated to the Queen with the verse: *"I am yours, Senhora, in all that I do."*[4] When Fontes Pereira de Melo died, Maria Pia had wept openly at his funeral. Thus, it was concluded they had to have been more than just friends. The Conde de Vale de Reis, the son of the Duke of Loulé and successor to the title, was a member of Maria Pia's household. He served her loyally all his life and was one of Maria Pia's closest friends, but given his swarthy good looks, gossip maintained there had to be more to their relationship than just a platonic friendship despite the lack of evidence to support this accusation.

A curious Maria Pia once asked of one of her ladies-in-waiting about the rumors concerning herself and the Conde de Vale de Reis. *"Why is it said that I like the Vale de Reis,"* inquired the Queen.[5] Her lady had responded, *"Those who accuse Your Majesty say that you very much like the bronzed type."*[6]

Maria Pia was clearly bothered by the rumors and falsehoods, but the manner in which she proudly conducted herself when faced with years of slander earned her a whole new set of admirers. Malheiro Dias, who venerated the Queen for the way she held her head high, wrote of his esteem for this *"figure of tragedy, whose red head rises above petty human misery."*[7]

Maria Pia had admirers aplenty and clearly she could have indulged in affairs throughout her marriage if she had the inclination; instead, she had always chosen to be faithful to the husband she had come to love. However, the late 1880s was an entirely different story as Luis's chronic and flagrant infidelities had finally driven a wedge between the couple. A part of Maria Pia still cared for her husband, but while her letters to Luis from this period are affectionate they lack the passion they two had achieved in the first decade of their marriage.

It was probably in 1886 that Maria Pia finally began her own affair with the handsome silver-haired Thomas de Sousa Rosa, three years her senior. Ironically, Thomas had led the defense against Saldanha's attack on the Ajuda Palace, and perhaps in recognition of his service Rosa had come to belong to Luis's Military House, which had brought him into closer proximity with the Royal Family.[8]

To this date no correspondence between the lovers has surfaced so we will perhaps never know the true depth of their emotions for one another; but human nature being what it is, attention from the handsome Rosa undoubtedly made Maria Pia feel desirable and attractive again after suffering private and public humiliation at her husband's hands and she can be forgiven for trying to find some personal happiness. The only documentation available to historians on this rather shadowy period of Maria Pia's life comes from Antonia's letters to her brother. Unfortunately, Antonia burned most of her correspondence before her death so we do not have Luis's letters to his sister on the subject, but Portuguese archives are full of Antonia's indignant writings to Luis on the matter.

When Antonia learned of the affair, she was outraged on Luis's behalf and in her affront developed a distinct animosity towards her brother's wife, of whom she had once been rather fond. In the beginning of their relationship the two women had been prepared to love one another as sisters for Luis's sake. During their engagement Maria Pia had written of her admiration for Antonia, whom Luis had described to his fiancée *"as a creature of affection."*[9] *"How pretty Antonia is,"* Maria Pia had commented alluding to a picture of the Princess. *"How good and kind she must be. I am sure I will love her as a true sister."*[10]

When the two sisters-in-law had finally met in person in 1883, Antonia had warmed to Maria Pia immediately, declaring, *"I cannot say how much Maria pleases me and I am regretful to see her depart."*[11] For her part Maria Pia had found her sister-in-law affectionate but in very poor health. Worried for Antonia's well being, Maria Pia believed Luis could raise his sister's spirits if he'd write to her more often with news of Portugal since Antonia had remained so attached to her homeland.

Maria Pia's kindness, however, would only be repaid by vitriol when Antonia learned from her brother of all the happenings in Portugal. Antonia, who had once happily called Maria Pia her friend, could now no longer even bring herself to write her sister-in-law's name. Starting late in 1887 Antonia would refer to Maria Pia only as 'X' in her letters.

The first mention Antonia made of her sister-in-law's affair occurs on October 26, 1887 when she wrote to her brother with shocking forthrightness, "*I found it extraordinary that X received as a present a glass box with a rose in the middle, the funeral of this person would not be such a bad thing.*"[12]

While Antonia absolutely condemned the Queen's behavior, her husband Leopold, having knowledge of Luis's own lifestyle, looked upon Maria Pia's conduct with relative benevolence, which upset and perplexed Antonia greatly.[13] "*Leopold does not believe well what I say to him about X, he always replies that he knows everything,*" she incredulously exclaimed when writing Luis. "*He would be the first to be terribly jealous if the same thing happened to him, certainly that is not the case with me, therefore it is not clear to me how he can still find reasons to excuse X; I can not tell you how eaten up with anger I am about this.*" As she continued to expound upon her anger she wanted her brother to vent his own frustration with Rosa instead of his more passive approach of sending Rosa on overseas diplomatic missions in order to get him out of the picture. "*You know what I would do with R? I would prohibit the sentries letting him in and when he went to the Queen's room they should send for you. Then you could say everything to him and have a reason not to live in the same house as her.*"[14]

Along with worrying about the affront to her brother's dignity, Antonia was also concerned at how Amelia and her nephews would handle the situation. "*Does Amelia ever talk to you about this,*" Antonia wondered. "*Does Carlos know anything about his mother? It seems that in time it will not be possible for her to return to Italy, or live in another palace like Cascais. As she is ill it would create a bad impression if you sent her away and would cause a scandal. Scandals are what you want to avoid. It would also damage your daughter-in-law, since for Amelia it would not be easy to live with a mother-in-law of this nature, and for your children it is not good either. What will they think when they see their Mother as she is?*"[15]

Maria Pia's affair was indeed common knowledge within the family, with Carlos and Amelia taking the same intolerant stance as Antonia. While the young couple hypocritically looked upon Luis's transgressions with amused tolerance, they outright condemned Maria Pia's behavior, with Amelia even going so far as to declare her mother-in-law a modern day Messalina.[16] Alas, it was the accepted norm of the period for men to conduct affairs, while women who sought pleasure outside of the marriage bed were considered immoral, and Amelia scrupulously adhered to this chauvinistic moral code. She would not, however, find it so amusing when in due course her own husband decided to follow in his father's footsteps. Although Amelia would eventually suffer the same pain and humiliation resulting from a husband's infidelity, she does not appear to have ever gained any greater understanding or sympathy for Maria Pia, nor did she ever relent in her harsh moralistic judgment of her mother-in-law.

Made more than aware of the double standard that her son and his wife held her to, Maria Pia couldn't help but now notice the change in Antonia's attitude and she confronted Luis with the situation. In her response Antonia contemplated on who could have been the Queen's informant and defended her convictions, which were just as uncompromising as those of Amelia. *"You have said here that X had said to you that I do not like her and that I do not think well of her, I have thought much on this, and I am certain that it was Rio Maior who told her."* Deploring affairs, Antonia gently scolded her brother about what she had recently learned of his own transgressions, but like Amelia she found similar behavior in a woman inexcusable. Such conduct she explained was *"bad in any woman, but in the position of X, doubly bad because it gives a bad example to all society and to all of the country."* Antonia even speculated on the political damage that could result from the gossip surrounding the affair. *"And this is good for the social democrats…this is what gives them pleasure when they can speak on royal people in this way."*[17]

Maria Pia would indeed be reproached with malicious gossip, which provoked her volatile temper. Furious that anyone would have the audacity to comment upon her behavior, she would indignantly protest, *"They can talk until they explode."*[18] With the scurrilous gossip at court combined with Antonia turning against her, along with her already troubled relationships with Luis, Carlos, and Amelia, Maria Pia must have begun to feel increasingly isolated within the royal family. She would, however, have one Braganza whose devotion to her remained unwavering, her youngest son Afonso.

By 1888 Afonso had grown into an uncomplicated young man. He was as described by one servant in the Ajuda Palace as *"very good, a little brusque, but always wanting to be useful."*[19] The Prince revered his mother, and out of respect for her wouldn't even curse in front of her.

Afonso was likewise devoted to his brother Carlos, who although quite fond of Afonso in return, was concerned with his lack of intellectual pursuits, and he complained to their mother about his teenaged brother's disregard for his lessons. Luis shared his eldest son's concerns and tried to enforce a strict atmosphere of discipline to promote a more academic mindset within his younger son, but to no avail. The King could become quite curt when thwarted by Afonso's disinterest, and Thomaz de Mello Breyner recalled an incident when the two friends had skipped their lessons whereupon Luis had become *"really angry, threatening the Prince with being sent to Alfeite without my company and with my being locked up in a very strict college."*[20]

However, despite his father and brother's censor Afonso's abiding interest would always remain in physical activity. From performing daring stunts on bicycles he advanced to automobiles. The Prince was the first to introduce automobiles to Portugal, and he would drive furiously through the Lisbon streets, shouting at startled passers-by to get out of the way.[21] These antics earned him the nickname "*O Arreda*" – "*the Speedy*" – or the one from whom you needed to move back from.[22] Thankfully, Afonso never hurt anyone for as one amazed pedestrian explained, "*The Prince drives like a cyclone, but he has eyes.*"[23]

On a more serious note, Afonso's love of daring did have its benefits. He admired the occupation of firefighters and eventually organized and installed a group of volunteer firemen at the court of the Ajuda Palace. It was a project that both Maria Pia and Luis disapproved of as he was putting himself in danger, but Afonso remained determined. The Prince trained alongside the volunteers, and would later prove essential in actual firefights. At the infamous Chiado fire Afonso had mounted the fire escape alone, and against all advice visited all the floors of the burning building, rescuing many people in the process.[24] So afraid was this intrepid daredevil of missing a fire alarm that he had seven different telephones installed in his apartments at the Ajuda Palace to be alerted of any outbreak.[25] Such was Afonso's dedication to this activity that in 1902 he was nominated the honorary commander of the municipal body of firemen in Lisbon.

When not occupied with fighting fires or his regimental duties, Afonso suffered the fate that befell so many second sons within a dynasty. He simply didn't have much to do. Afonso sought diversion at bullfights and the theater, but it was another of his amusements that would eventually alarm his mother. Like his father and elder brother, Afonso had an eye for the ladies. But Afonso resembled his maternal grandfather in that his preference was for women from the lower classes, and he was known to frequent the brothels of Lisbon. When the Ajuda Palace began receiving anonymous letters describing his amorous escapades, Maria Pia decided it was time to find the twenty-three year-old Afonso a bride.

The Queen and her son departed from Lisbon on July 30, 1888 – their tour included important destinations: Paris, Prague, and Vienna. Luis also left Lisbon on the same day but with a very different travel itinerary, with planned stops in Spain, Sweden, and Germany. This was to be Luis's last grand voyage and his visits to Sweden and Germany would be particularly poignant. In Sweden he was entertained by his good friend Oscar, now King, and in Berlin he was received with honors by the Kaiser. Afterwards Luis met with the Kaiser's widowed mother, the Empress Frederick, and he paid his respects to the deceased Wilhelm I's grave on which he laid a ribbon with the Portuguese colors. Once these formalities were taken care of Luis could enjoy a private visit with his sister in Sigmaringen, where Maria Pia and their son finally joined him. Given Antonia's animosity for her sister-in-law this must not have been a particularly enjoyable visit from Maria Pia's perspective. She doubtlessly felt relief when the trio could finally depart Sigmaringen for Vienna to visit the Emperor Franz Joseph. Maria Pia also used this portion of their trip to conduct some shopping for her ever-changing toilette. The Braganzas then departed Austria for Italy to attend the nuptials of Maria Pia's brother Amedeo on

September 11, 1888.

The American author M. E. W. Sherwood, a witness to the festivities, left a vivid account of the nuptials: *"I have seen a number of brilliant fetes in Europe, but I think the week at Turin which I spent looking at the mediaeval festivities, invoked in honor of that curious event the marriage of the Prince Amedeo, Duke d'Aosta, to his niece Letitia* [sic] *Bonaparte, was, perhaps, the most interesting in the way of sight-seeing. In the first place, the near relationship of the royal pair shocked us, but…Turin was very fond of Amedeo, for he lived there, and his manners were most attractive… Turin could not sufficiently decorate itself with banners, flowers, flags, ribbons, and roses. Triumphal arches opened every street…The bands of music, the files of soldiers, the illuminated evenings…all was beauty…Every day some royalty would arrive. Queen Maria Pia of Portugal…came first, with her husband and son. She, a striking Italian blonde, with red hair, shared the favor of the public with Amedeo, as one of the most regal of all this kingly race, both of manners and gracious courage."*[26]

In the controversial gowns she had purchased for the event – that had proven so distressing to her sister-in-law – Maria Pia at least publicly fulfilled her royal duty as she represented her exalted position to the masses with distinction. For the actual marriage ceremony, Maria Pia wore an elaborate ensemble entirely of blue with the author Mrs. Sherwood confirming that the Queen was adorned *"all in blue, with the arms of Portugal embroidered on her blue velvet train. She wore a net-work crown of sapphires in her red hair, and it was most becoming."*[27]

With her brother's wedding out of the way Maria Pia could now concentrate on finding Afonso a bride of his own. Luis's health, however, continued to deteriorate and he cut his portion of the trip short, returning to Portugal on October 15. Although Maria Pia was concerned for Luis, she was determined to fulfill her original mission. But she did worry about how her continued absence from Portugal would be perceived within the country, and asked her eldest son and husband to keep her updated on what was being said. Maria Pia was particularly concerned with their ministers' opinions, overall Barros Gomes, the Minister of Foreign Affairs.[28] *"This is in secret, what does he say…about Afonso?"* she questioned her husband. *"Does he see in this any inconvenience for our family and country?"*[29] Later Maria Pia would ask Luis to meet in secret with the President of the Council, Luciano de Castro, to solicit his opinion on the subject.[30]

Her delay in returning was indeed a source of discontent within Portugal as it was felt that the Queen was remiss in her duty by not returning with her ill husband. The President of the Counsel, Luciano de Castro, sadly explained to one diplomat: *"I know that this is another time the Queen is with the Infant! What nonsense! In a court as formal as this, what a sad impression is made by these travels in pursuit of a fiancee!!"*[31]

Despite Carlos's reports of the disapproval of their subjects, Maria Pia continued on with her journey. First she and Afonso went to Bavaria to look over the daughters of Prine Leopold, and then to Salzburg to inspect a daughter of the Grand Duke of Tuscany. This young lady made a favorable impression upon the

Queen, who reported to her husband, *"She is very lovely, fine and distinguished, she has chestnut hair, not tall, but nice. She pleased Afonso a lot; she converses very well, dresses with simplicity, knows music…She also pleased me alot."*[32]

From Salzburg mother and son traveled to Vienna to see the Archduchess Carolina, and then they went on to Paris. During this time Luis celebrated his birthday, and Maria Pia sent her husband an affectionate greeting, apologizing for missing his special day.[33] Still, she considered finding Afonso a wife her greater duty: *"But you know that I have another duty to fulfill and that is the search of a Princess for Afonso."*[34]

Finally, Maria Pia and Afonso traveled from Paris to Brussels to see the sixteen-year-old Princess Clementine, the youngest daughter of King Leopold II of Belgium. *"Afonso seems to me to find her very nice,"* Maria Pia informed Luis, but she wasn't sure of their son's preference. *"I do not know if he likes her better than the others. I know nothing more having only interrogated him a little on this subject."*[35]

Maria Pia, herself, had made a favorable impression upon the Belgium Royal Family, but Afonso appears to have given offence. Antonia would write to her brother what she had learned of the Braganzas' stay in Brussels. *"In Brussels she pleased very much and she was very polite, but they found that Afonso spoke very little, and that he had not visited Phillipe Flanders* [brother of King Leopold of Belgium and Antonia's brother-in-law, as his wife was Princess Marie of Sigmaringen-Hohenzollern, Leopold's younger sister]…*that scandalized Phillipe; know that I tell you everything since I always suffer to hear talk about people of whom I like."*[36]

Later Antonia would report to her brother the opinion of Archduke Albert on the search of a wife for Afonso. *"Afonso would have to make a trip, but alone to look for a wife, with Maria it is not possible, at least that's what Archduke Albert said to me."*[37] Albert was a first cousin of Maria Pia's mother, and as an adult the Queen maintained a close relationship with her maternal relations respectfully calling this particular cousin "Uncle." On his part Albert had come to love Maria Pia like a daughter instead of a niece, but he was aware of how the situation presented itself. By accompanying Afonso on this trip, Maria Pia gave every appearance of being the proverbial possessive mother, with Afonso allocated to the role of the weak willed younger son. While it is true that Maria Pia and Afonso were extremely close, with Afonso heavily reliant upon his mother's judgment, one could argue in this instance that Afonso was showing some strength of character by his resistance, as evidenced by his lack of following the social graces, of being pushed into a marriage for the simple sake of marriage.

While staying in Brussels, Maria Pia was struggling to come to terms with Afonso's apathy towards marriage, when she received even more disturbing news from home. She had in the past received several letters from Carlos imploring her to return home as she was receiving harsh criticism in the Portuguese newspapers, but it was in the letter that Carlos sent to Brussels on October 26 in which he told his mother that Afonso's pursuit of a wife was a source of ridicule to journalists and demanded she put a stop to her travels that infuriated Maria Pia.

Believing Carlos exaggerated the situation as Luis curiously maintained that everything was just fine in his own letters, she absolutely refused to be dictated to by her eldest son. Deeply hurt Maria Pia wrote to Luis in her first rush of anger: *"I assure that on the day in which I read everything I became horribly annoyed and terribly offended against all this. Especially them* [Carlos and Amelia]. *They do not know that; they may not and should not judge my actions, and even less to let others do that or listen to them. I suffered with that and I was very hurt…I do not admit anyone in this world [has the right] to judge my actions or what I think."*[38] She ended the letter to Luis by saying she would await an explanation from him.[39] When Maria Pia was calmer, she added a postscript. *"I am very sad and tired."*[40]

Maria Pia had not found a wife for Afonso nonetheless she decided in face of all the controversy that it was best to return to Portugal. Upon her arrival, however, Maria Pia further offended the Portuguese when she attended the Sao Carlos Theater with her son Carlos and daughter-in-law. The people, already angry with her for her prolonged absence, felt that it was inappropriate for the Queen to be attending the theater while her husband was ill, and they let their displeasure known by booing her. This must have been a horrible shock for Maria Pia as she had become used to being the recipient of the populace's adulation.

Immediately after this sorry event Carlos, in his name and that of his wife, tried to make amends to his mother for their past disagreements. *"Both of us were deeply upset at the sad scene that happened today in S. Carlos. We don't want to [take part] in intrigues, or make them catch on. Only we said some truths, knowledge of all that everyone was saying…If this pleased or not, we don't know, but what we know is that what we did is with a clear conscience because…we have done our duty and a duty that was sacred because it was for our Queen and for our mother."*[41]

There was another relationship of the Queen's, however, where amends were few and far between. The union of Maria Pia and Luis had finally come to a standstill. Although the couple had initially been able to obtain an affectionate, warm relationship in the early part of their twenty-six year marriage, for the past few years only their duties as King and Queen brought them together to present an united front to the public. Now, Maria Pia believed she could no longer endure the anguish of maintaining this facade, and she decided it was time to return to Italy to live with her sister. This decision would facilitate another kind of crisis for her husband. Luis felt that without his strong willed wife by his side he could no longer reign and he contemplated abdication.

In their partnership Maria Pia had always been the more forceful character. Although Maria Pia had been basically little more than a child when she had arrived in Portugal, it was she, according to the author Fialho de Almeida, who had taught Luis to be a king.[42] Maria Pia hadn't received as an extensive education as Luis, but she proved to have sounder instincts. Many believed she possessed better political sense than her husband, and her correspondence with Luis, particularly through the years of 1872–1886,[43] show her advice and recommendations to Luis on how to deal with political affairs. However, with her determined spirit Maria Pia would always be the stronger personality of the two, and she was the one who was far more adapt at handling difficult ministers as Vital Fontes, a server at the Ajuda Palace, relates, *"The Queen invited them to supper and later she spoke to them, finely or harshly, as she understood."*[44]

Maria Pia proved to be just as adroit at handling the rise of republican sentiments. By the 1880s Luis *"was the victim of some disrespects."*[45] Once when the Royal couple was on their way to a gala, protesters surrounded their carriage and prevented it from moving. *"It was the intervention of Maria Pia that changed the situation. She requested that the coachman open the door to the carriage so that she and her husband would be visible and that he initiate a salute to the King and Queen."*[46] Overcome by the bravery of Their Majesties in their willingness to face them, there was a conversion among the rabble. Maria Pia's quick thinking had transformed an adverse situation into one of the biggest manifestations of popular affection for the Royal Family.[47]

Perhaps Luis would have carried through with this intention of abdicating if it were not for the other strong willed woman in his life, his sister Antonia. When Antonia learned of what her brother was contemplating, she had become horribly distressed. Although Antonia, herself, had in the past on several occasions suggested that Luis and Maria Pia would be better off by maintaining separate residences, she would do her up most to dissuade Luis from abdicating:

"My Brother, I am distressed thinking about you...Dear Brother do not do such a thing, let her go but do not abdicate, that would wound...the heart of the Portuguese, that still now show you so much dedication and love, do not do this if you care for me, since that would make me terribly unhappy...I do not really believe that your position would be pleasant...in the country where you had reigned, after the step is taken it can not be withdrawn and there would be moments of great bitterness; your two healthy sons are certainly good, but when they are in power perhaps they will not be the same. Carlos is very ambitious, and those at times have little fine sentiment for others, do not do this then, you must be content; and you can be satisfied with the progress of Portugal."[48]

In February of 1889 the standstill between Maria Pia and Luis would be resolved when Maria Pia ended her affair with Thomas de Sousa Rosa. Old habits died hard for the Queen as Maria Pia followed a life-long pattern of sacrificing her personal happiness for the sake of duty despite the heavy emotional toll it would eventually take on her well being.

Although Antonia was relieved on Luis's behalf, and would eventually forgive Maria Pia for the affair, for now she still felt some rancor for her sister-in-law. *"How goes your X, still not eating?"* she inquired with contempt. *"Is she going to be ill with this? Or is she just longing for R; that life so extraordinary and little productive must be sad; and it must be unpleasant when one asks oneself at the end of the day what useful and serious things have been done, and one had only walked like in a dream all day long selling and ordering toilettes."*[49]

To say that Maria Pia was upset at her parting from Rosa is putting it mildly. Although Maria Pia had put her obligations before her personal happiness, it was still a bitter pill for her to swallow. Initially, she had sobbed in convulsions, before sinking into a decline, and in her depression she had no appetite. Nursed by the devoted Marquesa de Rio Maior, the queen slowly regained her equilibrium, and it was her strong sense of duty that eventually conquered her fragile emotional state. Maria Pia had made her decision and she would abide by it. She would remain by Luis's side untill the very end.

Chapter XI

Luis "the Popular"

By his late forties Luis did not enjoy good health – he had syphilis, but this was never publicly disclosed so as to protect the image of the King and his wife. Far less embarrassing maladies to acknowledge were his rheumatism and gout, which Luis made worse by consuming masses of meat and potatoes in the mistaken attempt to keep up his strength. Consequently, even walking had now become a difficult task for the King. When his great friend King Oscar of Sweden had come to Lisbon in May of 1888, Luis was not well enough to escort him around the city. It fell to his two sons to show the Swedish sovereign the capital. Deeply frustrated by the restricting side effects of his illnesses, Luis had later written contritely to Oscar, *"But…you forgive me because you know that my friendship is without limits."*[1]

Throughout the marriage Maria Pia, had always been concerned with her husband's well being. Twelve years earlier she had approached Luis about his excessive smoking, which she felt contributed greatly to his feeling poorly. *"I* [strongly] *recommend that you do not smoke,"* she entreated, *"I have so much fear of this for you…if you can not do without them at least reduce* [the cigars] *in number."*[2]

Even after their relationship had deteriorated Maria Pia continued to show an almost maternal concern for her husband's health. In December of 1887 she had written a letter full of advice to Luis, while he was staying at Vila Viçosa: *"Make conversation with your men…for you…to laugh a little, given that I am not there to read to you…Afterwards lay down early, don't conclude with smoking tobacco…close up the windows and doors, don't forget."*[3]

Just as her husband was failing in health, so too was Maria Pia's brother-in-law, Augusto. By October of 1888 the Prince was in torment from pleurisy. Although Antonia had fallen out with Augusto over his *"love for a coquette* [Elise] *so depraved,"* she still cared for him deeply.[4] *"The state of Augusto bothers me,"* the Princess wrote to Luis in concern. *"It seems to me that he is someone who isn't sensible in his health…I ask you…if he can walk or mount a horse or if he tires too much when making movement, perhaps…the Gymnastics in Baden-Baden will make him well, so many people that take treatment there for causes of illness of the heart…have come away with good results."*[5]

However, by the beginning of the following year Antonia anticipated the worst. *"I am prepared to receive the notice of the death of poor Augusto, you know that I have never sympathized with him but now that he is so gravely ill I feel how I care for him, thus I lose that disgust I had for him."*[6]

The comportment of the Countess of Edla with Augusto during his convalescence, however, remained a source of concern for the Royal Family. *"The Countess of Edla came here once and tired him so much that we feared a relapse,"* Carlos reported to his mother when relating a visit of Elise's to the patient recuperating at the Necissadades Palace. *"I was forced to throw her out on the street, and to forbid her from returning again (I ordered this because it is clear that she does not honor the hand extended to her...)...She has ordered all the newspapers to say that she is ill... because of this, that she is not able to go to the Necissadades."*[7]

Augusto, however, would not remain at the Necissadades Palace for long. Fearing how the impeding heat of a summer in Lisbon would affect their illnesses, both of the royal brothers retreated with their family to the cooler climate of the mountainous Sintra.

George Bailey Loring, the United States Minister appointed to Portugal in 1889, saw the Braganzas several times during this period at Sintra. Meeting the Royal Family for the first time at a reception held for Infante Afonso's birthday in July, Loring recorded his impressions of Prince Augusto and the royal couple: *"Dom Augusto has dragged on a feeble existence, broken down, as it is said, by the disease which attacked him more than a century ago. I met him at the reception given at the palace in Cintra* [sic] *on the birthday of Dom Affonso* [sic]*...and had a short conversation with him. He was very tall, and stooping. He bore himself like a feeble man and walked with difficulty."*[8]

At this party Loring also saw the King and Queen for the first time. *"I was introduced by Senhor Barros Gomes, the Minister for Foreign Affairs, to His Majesty, who sat during the reception and offered me a chair by his side. He is a gentleman of taste and talent and culture, speaks well many languages, is a good musician, a first rate English scholar, and a judicious statesman. My conversation with him was interesting, and we discussed the affairs of his kingdom with allusions to the literature of the United States. He very civilly excused his inability to receive me formally on account of his ill health, and assured me that the informal interview we were having would be sufficient to establish my official relations with his government, while my presentation would come hereafter."*[9] Loring was then presented to Queen Maria Pia, whom he found to be *"a stylish and anxious woman with a pomp of golden hair."*[10]

Later, the Queen officially received Loring:

"We drove to the palace and strolled between files of soldiers up the wide staircase to the Queen's salon...She occupied the same sofa on which she sat during the birthday reception. She was alone and most dignified and attractive in her appearance. She has a pleasant face, tinged with sadness, [but]...lightened by a smile. Our talk was mainly on the health of the King, the antiquity of the palace, the attractions of Paris, and the glories of Worth. The quiet, gentle manner of the Queen reminded me of those admirable old ladies of Salem, now gone, who in their lives never knew the back of a chair, and were models of kindness, dignity, and sincerity. We retired from her presence with our respect for her good qualities greatly increased."[11]

On one other occasion before the Braganzas' departure from Sintra Loring met separately with Maria Pia, though throughout the reception she would be preoccupied by her husband's health. One Sunday Loring was *"suddenly informed that the day was the Queen's name-day and her majesty was receiving...When we reached the palace we...were at once presented to the Queen by the grand Chamberlain. The interview was short. The condition of the King's health cast a shadow over the occasion, and created in the Queen an air of sadness and nervousness which...was touching to contemplate."*[12]

Although Luis did enjoy some improvements during his stay at Sintra, his sufferings had left him very weak. Luciano de Castro, who saw the King at Sintra, commented on his sovereign's improvements, but overall he noted the effect Luis's long torment had had upon his spirits. *"I went yesterday to Sintra ...to see the King. I found him very depressed. He had slept well and looks better, but he is very weak and very dispirited."*[13] Maria Pia, however, was pleased with the advances in her husband's health and was in a good mood during Castro's visit. *"The Queen shows much animation with the improvements of the last days,"* de Castro confirmed.[14]

These improvements, however, were fleeting. At Sintra Luis eventually became paralyzed from the waist down; moreover, an ulcer was discovered that wouldn't heal.[15] As his strength continued to fail him, Luis naturally turned his attention to Cascais as he had never forgotten the sea nor lost his love for the sea-life.[16] That September the King resolved to depart for Cascais.

In the early hours on the morning of September 23 the caravan carrying the King left for Cascais. Their Majesties' departure was carried out in strict secrecy so as to avoid observation and conducted in the early hours of dawn to protect Luis from the heat of the day. Maria Pia had directed all the travel preparations, sending servants ahead of the caravan to clear the road of any debris that could cause the carriage transporting Luis unnecessary jolts.[17]

Due to these precautions the King arrived to his destination in good condition, and he settled into the Cidadel, a fortress built by King Afonso VI in 1681, which had been converted into a comfortable summer palace by the present sovereigns. It was here by the sea that Luis breathed with more ease and his health briefly saw some improvement.[18] He enjoyed being wheeled out onto the Cidadel's terraces to view the sea until the return of the pain of his malady forced him to retire to his bed.

Maria Pia followed Luis's sufferings *"moment by moment,"* never leaving his side.[19] In the rare moments she did rest, the Queen slept behind a screen set up in the King's room so she could hear if he called out for her. It was during this time and also during their previous sojourn at Sintra that the relationship between Luis and Maria Pia underwent a change. Seeing how Luis suffered had erased the old hurts of the past for Maria Pia, enabling her to return to a loving relationship with her husband.[20] Luis was likewise able to set aside their past differences and now he looked upon Maria Pia only with love. Once it was reported that Luis, gazing at the wife, who had never abandoned her post at his sickbed, had captured her hands and bringing them to his lips kissed them touchingly.[21]

As an unfailing nurse to the King, Maria Pia's image had also undergone a change with her subjects. Due to her untiring devotion in nursing her ill husband, the populace decided to overlook her recent transgressions and let bygones be bygones. They quickly resumed their reverent worship for their Queen, while the journalists so quick to condemn Maria Pia in the past months were now unanimous in their praise: *"The King continues in agony and next to his bed she remains unshakable, with the firmness of a martyr and the gentleness of a sister of charity, Her Majesty senhora D. Maria Pia. She is the image of dedication seeking to remove with her presence the image of death…Her duty of wife, so religiously fulfilled in her office of devoted nurse, puts on her head a crown more beautiful than a crown of Royalty."*[22]

But Maria Pia's dedication to keeping the hand of death at bay could not prevent the inevitable demise of the Braganza royal brothers. Of the two, the youngest was the first to die. On September 26, 1889 Prince Augusto passed away at the age of forty-two in the Necissadades Palace, to which he had been carried but a few days before his death.[23] The Countess of Edla soothed his final hours; Maria Pia had benevolently allowed her to be at his side.[24] This was the first and only time the Queen would make any concession in regards to the Countess, but Maria Pia was too kindhearted to deny Augusto this final comfort.

When Antonia learned of Augusto's death, she was devastated and even more terrified at the thought of losing her sole remaining sibling, her great favorite Luis: *"My Good Brother of the heart! Of the 7 siblings that are left we 2 are more friends, we suffer together the blow, the loss of our dear Tubinho* [Augusto], *it seems to me that it is all a bad dream; you are also not well, and I am very concerned…(W) hat will happen to me if you die…I must see you even if I have to crawl on my knees. Please let me know your children are near you…   Your sister and best friend."*[25]

It is doubtful Luis even had a chance to read this letter as his own condition was rapidly deteriorating, and the news of his brother's death was withheld from the King as long as possible by his wife and sons, as they were afraid of the effect the sad notice would have upon his own health. In fact on the day of Augusto's funeral, Luis had to undergo an operation to remove gangrene from his paralyzed legs. Dr. Oliveira Feijao cut away large portions of decaying flesh from both legs, but the procedure brought no relief to the King and the gangrene continued to progress throughout his body eventually invading even his face.

On October 15, Luis briefly lost conscious. When he came to, Luis tried to kiss Maria Pia but he was too weak to carry out this act of affection. The end was obviously near, and Maria Pia and her sons kept a constant vigil by his side. Only Amelia was absent, but through no choice of her own. The Duchess of Braganza had arrived in tears from Belem, but heavily pregnant with her third child, Amelia was denied entrance to the Cidadel by Maria Pia and the King's physicians, as they feared the highly charged emotional atmosphere could cause Amelia to once again go into premature labor. Luis's ministers, who had a vested *"interest in prolonging the life of King,"* were, however, permitted onto the premises.[26] From the Cidadel's salon, the ministers waited for news from the King's quarters, all the while maintaining that Luis was recovering despite the appalling evidence to the contrary.

On the morning of October 18, Luis's condition worsened. As a crying Maria Pia went to make a dressing for the King, the depleted Luis murmured, "*Leave it.*"[27] These words were to be his last. After a prolonged agony an exhausted Luis died the following morning at 11:05. When he had drawn his last breath, Maria Pia kissed her late husband's face and her two sons had quickly followed suit.

Then "*more white than ever and looking like a specter,*" Maria Pia went to the door of the death chamber.[28] Addressing the awaiting assembly, she stoically declared, "*The King is dead. Long live the King.*"[29] Afterwards she turned to her eldest son Carlos, now King, entreating, "*May you be as good a king as you have been a son.*"[30]

From Sigmaringen, Antonia, inconsolable upon learning of Luis's death, immediately telegraphed asking her sister-in-law for a lock of her brother's hair, which had turned white during his long ordeal, and for a photograph of the death chamber. Knowing Antonia suffered "*with a pain similar to mine,*" Maria Pia willingly complied with this request, though she was aware of Antonia's animosity toward her.[31]

Antonia remained desperate to receive these cherished mementos of her favorite brother. "*I did not receive the photo of his room yet…do not forget to send it,*" she wrote anxiously. "*I am quite grateful to you for sending me his hair, as well as Augusto's and my father's rings. They are doubly precious now…I can see you have a heart, as has your poor sister.*"[32] Appreciative of Maria Pia's continued kindness towards her even after her intolerant conduct, Antonia's harsh stance towards her sister-in-law was beginning to soften.

On October 21, the mortal remains of the King was borne from the Cidadel first to a monastery in Belem and finally to St. Vincent's for burial. Accompanying her husband's corpse for his final journey, Maria Pia proclaimed upon leaving the Cidadel that she would never return to this palace "*where she had attended, days and nights, to the macabre decomposition of her husband.*"[33]

The Minister George Bailey Loring, who witnessed the Royal funeral, left a detailed account of the proceedings:

"*The funeral of the King was very imposing. He lay in state at Cascais for a few days, and was then borne to the beautiful Igreja e Mosteiro de Santa Maria de Belem…the Convent of St. Jerome. It was on this spot that Vasco de Gama passed the night before his departure on his famous voyage of discovery, in a small chapel, asking for God's blessing on his perilous undertaking…From this beautiful and historic church the body of the King was borne to its final resting-place in St. Vincent in Lisbon, on Saturday, October 26, attended by a long procession of the representatives of many of the courts of Europe…among whom were the Duke of Edinburgh, the Duke of Montpensier…General Werfen, representing the Emperor of Germany, the Prince of Hohenzollern [William, the eldest son of Antonia], peers of the realm, and councilors and ministers of the state…I think every European nationality was represented, together with the United States, Japan and China, Brazil, and the Republics of South America. At eleven o'clock we drove through the crowded streets filled with a noiseless multitude dressed in black; even the poorest peasants were in mourning, for Dom Luis had been a good king and much beloved. Every quarter of an hour for eight days and nights the great guns on the ships on the Tagus had been firing; as they were continuously during the procession, making it almost impossible to sleep in Lisbon. When we reached the church of St. Vincent we entered a side door...The church was hung with gold tapestries edged with black velvet. Three stationary cantaloupes had been erected along the nave, covered with gold and black, on each side of which eight candles, six feet high, burned in golden candlesticks. The first catafalque was near the door, and there the coffin was placed while a chant was sung. It was then borne to the second, in the center of the church, at the head of which stood the cardinal in his scarlet robes holding a high gilt cross, many archbishops and bishops being around him. The coffin was borne thence to its last resting-place – in the church in front of the high altar. A black velvet pall with a large white satin cross embroidered with gold was thrown over it, and the crown of the Kings of Portugal on a satin cushion was placed at the foot. Dom Carlos, the new king, dressed in full uniform and covered with jeweled decorations, walked alone at the head of the procession. Behind him came the Duke d'Aosta, the Duke de Montpensier, and Dom Affonso* [sic]. *Every one was in uniform, and the church was soon filled with a glittering throng of courtiers and officials. In the royal box sat the widowed queen hidden behind her long crape veil, through which gleamed the pink satin ribbon of the royal Order of St. Isabel worn across her breast. By her side sat the Princess Letitia Bonaparte, the Duchess d'Aosta. The King stood through the service in front of the box. As the mass progressed numbers of lighted candles were brought in and distributed until nearly every one standing on the floor held one. Their light made the gold hangings and the uniforms brilliant, while high up in the vaulted roof long rays of sunlight were streaming through the oriel window across to the gleaming altar. The effect of the whole scene was wonderfully grand and imposing. At the end of the service the cardinal, followed by all the other high clergy, walked twice around the coffin, swinging upon it a great censer, and then proceeded to the Pantheon, the royal tomb, the priests chanting, the organ pealing, and heavy salutes of cannon being fired as they moved on. The widowed Queen followed the coffin on the arm of Dom Carlos. The cardinal patriarch officiated, and at the close of the high mass pronounced a short eulogy on the character of the King. Accompanied by funeral chants by the choir of the royal chapel, the body was borne into the Pantheon to rest with the long line of Braganza kings entombed there. By the terms of the royal decree, the grand marshal of the palace, before delivering to the cardinal the mortal remains, took the oath required by law that body was that of His Majesty Dom Luis I. He presided at the ceremony of interment, and kept a key of the coffin, which, with a copy of the process verbal, is to be deposited in the archives of the Pantheon. All the high personages present signed the process verbal, and a duplicate key was given to the cardinal. Amidst heavy salvos of artillery the body was deposited in its last resting-place, and the apartment of the royal dead was closed."*[34]

As George Bailey Loring had stated Portugal was in deepest mourning for Luis as he had been a beloved constitutional monarch, earning him the epitaph *"the Popular."* It was deserved as Luis himself had loved his subjects *"like a family;"*[35] he had displayed a genuine concern for their welfare, and although he had not believed their governing council or other administrative institutions were ready for *"all* (the) *reforms...which a state always needs"*[36] his reign, nonetheless, was one of modernization for Portugal. Noteworthy reforms during his rule were the abolition of the death penalty and of slavery in Portugal's oversea domains.[37]

The King's personal interests were also of great benefit to the nation. With his love of literature he had introduced Portugal to Shakespeare. His other grand passion had been for the sea. While Luis, as King, could no longer serve the country he loved in the capacity of a naval officer, he did everything in his power to improve the lives of his former comrades by implementing reforms in the nation's sea force. Never forgetting his love of the sea, Luis also turned his attention to the study of oceanography, investing a large amount of his private fortune into funding research boats to collect specimens from oceans around the world. These research efforts resulted into the opening of Portugal's first sea aquarium.

The King was mourned not only by his people but by his family. Although Luis was a more controversial figure as a husband than as a King, he and Maria Pia had been able to make peace with one another in the end, and she would sincerely mourn his passing despite painful reminders of his past transgressions. Luis's funeral was not yet concluded when Carlos wrote to his physically exhausted and emotionally drained mother on a matter *"grave and serious."*[38] A hurt Maria Pia had torn this letter to shreds but it is possible to piece the sections together to make sense. Carlos was certain there was a second secret will drawn up in 1876 which would *"contain embarrassing clauses which can in no way be made public without serious drawbacks to the good memory of our good and always dear Papa."*[39]

Although deeply pained by this evidence of Luis's unfaithfulness, Maria Pia, with her typical strong will, made up her mind to concentrate on the happy times she had spent with Luis and for the rest of her life she spoke of him in only loving terms as witnessed in her correspondence. A letter written in May of the following year to her Hohenzollern-Sigmaringen brother-in-law Leopold thanking him for his support during the King's long ordeal particularly stands out:

"Dear Brother, I...return your...letter to thank you profoundly...for the part that you have taken in my grand misfortune of the loss of my...love...the King your brother...I have also written this to Antonia and your son William to think him again for his assistance during those terrible days ...That affection for us is doubly dear. The resolve of dear Luis was...supported with courage and resignation. He died never complaining...I always hoped that he would...recover but then all...of September he worsened and...was in torment...I have suffered horribly...also...for his sons, and for our people!...I know that I speak to a good brother that Luis also loved...I am your affectionate sister, Maria Pia"[40]

At the time of Luis's death Maria Pia was only forty-two years old, and for twenty-seven of these years she had been a wife and Queen. Now, the still relatively youthful Maria Pia was entering a new phase of her life; widowhood.

Chapter XII

The Long Widowhood

Although in the first throes of grief for her husband, Maria Pia was holding up better than her eldest son had anticipated. *"The poor Queen thankfully reacted better than I expected,"* Carlos marveled in a letter to his wife. *"Not too depressed and even now told me she wanted to see you and be with you when you expect the happy event we await so eagerly. Happiness is a real consolation for her to talk about."*[1]

Fortunately, Maria Pia did not have long to wait for the happy event. Exactly two months after the death of Luis, the Braganzas could take joy in the birth of Amelia's third child. Advised by telephone of the impending arrival, Maria Pia had rushed from the Ajuda Palace to Belem to assist Amelia with the birth. It was an understandably anxious time for the Royal Family as Amelia's last pregnancy had resulted in tragedy, but finally at 4:45 in the morning on November 19, 1889 Prince Manuel was safely delivered in the presence of his grandmother. The newborn Prince was given the title of the Duke of Beja, which had been formerly held by his elder brother *"Little Luis,"* who upon their grandfather's death and their father's accession to the throne was rendered the Duke of Braganza.

Ironically, on this very same day the proud father received word that the Braganza monarchy in Brazil had been overthrown. As Carlos received news from Brazil, he kept his mother updated on the situation by tersely telegraphing: *"Finish of the revolt of the Brazilian army. Situation in Rio de Janeiro awful…I've ordered the Portuguese legation in Rio de Janeiro to give hospitality to the Emperor and the entire Imperial Family. I've ordered the* Bartolomeu Dias *to leave with all the available force for protection that will be necessary."*[2]

The Brazilian Braganzas eventually landed in Lisbon, where they were shown great deference by their Portugese cousins. Not wishing to be a burden to his nephew, Emperor Pedro II quickly left the capital and settled temporarily in Oporto, Portugal's largest northern city. Sadly, however, the Empress Teresa Cristina died soon after the exiles settled in Oporto. Emperor Pedro II eventually left Portugal and settled in Paris, where he died in December 1891.

Maria Pia and King Carlos, mother and son, had always been comfortable discussing politics. Before Carlos was rendered King, Maria Pia had written to him with the her advice and hopes for his reign: *"Never resort to violence, this is the wrong way, it is better to succeed with persuasion and a strong will…I hope that you will never have trials or sorrows in this world because this is very sad and I wish I could keep them away from you. Because I want you to be happy…and…loved and respected in our dear country, as well as Amelia."*[3]

While Maria Pia would do her utmost to alleviate her son's troubles and was happy with the recent addition to the family, she had her own sorrows to endure. Maria Pia was still grieving for her husband and barely a month after her grandson's christening she would suffer another loss. While attending Luis's funeral Maria Pia's brother Amedeo had contracted influenza, which would prove fatal. The former sovereign died in their brother, King Umberto's, arms on January 18, 1890.

Fortunately, Maria Pia's mourning for her husband and brother would not be compounded by having to adjust to a new home as Carlos, who did not want to turn his mother out of the Ajuda Palace, decided with his wife to make the Necessidades Palace their new official residence.[4] Upon learning Maria Pia would remain in the Ajuda Palace, Antonia had quickly written to congratulate the Queen Dowager on her good fortune in being able to stay in the palace that held so many memories for her. "(I)*t would be too cruel for your heart…to leave…the apartments where you spent so many years with Luis.*"[5]

It was the first of many letters between the sisters-in-law. By now Antonia had completely forgiven Maria Pia for her indiscretion, and writing to her sister-in-law was also of a comfort to Antonia as it helped her to keep the memory of her brother alive. The Princess's letters to the Queen Dowager show a genuine concern for Maria Pia and her sons' welfare, but their correspondence is also of a political significance as both women were well versed in the politics of their day, particularly, when it concerned their family or their homelands.

Unfortunately, barely three months into Carlos's reign political worries were already beginning. The late 1880s and early 1890s was the period of the European powers' partition of Africa, and in this scramble to divide and rule Portugal cherished a *"contra costa"* dream, which entailed linking their colonies of Angola on the Atlantic Ocean to Mozambique on the Indian Ocean, thus creating a vast Portuguese empire in Southern Africa. Great Britain, however, cherished a similar dream for the African continent in their *"Cape to Cairo route,"* which could not be made possible without gaining possession of the territory that lay between Portugal's Southern African domains. Thus on January 11, 1890 Great Britain, Portugal's oldest ally, demanded that the Portuguese withdraw from their African territory of Mekolols and Mashonas, located on Angola's eastern border, or they would sever all diplomatic ties.[6] This demand would end forever Portugal's territorial ambitions for Southern Africa, but Carlos had little choice but to acquiesce to the ultimatum as Great Britain could easily seize all of Portugal's overseas colonies if they so desired.[7] However, in the eyes of the public, press, and a number of politicians this capitulation was regarded as transforming Portugal into a vassal of Great Britain, and it did such damage to the prestige of the monarchy that Carlos's cabinet was forced to resign.[8]

Antonia was furious at the greed of Great Britain and fired off an angry letter to Maria Pia: "*England has* [acted] *in a wretched way…towards our dear fatherland. I suffer from it because I am Portuguese to the bottom of my heart; it is a lack of courage and nobility to attack a country which cannot defend itself against a great power. Carlos begins his reign heavily.*"[9]

Maria Pia, herself, planned a trip to England to meet with Queen Victoria over the dispute in the hopes that in direct contact with the Queen she could negotiate a better deal in favor of Portugal. But Carlos not wanting to push their luck put a stop to his mother's plans, using Maria Pia's poor health as the excuse for the canceled visit. Queen Victoria had responded contritely commiserating with Maria Pia over the recent loss of her husband, but the Queen absolved herself of any responsibility from the political situation:

"My dear Niece, It is with all my heart that I thank you for your kind and amiable letter which greatly moved me. I understand well all that you must have suffered, and how much you must have found yourself alone since the loss of our dear Louis [sic]! You know, I am certain without my telling you, how much I regret the difficulties that disturb the good harmony between our two Governments, alas! I cannot do anything, and I can only hope that in a little while the painful affairs will be settled. I hope that your health is good now and that I will have one day the pleasure of making your acquaintance personally. I am, forever, my dear Niece your good affectionate Aunt, Victoria R.I."[10]

But painful affairs in Portugal would not be settled anytime soon. After the setback in Anglo-Portuguese relations, Antonia continued to worry over the worsening political climate in Portugal and confessed to her sister-in-law that she feared the nation would become a republic. Sadly, her fears were well founded and tragically both women would live to see them come true.

Within a year of Antonia's prediction a Republican revolt took place in Oporto. Republican conspirators had exercised little influence in the past, but now hoping that the recent discord resulting over the British ultimatum would aid their cause, they proclaimed Oporto a Republic on January 31, 1891. Their uprising, however, was poorly organized. Moreover they did not have the support of the masses.[11] Consequently, the insurrection was easily put down by the Municipal Guard of Oporto.

With this latest development Maria Pia and Antonia once again discussed their political concerns, with Antonia offering what comfort she could: *"My beloved Sister! Thanks...for your...affectionate letter that I received yesterday, and for your details on this unfortunate affair at Oporto...have hope that this harsh trial will cool down."*[12]

For the time being matters did settle down, although discord continued to seethe under the surface. Nonetheless, the overthrow of the Braganza monarchy in Portugal was still about a decade away, and in the meantime Maria Pia was still adjusting to life as a widow. Just two years after the death of King Luis, Carlos and Amelia had resumed the custom of residing in the Cidadel, where Maria Pia had vowed to never return. Amelia understood the memories within this palace were still too painful for her mother-in-law to return to and had written sympathetically to Maria Pia upon her first stay at the Cidadel: "[My] *first thought on arriving here was for you, for all that you had suffered here."*[13]

True to her word Maria Pia would rarely reenter this palace with the exception of one visit in 1892 for the sole purpose of praying for her husband's soul in the room where he had died. Still, Maria Pia missed the sea and she often rode her bicycle to the shore to gaze upon the sea that both she and Luis had also loved so much. Due to this love Maria Pia eventually decided to establish a residence in Estoril, a seacoast town west of Cascais, where the sea was less wild.

In 1893 Maria Pia purchased a chalet on the bay in Estoril. Here she lived with a reduced entourage, and could conduct herself in a more informal manner. She loved to indulge in target practice on the beach by sitting in the sand and tossing bottles into the sea then shooting them as they reemerged, rarely missing her target in the process. Another one of Maria Pia's greatest newfound enjoyments was dining on the beach. However, always ensconced in a large tent, the Queen Dowager did not realize the difficulties her servants would encounter with the sand. It *"was a punishment for us,"* the server Vital Fontes dramatically recounted, *"buried in the sand, always afraid that some spoon of silver was lost."*[14]

The Royal Family, however, would enjoy the break from the rigid court protocol when visiting Maria Pia while she resided in Estoril. To her delight her grandsons were frequent visitors, while Carlos dropped by weekly and Afonso daily. But Maria Pia was soon to lose Afonso's companionship when political difficulties once again erupted in Portugal's oversea domains.

In 1895 a revolt arose in Portugal's Indian possessions, when the indigenous Mahratta soldiers, who had been trained to fight for the Portuguese, objected to a decree requiring them to leave India for service in Africa.[15] Rebelling against the order, the Mahratta soldiers kept the colony of Goya in a state of turmoil, culminating in the seizure of the Nunez fort.[16] That October Afonso, as the commander of the 1st Regiment of Artillery, was sent to India to put down the rebellion.

While Maria Pia naturally worried about her son's safety, she was also highly patriotic and elated that Afonso had the chance to be of service to Portugal. *"I am delighted that the Infant has the opportunity to be able to serve his country, our dear country,"*[17] she proudly wrote to the minister Hintz when requesting to be kept abreast of all the political details concerning the rebellion.

Afonso, however, was decidedly less than delighted with his opportunity. In the ensuing combat, Afonso inevitably became the focal point of local political intrigues, in which he was portrayed as an opponent of his brother's policies. Detesting politics, Afonso was eager to return home and as soon as December he began to entreat his mother to intercede on his behalf and that of his troops. Afonso even went so far as to plan the entertainment for their return, suggesting they should be allowed to spend three days in Nice so that *"we can amuse ourselves a little after such work."*[18]

But relief was not forthcoming and the condition of his troops became increasingly worrisome for Afonso. Throughout his maneuvers Afonso assailed his mother with demands for their return, insisting that the majority of his troops had come down with fevers and intestinal illnesses due to the climate, leaving only 250 out of the 500 men in his unit capable of service.[19] He also recounted what he had discovered about the political intrigues. The Captian Gomes da Costa, a member of the governing Council of Goya, had reportedly told the Duke of Oporto that the Governor Rafael de Andrade *"has a hand in this."*[20] Afonso, however, found the behavior of the captain, who was otherwise lauded for his heroics in combat, to be rather suspicious, and he was convinced that it was the Gomes de Costa who had supposedly posted a note of surrender from the *"brother of the King of Portugal"* on a door in the disputed Nunez fort.[21]

Despite these intrigues Afonso was appointed Viceroy of Portuguese India on March 19, 1896, and in this new capacity Afonso was finally able to reconcile the differences between the quarrelling factions. He granted amnesty to the rebels and reversed the decree of the Council of Ministers, allowing the Mahratta soldiers to remain in their native India.[22] His decision he declared was *"indispensable for the good of India and the honor of Portugal's name."*[23] Having resolved the issue, Afonso's tenure as Viceroy was brief and his rule ended, to his great satisfaction, on May 27 thus enabling the Duke of Oporto to return home.

On the home front Maria Pia had been drawn into her other son's troubles. Carlos and Amelia had married for love, but their relationship was not progressing smoothly for the King, like his father before him, had a roving eye. When Carlos traveled to Europe for a good will trip in September of 1895 Amelia, realizing the side benefits he would indulge in while on his journey, was *"astonished and preoccupied."*[24] After her husband's prolonged stay in Paris, Amelia appealed to her mother-in-law, asking Maria Pia to telegraph Carlos to return home. Knowing all too well what her daughter-in-law was going through, Maria Pia sympathetically complied, despite the distinct lack of compassion shown to her by Amelia under similar circumstances. Her telegraph, however, had no effect whatsoever on her headstrong son, who soon wrote to his wife that he was extending his trip for a voyage to Italy.

A son's tribulation is never easy for a mother to bear, but Carlos and Afonso's difficulties during the early 1890s did help distract Maria Pia from her grief. By this time she was finally ready to move on. The Queen Dowager *"has thrown off her widow's robes,"* commented Sister Mary Magdalene MacDonnell, an American nun stationed in Portugal, of Maria Pia's emergence from mourning, but she could not resist adding that Maria Pia was again *"spending money like water."*[25]

While Maria Pia was resuming her extravagant ways, she had always maintained her charitable inclinations. In 1892 she had held a grand Kermess to benefit the victims of shipping disasters, inundations and strikes.[26] Her next project was to set up soup kitchens to serve the poor, but Maria Pia met with some resistance from her son, who appears to believe that in her generosity his mother was perhaps too easily moved by a sob story. *"In fact I believe workmen in Lisbon without work are very few,"* Carlos hedged. *"Almost everyone begging in Ajuda and Belem are rogues with very long prison records. Your idea is good, and Amelia is willing to assist you, but it needs to be studied, and only then can I let my good Mother do as she wants."*[27]

Maria Pia, however, prevailed as she and not her son had judged the situation correctly. With the assistance of her daughter-in-law, Maria Pia set up fuel saving stoves to help the out of work laborers. Free tickets entitling the unemployed to food were issued with the entire cost undertaken by the two Queens.[28]

Unfortunately, their shared philanthropic endeavor brought no greater understanding between the two women. Amelia still disapproved of her mother-in-law's behavior, especially with her extravagance and friendships with the opposite sex. She was convinced that Maria Pia was having an affair with her faithful attendant Joao Benjamim Pinto, who in his broad shouldered handsomeness was playfully referred to as the grotesque. On her part Maria Pia would tolerate no one, let alone her daughter-in-law, commenting on or judging her actions. Of their relationship the nun Sister Mary Magdalene, relaying the gossip in Lisbon, went so far as to write to her superiors in America that Maria Pia hated her daughter-in-law. While hate is actually much too strong of a word to describe the emotion Amelia inspired in Maria Pia, there is no denying there was tension between the two women.

The primary cause of tension between Maria Pia and her daughter-in-law remained the great popularity of the Queen Dowager to the deterrent of Amelia. While the Queen had gained popularity in some quarters due to her charitable work, particularly in her crusade against tuberculosis in which she *"sponsored a private foundation of free clinics, hospitals, and sanitariums"*[29] for victims of the disease, Amelia had never fully gained the trust of the Portuguese, who felt that she was overly religious. Whereas Maria Pia carried out the religious duties of her Catholic faith that were relevant without fanaticism, Amelia, according to British author Francis Gribble, was encouraging the reestablishment of religious order in Portugal.[30] *"There is unhappily,"* explained Gribble, *"only too much evidence to show that, when religious orders come in at the door, all prospects of thorough-going reform fly out the window. Or that, at all events, was the view of the new school of reformers then arising in Portugal:…the anti-clericals from the University of Coimbra."*[31] *"The Queen, whose piety…had never won her any popularity,"* added the diplomat George Young, *"was suspected of being in the hands of the Jesuits, those traditional traducers of Portuguese national liberties."*[32]

After a visit to Portugal the French journalist Jean Finot wrote of the people's continuing preference for the Queen Dowager. Maria Pia was a *"true queen. Above all, she is majestic. A true daughter of kings, she is good-natured and generous. The other queen? Still young and distinguished-looking, she brought with her to Lisbon a royal, a divine beauty. She is without doubt the most beautiful woman who has ever reigned over Portugal. Ever since she came she has tried to win all hearts. Amiable and prepossessing, she is careful to ignore, not to accentuate, distinctions in rank. She is as economical as the dowager is prodigal. Nevertheless, the Portuguese prefer Maria Pia. Queen Amelia is a Clerical, which offends the people."*[33]

Amelia, as Finot had noted, was at the height of her beauty, but she was also at the height of her ambition, and she was not unnaturally jealous of the favoritism shown by the Portuguese to Maria Pia, whom she felt was undeserving of the populace's adulation. Amelia's relatives shared this resentment after hearing her speak disparagingly of her mother-in-law. *"The Queen Maria Pia is a spendthrift, with many lovers,"* Amelia's sister, Infanta Louise of Spain, would complain, *"and there is poor Amelia, a true saint,* [who] *has never managed to make herself loved."*[34]

While dealing with the resentment of her daughter-in-law, who was aforementioned at the height of her beauty, the aging Maria Pia was adjusting to the fading of her own good looks, which perhaps added another element of tension between the two women. By this time Maria Pia had gained a considerable amount of weight, and while she was fighting a downhill battle with the extra pounds, Maria Pia would make a valiant attempt to preserve other aspects of her appearance. Perhaps the most difficult aspect of aging for Maria Pia was that her crowning glory, her red hair, was turning white, and she began to dye her hair to try to recapture its original hue, but with disastrous results. The Englishwoman Matilda Lucas, who witnessed one of these misguided efforts of the Queen Dowager's at a garden party in Rome in 1893, recalled in amusement, *"Maria Pia…the King's sister…was wonderful to behold. She has a good face, but the hair that was red in her youth is now transformed by art into a dark orange with shades of crimson. It is said that the King burst out laughing when he met her at the station."*[35] Maria Pia appears, however, to have taken her brother's amusement over her hair good naturedly, ruefully admitting she had felt it a necessity to dye her hair. And with her typical self-confidence she would continue to dye her hair regardless of what others thought for the rest of her life.

Amusing incident aside, this visit to Italy in 1893 was not for pleasure as Maria Pia was there on a secret diplomatic mission for her son. Unlike his wife, whatever jealousy Carlos had experienced as Hereditary Prince over his mother's popularity dissipated once he was in power, and no longer feeling the need to compete with her the King quickly realized that in Maria Pia he had a great asset. When Carlos first came to the throne he had little influence on the world stage, but Maria Pia still had great influence with her surviving brother, who as the King of Italy was a part of the Triple Alliance with Germany and Austria-Hungry. Consequently, Carlos would never directly negotiate with his uncle, instead relying upon his mother to broker deals with her brother in favor of Portugal.

At this time, Maria Pia was to meet with representatives of the Triple Alliance, including the Kaiser himself, to negotiate credit for Portugal's foreign debts. On her way to Italy she sent an optimistic letter to her son expressing her hope for favorable results for their country and dynasty and her joy in being able to assist their nation. Once she arrived in Italy, Maria Pia expressed her satisfaction that no one there knew Portuguese so if their correspondence was interfered with then at least no one could understand it.

Soon she was able to communicate good news. To Hintz, the President of the Ministry, she elatedly telegraphed the favorable results on the business of their foreign debts, crediting the goodwill of the King of Italy and the Kaiser, who in her own words *"helped a lot"* with the outcome. She modestly added, *"I am happy...to have been able to contribute."*[36]

Upon her return to Portugal she was drawn into another diplomatic crisis. In May of 1894 there was a break in diplomatic relations between Portugal and Brazil, and once again Carlos turned to his mother for a solution. After informing her brother of the situation, Maria Pia telegraphed Hintz briefly explaining how they resolved the issue: *"The King of Italy was made aware of everything concerning the question and why it was done this way. Someday when you come here I'll show you what I wrote him."*[37]

Unfortunately Carlos's reliance on his mother's political acumen and services only increased Amelia's rancor for Maria Pia. She bitterly complained in her diary that Carlos kept her away from political affairs, while spending days at a time with his mother. Resentful of the close bond between Carlos and Maria Pia, Amelia began to make scenes whenever she discovered her husband's intention to visit his mother. Consequently, Carlos and Maria Pia had to learn to carefully plan their meetings in order not to offend her. During one of his wife's absences, Carlos wrote to Maria Pia with the request, *"As Amelia is going to the procession... and coming home late...I beg you to write me a note saying 'since Amelia is gone you are inviting me to dine with you alone.' It is better this way because we can avoid histrionics."*[38]

On another occasion when Carlos was in the Algrave to view some naval maneuvers and Maria Pia expressed interest in joining him, Amelia strenuously voiced her objections to her mother-in-law's presence. Carlos, who believed his mother deserved to unwind after very serious work was appalled by his wife's reaction. Usually quite amiable when addressing Amelia, he for once ceased to be placating and not mincing words, wrote in a temper, *"Your letter disgusts and amazes me."*[39]

By now conjugal relations between Carlos and Amelia had ceased and unable to work together they took to battling each other in vain, creating two distinct parties within the court.[40] The King tried to keep Amelia's role in politics to a minimum by confining her to ceremonial duties, while the resentful Amelia according to the Portuguese historian Rui Ramos worked actively against her husband, never hesitating to encourage leaders in opposition to the King.[41] Plotting against a spouse was not unheard of within the Braganza dynasty, but a relationship such as theirs noted Maria Antonia Lopes, Maria Pia's most recent Portuguese biographer, had not existed since the time of Joao VI and Carlota Joaquina.[42]

Unfortunately, we do not have a record of what Maria Pia thought of Amelia's political machinations against her son. With the exception of the letter where she complained to Luis about both their son and daughter-in-law's behavior, Maria Pia appears to have taken the high road where Amelia was concerned at least in her correspondence. But she could not have approved, and her son, who knew he could trust his mother to have his best interests at heart, not surprisingly continued to turn to Maria Pia for political assistance instead of his wife.[43]

And he would have need of her support in due time. In September of 1895 Carlos announced his intention of officially visiting Rome. Since the city's seizure from the Pope by the Savoys Catholic sovereigns had avoided the capital. Carlos's official visit could start a new precedent, however, in the eyes of the Vatican it would be a dangerous one, and when the Holy See learned of Carlos's intended trip he threatened to sever relations with Portugal. After consulting with his cabinet, Carlos decided that it would be wise to postpone his visit indefinitely.

While the Vatican was satisfied with Carlos's turnaround, the Italian government was naturally furious. Maria Pia wrote to her brother Umberto to try to soften the blow of her son's defection, but to no avail. Umberto's excitable, despotic Prime Minister Francesco Crispi was so furious that he went so far as to express the desire that Portugal as an "*unimportant country*" should get rid of its "*miniscule monarchy.*"[44] Within a few days the Italian minister to Portugal was withdrawn, while the Portuguese minister in Rome was not received at court, until he too was recalled home.[45]

A year would pass before Maria Pia could set things right between the two countries. Her opportunity finally came in October of 1896 at the wedding of her nephew Victor Emmanuel, Umberto's diminutive heir, to the ironically statuesque Princess Elena Petrovich of Montenegro.

When Maria Pia, accompanied by the ever devoted Afonso, arrived in Italy for the festivities, she was welcomed by her sister-in-law, Queen Margherita, who later commented, "*Poor woman, she has remained so attached to our country… and is satisfied to be coming here.*"[46] But Margherita was obviously irritated that her nephew Carlos was still avoiding Rome and she forcibly condemned his continued absence. "*My nephew is a beast, an imbecile. Last year I would have beaten [him] up and now he should have come.*"[47]

Despite the rancor still felt for Carlos in Italy, Maria Pia was finally able to reconcile the differences between the two countries. It was through the Queen Dowager's good offices that Carvalho de Vasconcelos, the former Portuguese ambassador to Rome, was welcomed back to the Quirinal Palace, while Maria Pia's brother King Umberto sent to Lisbon as Italy's representative, Carlo Alberto Gerbaux de Sonnaz, the son of a heroic general of the Risorgimento.[48]

With the diplomatic crisis resolved Maria Pia could now relax and enjoy the nuptials of her nephew, though his wedding would not be without an embarrassing incident of its own. When the officiating priest inquired, "*Is Your Royal Highness Victor Emmanuel of Savoy, Crown Prince of Italy, content to receive as your legal wife Princess Elena Petrovich, according to the rites of the Holy Mother Church,*" Victor Emmanuel had turned to Umberto and asked, "*My Father, do you permit me?*"[49] Unfortunately, Umberto distracted by the heat of the day did not hear the request and had remained silent. While the bride anxiously looked on, the groom repeated his request, "*Father, do you permit me?*"[50] Finally, Victor had his father's attention, and Umberto had enthusiastically if belatedly replied, "*Certainly, certainly!*"[51] But the damage had been done. Margherita was humiliated by her husband's lapse of concentration during the ceremony, finding such behavior not sufficiently royal.

Although Umberto, himself, was quite satisfied with the proceedings, the embarrassing incidents weren't over. In the subsequent celebratory festivities royal small talk treaded into dangerous territory. Maria Pia's Austrophile nephew the Count of Turin, the second son of her brother Amedeo, went from relating anecdotes of his travels to discussing the unnecessary blood shed for the unity of Italy. For her part Maria Pia conversed only on formal topics.[52] Having solved one diplomatic crisis, she was not about to become involved in another.

When the newlyweds departed for their honeymoon, Maria Pia left Rome with Umberto and Margherita for Monza, the Italian sovereigns' favorite Alpine retreat. It was fortunate that Maria Pia was able to reconcile the differences between their two governments when she did for Monza would be the site of the King's assassination just four years later.

Although Umberto had already survived two previous assassination attempts, he had dismissed these attacks as *"risks of the trade,"* and refused to allow special precautions to be taken for his safety.[53] Maria Pia, however, could never be so nonchalant about the danger her brother faced. Whenever Maria Pia heard of republican conspiracies being organized in Italy, she would telegraph Umberto entreating him not to visit regions where his life might be endangered.[54] The King, however, always shrugged off his sister's warnings, having come to the conclusion, *"If it is destined that I am to die like Alexander II* [of Russia], *of what importance are precautions?"*[55]

Thus when the King attended a gymnastic competition in Monza on July 29, 1900 he had taken no especial precautions and was transported to the event by a carriage with the top down. When the contest was over, Umberto boarded his carriage, taking the seat closet to the spectators, who gathered to send the King off with a cheer.[56] This enthusiastic crowd, however, harbored one sinister onlooker, the Italian born anarchist Gaetano Bresci, who had received his deadly training in the United States. Seizing his opportunity, Bresci emerged from the crowd, took aim at the King and fired four shots, three of which unfortunately found their mark.

The King's entourage raced their injured sovereign to the safety of the royal villa, but Umberto would be dead upon arrival. His wife Margherita, however, at first believed Umberto to still be alive and had insisted that he be revived. *"Have pity on me, save him!"* she implored an attending physician.[57] When Margherita could no longer deny the terrible truth, she had dropped to her knees in a paroxysm of tears and had fairly screamed:[58] *"They killed you, you who so loved our people! You were so good; you brought harm to no one and they killed you! This is the crime of the century!"*[59]

Fortunately, she quickly gained her usual self-possession. As her son Victor Emmanuel, who was now King, was sailing on his yacht in the Aegean Sea, Margherita insisted that Umberto's burial be delayed until his arrival. Consequently, she had to take measures to preserve her slain husband's remains. Margherita ordered the royal corpse to be packed with ice, and had an electric fan brought into his room to distribute the cold air in a fashion.[60]

Maria Pia and her son Afonso would be the first relatives to arrive as they had been staying close by at Aix-les-Bains. While Maria Pia did her utmost to support to her widowed sister-in-law, she herself would be prostrated by the death of her only remaining brother.[61] The two had been more than just siblings, they had been political allies, but even more importantly they had been friends.[62]

From Lisbon Maria Pia's thirteen-year-old grandson Luis Filipe, who adored his grandmother, was full of concern at how she was coping with the loss. He had immediately written to her: *"Dear Grandmother, When I heard yesterday that Uncle Humberto* [sic] *had been killed, I was immensely sorry and straightaway thought on the great sorrow you have…I hope that such a great shock has not harmed your dear health. I ask you to give on my part my deepest condolences to…all of his family. Your grandson who respectfully kisses your hand Luiz* [sic]."[63]

On the Aegean Sea Victor received a vague dispatch concerning his father's health, and he had quickly changed course for Italy. When he came ashore in Naples on the first of August, Victor was met by his maternal uncle the Duke of Genoa who confirmed Umberto's death. In stunned disbelief, the new king could only mutter, *"I feel as if it were all a bad dream."*[64] The populace mirrored his bewilderment, and shock soon turned outrage.

The journalist Henry Wickham Steed remembered the highly charged emotional atmosphere in Italy in the wake of Umberto's assassination and subsequent funeral:

"*A great revulsion of feeling followed the assassination. King Humbert* [sic] *had been sincerely devoted to his people and, if his intelligence was not of the highest order, he was courageous to a fault. During the floods at Verona in 1882, the earthquake at Ischia in 1884, and the cholera epidemic at Naples in 1885, he had shown exemplary fearlessness. His generosity was remarkable, all the more because he was by no means a spendthrift. When his body was brought from Monza to Rome for burial in the Pantheon, millions stood bareheaded along the line of railway and tens of thousands waited all night in the streets of Rome. One incident in the funeral procession remains in my memory. Fear of another anarchist outrage was in all minds: and a panic arose at the collapse of some planks on which spectators had taken their stand. For a moment, the crowd disturbed the procession. King Victor Emmanuel III, who, surrounded by the representatives of foreign reigning houses, was following the bier, paid no heed to the noise and the rush: but his father-in-law, Prince Nicholas of Montenegro, a man of great bulk and stature, drew his yataghan* [shield] *in a flash and held it aloft covering his son-in-law until order was restored.*"[65]

Unfortunately, these were dangerous times for Royalty and other world leaders, and soon Maria Pia herself, according to the *Chicago Tribune*, would be threatened by the same anarchical organization that had trained her brother's assassin. A correspondent of the *Chicago News* reported shortly after the assassination of President McKinley of the United States in late July of 1901:

"[Paterson] *the 'silk' city of New Jersey is the capital of all the 'reds' in the United States. It is the seat of a kind of university for training of regicides. Here Bresci, the killer of Humbert [sic], was trained. When the assassin's knife sunk into the breast of Elizabeth of Austria, in Geneva, the secret service bureaus of the world sent extra men to Paterson. Recently, the life of Maria Pia, the Queen of Portugal was threatened...At 355 Market* [Street], *on the top floor back, you will run down the king creature, the leader of the 3,500 Italians comprising the society called Dritto All' Esitensa (Right to Existence). This chief of Italians is a Spaniard named Pedro Esteve. In his rooms on the top floor back is published La Questione Sociale. Editing this weekly paper is Esteve's ostensible occupation. His real life work is sharpening the knives of regicides and fattening the purses of royal undertakers...The day the news was received of the attempt upon the life of Maria Pia of Portugal Pedro Esteve was found in his office on the top floor back, type cases to the right of him, portraits of Herr Most to the left of him."*[66]

However, the *New York Times* quickly published an article on August 1st disputing the story: *"Aix-les-Bains July 31 – the Authorities here, when questioned today regarding the report circulated in the United States that an attempt was made upon the life of Dowager Maria Pia of Portugal previous to her departure from here to Rome, denied that any such attempt had been made. Queen Maria Pia was about town on Friday, and before her departure for Rome on Saturday took a long walk on the boulevards."*[67]

Despite the conflicting reports an arrest was made in the case, although the *New York Times* expressed doubt as to guilt of the culprit:

"August 2, 1901, The Anarchist Galliotti: Man arrested in Switzerland; Not known to have tried to kill anyone. Berne, August 1 – An Investigation of the Report; published in the United States, that the anarchist, Galliotti, who was arrested at Viedikon on Tuesday night by order of the Prosecutor General, is charged with being connected with the alleged attempt on the life of Queen Maria Pia at Aix-les-Bains, shows that there is no foundation for the story. The Public Prosecutor's office is authority for the statement that Galliotti was arrested for dispatching anarchistic writings in Switzerland. The prisoner, who was born in 1871 at San Sofia in the vicinity of Florence, Italy, is known as one of the most fanatical of anarchists. He has undergone several terms of imprisonment in Italy, but there is no record of his having been in any attempt at assassination."[68]

This is the only reference, fictional or otherwise, made of an attempt upon the life of Maria Pia. But these were still dangerous times for the Portuguese Royals, as Maria Pia's son Carlos would soon become the focus of the ire of revolutionaries.

Chapter XIII

Regicide

Carlos's reign had not begun auspiciously and unfortunately matters would only become worse. The dismissal of the King's old cabinet only temporarily placated Carlos's opposition. *"In February of 1895 the Spanish minister in Lisbon reported to his government of a rumored conspiracy to take down the king, due to the dissatisfaction with his new cabinet led by the politicians Hintz and Franco. According to this Spanish minister Carlos would be substituted by a Regency headed by Maria Pia, backed by the support of the Italian representative in Lisbon. The Portuguese millionaire Conde de Burnay, an intimate of the Queen Dowager, was said to be one of the main conspirators."*[1] These rumors proved false, nonetheless, faced with the gossip Carlos was again forced to replace his cabinet.

While this particular regency never materialized, Maria Pia would act as regent twice for her son while he traveled abroad in 1902 and 1904. She would be criticized, however, during both of her regencies for her extravagance. According to the author Fialho D'Almeida the numerous festivities and balls thrown by Maria Pia during her regencies tarnished the wings of this *"angel of charity."* On a brighter note, it was observed she worked as hard as she played, as she officially visited numerous hospitals, prisons, schools, barracks, and arsenals.

Fortunately, Carlos's goodwill travels abroad would prove highly beneficial for Portugal. The affable Portuguese King was greatly esteemed among his peers, which resulted in Portugal hosting many royal visits in return. The sojourn of the Kaiser to Portugal in March of 1905 would inspire a particularly poignant exchange between Maria Pia and Antonia, who had recently lost her husband and was suffering from ill health. Travel abroad was now difficult for Antonia, and Maria Pia knew that her sister-in-law might never see her beloved Portugal again. With this in mind Maria Pia had thoughtfully documented the Kaiser's travels throughout the Princess's native land. The deeply touched Antonia had responded gratefully: *"My dear sister! Receive my sincere thanks for your dear kind letter which is a consolation in my great affliction and accept at the same time my profound gratitude for the album with the beautiful photographs…of the visit of the Emperor Guillaume* [sic] *to Lisbon. Allow me to say how much they recalled dear memories of my youth and my native land Portugal…I embrace you tenderly Antoinette* [sic]*"*[2]

Unfortunately, Portugal would not act as a host to Maria Pia's nephew King Victor Emmanuel III. Having never cultivated a closer relationship with his Savoy uncle, Carlos followed the same pattern with his cousin, instead relying upon his mother to maintain good relations with the Italian relatives even though he would be in dire need of his cousin's assistance with it came to Portugal's foreign creditors.

Hearing grumbling that the Kaiser was opposed to helping Portuguese interests any further, Carlos had dispatched his mother to Italy in 1901 on the pretense of attending the baptism of Victor Emmanuel's first child, Jolanda. As the Kaiser was also attending this event with a secret agenda – he wanted to ensure the unenthusiastic Italian King's continued participation in the Triple Alliance – it was hoped Maria Pia could use Germany's need of Italy to Portugal's advantage.

Maria Pia did not disappoint. Eight days after her arrival, she was able to relay the good news of the Kaiser's willingness to continue to lend his support to Portugal. Carlos, however, would receive all the accolades for this diplomatic feat. *"The diplomacy of King Carlos saved the country from disaster,"*[3] the Marques de Lavradio crowed, without acknowledging that it is was Maria Pia who had actually carried out the difficult task of negotiating with the capricious Kaiser.

While Maria Pia believed in giving credit where credit was due, she herself never needed recognition for her political services. As evidenced in the letter Maria Pia had written her father decades earlier where she had informed him of her discrete networking behind the scenes, she continued to prefer to conceal her work in the political arena, and was thus quite happy to let Carlos have all the glory for her diplomatic successes. As Queen Dowager, Maria Pia personified discretion, always putting the good of the Braganza dynasty before her own ego.

However, looking to the future Maria Pia knew she could not always act as a buffer between her line and that of her Italian relations in matters of state. Her son may have chosen not develop closer ties with the Savoys, but Maria Pia would try to rectify this situation with her grandson. As Victor Emmanuel and his wife Elena continued to have more children, Maria Pia viewed their subsequent christenings as an opportunity for Luis Filipe to get to know the Italian Royal Family better. Unfortunately, Amelia would put a stop to Maria Pia's plans. Amelia stubbornly refused to allow Luis Filipe to accompany Maria Pia to these events, always putting her dislike of her mother-in-law before the good of the country.

Fortunately, one relationship Carlos chose to cultivate was with King Edward VII of Great Britain. During his travels abroad, Carlos had formed a crucial friendship with Edward while he was still the Prince of Wales. Consequently, relations with Great Britain would vastly improve with the ascendance of Prince Edward to the British throne in 1901.

The new King extended his hand of friendship to Carlos's sons. In 1902 Edward named the fifteen-year-old Luis Filipe a Knight of the Garter. Delighted with the recognition shown to her son, Amelia thankfully approved of this budding relationship and took no steps to hinder its development.

As Luis Filipe matured King Edward was anxious to solidify the renewed good relations between Great Britain and Portugal by uniting the Hereditary Prince in royal matrimony with one of Britain's Princesses, preferably one of his nieces Margaret or Patricia, the daughters of his brother Arthur, the Duke of Connaught. In 1905 Edward ordered his brother and his family to delay their trip to Egypt by first visiting Portugal, though they thought this was a great bore on account of the extra expense in which it would involve.[4] And despite the warm reception they received from the Braganzas, the Connaughts remained resentful. Consequently, Luis Filipe made little impression upon Princess Margaret or Princess Patricia.

While the Connaught Princesses failed to appreciate the charms of the Portuguese heir, Luis Filipe had matured into a promising, talented young man who possessed boyish good looks. Tall and blond in the Nordic way, Luis Filipe enjoyed sports, mainly motoring and hunting.[5] According to his brother Manuel's secretary, the Marques de Lavradio, the Hereditary Prince *"was more intelligent than average, being at the same time the most loyal, the most honest, the noblest, the bravest man I have ever met. He did not speak much and when he did, it was always slowly; he always paid attention to what was being said. He was considerate and polite to the King, his father, whom he tried to emulate in every possible way and who he, very movingly, admired passionately. To him, no one in the world could be compared to the King, in either intelligence or culture or artistic talent; no King would ever be equal to him."*[6]

Luis Filipe's resolute character was lightened by a keen sense of humor with a love for practical jokes. He liked to tease his naïve younger brother Manuel, but could take a good ribbing himself as demonstrated in one of his letters to his mother: *"Yesterday I failed to shoot a very wild boar, and you, my mother, can not imagine how ridiculed I was by everyone...At dinner, I received a letter from my friends. Father gave it to me. It was a picture of a sad boar, a happy boar, and a third boar looking me in the eyes. This last one said 'with all my thanks!' To Your Majesty the Queen, from the Number 1."*[7]

Both Amelia and Carlos were extremely proud of their accomplished eldest son, and Their Majesties began to entrust their heir with more and more political duties at home and abroad. In 1905 Luis Filipe acted as Regent while the King paid a state visit to France. The following year he represented his father at the wedding of King Alphonso XIII of Spain to Princess Victoria Eugenie "Ena" of Battenberg. Unfortunately, in this capacity Luis Filipe would witness the assassination attempt upon the newlyweds. *"You cannot imagine what the assassination attempt was like yesterday,"* Luis Filipe wrote when informing his mother of the horrifying event. *"We were about to arrive at the Palace when a terrible noise was heard. At first I thought it was a gun salute but soon I could see what really happened. The King's coach was completely destroyed, there were corpses, a lot of injured people, dreadful! Fortunately neither the King nor the Queen was wounded but what a fright! Poor people! Seventeen people have been killed and about one hundred injured."*[8]

The Hereditary Prince's next trip abroad was much more satisfactory. In 1907 Amelia arranged for her son to tour the Portuguese colonies in Africa. Luis Filipe's visit was a huge success, with one Portuguese official affirming, *"You can not imagine the good impression that the Prince caused here, as much in the Portuguese as in foreigners, there is an Englishman that said to me...it seems impossible that in Portugal there are Republicans with a prince like this; an old Portuguese said to me: he will be another Pedro V."*[9]

Tragically, Luis Filipe was destined to die young just like King Pedro

V, and the cause would be due to the very existence of Republicans in Portugal. Republicanism grew from the discontent of a select group of the Portuguese people over the exorbitant cost of maintaining their hereditary leaders.[10] The overthrow of the Brazilian Braganzas had made a significant impression upon this segment of the population, especially in light of the fact that the republic in Brazil cost substantially less to operate than the old monarchy it had replaced.[11]

By 1906 the country's leading two party monarchist system, consisting of the Progressives and the Regenerators, had proven incapable of improving the nation's financial problems. All they did was argue among themselves and divide the spoils of office from time to time.[12] Capitalizing upon this dissention within the cortes, the small republican contingency within its ranks was rapidly gaining ground.

The Regenerator leader Hintz, once again prime minister in 1906, believed that the only way to ensure the continuation of the monarchy was to declare an *"instant dictatorship,"* and proposed himself for the position.[13] Although the King was aware that the government needed to be infused with new ideas to be effective, he was not prepared to take such a drastic step at this time as he felt this measure would alienate his monarchist supporters. Declining Hintz's recommendation, Carlos explained, *"It does not appear convenient to me to close the cortes, because this would lead to a revolt of public opinion; not only of the republicans – that would be natural – but also of all the monarchists who are not with you on the present occasion. This would be certain, and we should not have any illusions about it. All we would do would be to add to the number of malcontents."*[14]

An incident shortly thereafter, however, led Carlos to reconsider his decision. On April 8, 1906 sailors of the Portuguese navy mutinied calling for the King's abdication in favor of the Hereditary Prince Luis Filipe.[15] Carlos believed only a strongman could preserve his crown and he began to look within his Cortes for a *"really honest man – a patriot who would put the honor and interest of Portugal before his personal interest and those of his adherents! How gladly would I delegate to him all the authority which I have in order that he might introduce the era of reform which I and the Portuguese people equally desire."*[16] Carlos became convinced that the best candidate was the independently wealthy politician Joao Franco, who as such would be above corruption. In May of 1906 Carlos appointed Franco as prime minister with full dictatorial powers.

Franco was well intended, but he eventually succumbed to two temptations that plague almost every dictator, the use of violence and financial corruption,[17] although it must be noted that Franco did not profit personally from the latter as his questionable financial dealings were purely on behalf of his King. While Carlos led a more bourgeois lifestyle than his parents had during their reign, Carlos came by his extravagance naturally as he had had his mother for an example, and now he, too, was hopelessly overdrawn from the Civil List. Franco's shady dealings to get the Royal Family out of debt, such as having the King sell to the nation by Royal decree the Royal Yacht and some unused property at inflated prices,[18] and then turning around and increasing Carlos' annual allowance, did nothing to improve the monarchy's image, but it was also damaging to Franco's own reputation. He was vastly unpopular with the people, who resented his abuse of power and now saw him quite rightly as a hypocrite. But Franco would not tolerate any criticism of himself or his King, and he began to censor the newspapers, suppressing the revolutionary ones and imprisoning their journalists.

He was just as unpopular with the remaining Braganzas, excluding the obviously grateful Carlos. Of the Royal Family Amelia, in particular, was resentful of the power and confidence her husband had placed in Francco, as she herself had no influence with the King. *"Franco is in the right,"* she was once grudgingly conceded of the dictator's domineering policies, though she could not resist adding: *"but he has no tact."*[19]

It was Franco's brutality, however, in putting down republican uprisings that would be the downfall of the Braganzas. When Franco convinced the King to sign a decree to transport individuals seen as a threat to the monarchy, Carlos was signing his own death warrant.

While Carlos, Amelia, and Luis Filipe – Manuel had already returned to Lisbon to resume his schooling – were on their annual winter vacation in Vila Viçosa, a republican uprising was foiled in Lisbon resulting in the arrest of ninety-three conspirators. Franco immediately drew up a decree to deport the implicated individuals to exile in Portugal's African colonies. On January 31, 1908 Carlos signed the edict, though he is reputed to have said, *"I fear that in singing this decree I have also signed my death warrant but that is what you what me to do."*[20]

Carlos was marked for assassination by a small group of extremists who had decided to have him killed as a result of the failed Republican uprising.[21] This small group's leader was the thirty-year-old Manuel Buica, an ex-sergeant of the 7th Cavalry, who was such an excellent shot that he had ironically once received a rifle from the King as a prize in a shooting competition.[22] There were other conspirators, but the only other confirmed member was Alfredo Costa, the editor of a revolutionary paper.

The planned assassination was an open secret within the country. Rumors instantly spread in Lisbon that the pig was going to be killed, a crude reference to the now corpulent King.[23] When he heard of the terrifying gossip, Carlos's childhood friend Thomaz de Mello Breyner, now one of the physicians to the Royal Family, sadly recorded in his diary, *"They want to kill my dear King, who is so good to everyone."*[24] Luis Filipe was also aware of the rumors and was determined to protect his father, whom he worshiped. *"When I go out with my father, I always carry a gun,"* the Hereditary Prince announced. *"Should anyone try anything against him, I'll shoot. If I am too late, I'll shoot to kill."*[25]

While Franco had taken to sleeping in a different residence each night in fear for his life, he assured the King that the capital was safe, though he had perversely arranged little police protection for their return. Carlos never lost his faith in Franco and on February 1 he returned with his family to Lisbon. They were expected to arrive around 4 o'clock. that afternoon, but their train from Vila Viçosa had been derailed, delaying their journey for about an hour and a half. From the Barriero train station, they Royal Family took the ferry *Dom Luis* across the Tagus before finally disembarking at Black Horse Square. This square, one of Lisbon's largest, was lined with arcaded three storey buildings, mostly ministries and Government offices, and distinguished by the classical equestrian statue of King Jose I, which stood at its center,[26] all of which combined unhappily provided the perfect hiding places for those with nefarious intentions.

A reception party, consisting of Infante Manuel, Infante Afonso, Franco, and other palace officials greeted the returning royals with a goddaughter of the Queen presenting Amelia with flowers. Court dignitaries suggested the use of cars for the remainder of their journey, but Carlos felt that with the recent unrest it was important for the people to see the Royal Family, and he insisted upon open carriages. The King it seemed fully abided by his Uncle Umberto's adage that there was nothing to do but *"open your eyes wide and look into the faces of your people."*[27] Unfortunately this maxim, which had proven so fatal for the former, would have just as of a tragic result for latter.

The King was the first to board the provided carriage, taking the seat in the back on the left. Then his sons boarded with Luis Filipe taking the seat across from his father, while Manuel sat to the right of his brother. All three men stood for Amelia, who clutching her bouquet of flowers, took the remaining seat to the right of her husband.

The carriage, followed by a conclave of other carriages containing the Royal Family's retinue, began its departure from the square heading towards the left corner of Terrio do Paço connecting to Arsenal Street. Just as the procession began to pick up pace the assassin Manuel Buica emerged from a crowd of onlookers. Kneeling, Buica withdrew his prize rifle and took aim at the King. His shot entered Carlos in the spine killing him instantly. The second assassin, Alfredo Costa, jumped onto the left hand side of the carriage pumping two more bullets into the King, who was already dead.

Both Amelia and Luis Filipe rose to defend their family, with Amelia brandishing her bouquet of flowers while Luis Filipe drew a more deadly weapon in his revolver. Costa chose the Hereditary Prince as his next target, shooting him in the chest. The bullet entered through the breastbone and exited out his back, but Luis Filipe was able to fire four shots in rapid succession into Costa causing him to fall off the carriage. True to his pronouncement Luis Filipe had fired to kill.

However, by standing Luis Filipe became a target for the first assassin. Buica changed position, now aiming at the Hereditary Prince. His shot entered Luis Filipe in the face in the left check from where the bullet traveled through to the brain, before finally exiting from the back of the skull, shattering it in the process.

Chaos reigned in the square where the terrified crowd became an angry mob intent on apprehending the assassins. Both Buica and Costa were subdued, the latter in large part due to the Hereditary Prince, and killed, but another anonymous assassin was able to escape in the ensuing confusion, and unfortunately many innocent bystanders were injured while one was even killed. During the exchange of gunfire, Manuel and the coachman were also shot, but the wounded coachman was able to keep his wits about him and rushed the carriage to the nearby Marine Arsenal where medical facilities were available.

At the arsenal attendants from the following carriages bravely made an attempt to protect the Braganzas. Ignoring their Queen's cries of *"Go away or they will kill you too,"*[28] the Condessa de Figueiró, the Conde de Figueiró, and the Visconde de Asseca jumped onto the carriage to shield the Royal Family. Screaming, the Condessa de Figueiró could do no more than cradle the disfigured Luis Filipe in her arms.

The Marques de Lavradio, part of the royal party who had been making his way home on foot, had heard someone shout, *"They're shooting at the royal carriage!"*[29] Immediately, the Marques had run to the Terreiro do Paço; he couldn't see the carriage, but now heard the shout: *"They've killed the King."*[30] He continued around the corner and proceeded down Arsenal Street until finally he caught up with the carriage at the entrance of the Arsenal's doors.

In his memoirs the Marques vividly recorded the horror he felt at his discovery: *"Never will I forget the spectacle that was revealed to me: the King, with his head inclined on his chest…with a trickle of blood dripping from his nose and mouth which left no illusion…on his state. The Queen…with a look of terror could only say: 'They've killed the King and the Prince!' The Royal Prince, fallen on the right hand side, displayed in his left cheek an enormous wound…*[there was] *little hope… The pale Infante, searched* [for a handkerchief] *to dry the blood of his brother. Near the royal carriage there was only the Condessa de Figueiró, a lady-in-waiting to the Queen…who supported the Prince and, behind the lieutenant of the cavalry Francisco Figueira, injured, with a rifle in hand, and the Visconde de Asseca. Only when we entered the Arsenal, helping to transport the bodies for the medical post, did we loosen the collar of the suit of the Prince. The heart was still beating, but a few moments later stopped."*[31]

It was months before Manuel could bring himself to record his memories of the incident. Finally, on May 21 he was able to put his thoughts to paper:

"I was looking at the statue of Dom Jose and I saw a black bearded man wearing a big coat. I saw this man open his coat and draw out a carbine. I was so far from imagining something as terrible as what happened that I later thought to myself, 'What a stupid joke.' The man stepped off the pavement and started shooting…When I saw this bearded man, looking absolutely terrifying, take aim at the carriage well, I realized what was about to happen…What happened, only God, my mother and I myself know; even my beloved and deeply mourned brother only saw a few minutes of it before he himself was shot down. How I miss them, my God! Give me strength, Lord, to carry this heavy cross to Calvary! Only you, my God, know how much I have been suffering! Soon after Buica had started shooting…a real shootout started, like a hunting party! Terreiro do Paço was empty, no security steps had been taken! This

is what I cannot forgive Joao Franco for. Immediately after Buica started shooting, another man got out from under the Arcada do Ministerio and fired at my poor father at close range...Bastards! To round up their evil doings and their awful cowardice, they fired at him through his back. After that I do not remember much of what happened; it was so quick! I remember perfectly seeing my adored and heroic mother standing in the carriage still carrying her flowers and shouting at those evil beasts: 'Monsters, monsters.' There was enormous confusion. I also remember, and I will never forget, coming to the corner of Tereiro do Paço and Rua do Arsenal and seeing my brother standing in the carriage with a gun in his hand. About him, I can only say what Canon Aires Pacheco said at his funeral...: 'He died a hero's death, next to his King!' My God, how terrible! Whenever I think about the enormous tragedy, it still seems like a nightmare to me! When we were already at Rua do Arsenal, I suddenly looked at my dearest brother. I saw him lying on his right side with an enormous wound in his left cheek from which blood poured as if from a spring! I got a handkerchief from my pocket to see if I could stop the bleeding; but what could I do? The handkerchief was soon completely soaked. In the middle of all that chaos, we were in doubt about where to go; we thought about the hospital at Estrela but it was decided to go to the Arsenal. At Rua do Arsenal, I was hit in the arm by a bullet. It felt a bit like being struck, a bit like a blow with a whip: it was in the upper right arm. Now that I think still on this dreadful day and on the terrible attack it seems to me almost certainly...that I escaped by making a movement instinctively for the left side...In the second carriage was the Conde de Figueiró and the Marques de Alvito and in the third the Visconde de Asseca, the Vice Admiral Guilherme A. de Brito Capelo and Major Antonio Waddington. When we came to the entrance of the Arsenal the Condessa de Figueiró got into our carriage and I also remember that the Visconde de Asseca and the Conde de Figueiró got onto the side of the carriage. Inside the Arsenal I got out of the carriage first and afterwards my adored Mother...How I then passed those hours in the Arsenal no one can dream! The first thing that I lost completely was the notion of time. I grasped my poor and so dear Mother by an arm and I wouldn't let go and I asked the Condessa de Figueiró not to leave us. There was still doubt (unhappily short lived) if those two beings so dear still lived! Within minutes doctors arrived...Dr. Bossa (who seemed to me to be the first to arrive), Dr. Moreira Junior and Dr. Antoino Lencastre...As soon as Dr. Bossa arrived he lighted a match and still their pupils retracted. However, when the test was repeated not even this small sign of life remained. At the Ajuda Palace, my poor grandmother had been told to come to the Arsenal. I was not there when she arrived. I was having my arm attended to."[32]

Maria Pia had been informed over the telephone that her son had been injured. On the way to the Arsenal she was told that Carlos was dead, but nothing was ever said then or before about Luis Filipe. Upon entering the Arsenal, Maria Pia had immediately thrown herself down beside the corpse of her son. Then she rose and embraced Amelia, crying, "*My son has been murdered.*"[33] But Amelia gave the answering cry, "*And mine too!*"[34] Only then did Maria Pia realize there was a second lifeless body. According to some sources the shock of seeing the mutilated remains of her grandson was too much for Maria Pia and she had fainted. When she was revived, Maria Pia was still in a state of shock. The Dowager Queen could be heard crying over and over again, *"My little one, where is he?"*[35]

After Manuel's arm was attended to, preparations were made for the Braganzas to safely depart the Arsenal. At 7 o'clock that evening Maria Pia, Amelia, and Manuel left the Arsenal for the Necessidades Palace under heavy guard in a closed carriage escorted by a squadron of the cavalry of the Municipal Guard. The Count of Sabugosa, detached to accompany the Royal Family in the carriage, received a revolver for their protection. Maria Pia also wanted a handgun, asking for a pistol, which to her disappointment, but to everyone else's relief due to her almost catatonic state of shock, she did not receive.

When the Royal Family arrived at the palace, they found their devoted attendants, including Thomaz de Mello Breyner, awaiting them. *"It was a horrible scene!"* recalled Manuel. *"All cried in distress…very slowly we wandered up stairs…I accompanied my poor and adored Mother up to her quarters and left my poor Grandmother in a salon."*[36]

There the stunned Maria Pia remained for the most part alone, nursing her grief stoically in silence. *"The old Queen sat in a chair, without a word, without a tear, her glassy eyes fixed on the wall,"* noted the diarist Raul Brandou in his memoirs. *"And in this manner she stayed for hours, as unmoving as a rock."*[37]

At nine o'clock that night the remains of her son and grandson were brought to the palace and the improvised manner of their transport could not have been more macabre: the corpses of the King and Hereditary Prince were transported in carriages seated upright.[38] The Conde de Sabugosa had returned to the Arsenal to escort the King, while the Marques de Lavradio and Visconde de Asseca accompanied the Hereditary Prince. When the remains arrived at the palace, rigormortis had already set in making the corpses extremely difficult to remove, especially that of Carlos due to his excessive weight.

The shock of the regicide reverberated around the Royal Courts of Europe.[39] Archduke Franz Ferdinand, whose own assassination would spark World War I, had exclaimed, *"They are shooting us like sparrows from the roofs."*[40] Great Britain was particularly struck hard by the news. The stunned King Edward had cried in disbelief, *"What! Two Knights of the Garter shot in the street in broad daylight."*[41] *"Everyone shaken to the core here,"* confirmed Count Mensdorff, the Austrian ambassador to Great Britain. *"The King and Queen feel it very badly. Everything has been cancelled."*[42] In honor of his dear friend King Edward with his wife Queen Alexandra had attended a requiem mass at St. James's Church, a significant gesture as this was the first time since the Reformation that a British sovereign had attended a Catholic service.

Royal representatives were sent to the official funeral held in Lisbon on February 8, but not without trepidation. The Kaiser even dispatched a contingent of soldiers to protect his representative, his second son Prince Eitel Frederick. The funeral service was held in the chapel of the Necessidades Palace despite rumors that revolutionaries would open the door of the church and throw bombs to end the life of the remaining family members. For their protection the mourners were seated on podiums almost reaching to the ceiling of the church. The gallery in the chapel was prepared with six rows of seats for the royal attendants. In the first row sat the young king between his mother and grandmother. From time to time Manuel could not suppress a sob and tears rolled down his cheeks, but aware of the two queens' equal distress he would periodically squeeze their hands in reassurance.

After the mourners had paid their last respects to the slain monarch and his heir, it was time to transport their remains to St. Vincent's for interment. When the coffin containing Carlos's remains was lifted from the catafalque, people expected to hear the accompanying grunting made by the effort to support his excessive weight, but it was a blood-curdling scream that caught everyone off guard. It had come from Maria Pia. Having finally lost control of her tightly reigned emotions, the Queen Dowager broke through the file of mourners and disappeared into the palace. Her ladies-in-waiting eventually found Maria Pia in a small room located near the entrance hall.[43] She had momentarily fainted, but when she came to, Maria Pia, with smile full of melancholy, assured her ladies-in-waiting that she felt better.[44]

The next day the Marquesa de Rio Maior called upon Maria Pia at the Ajuda Palace. Maria Pia again assured her lady-in-waiting she felt better, but the Maquesa knew that the Queen Dowager didn't want anyone to speak of what had happened.

Maria Pia, however, was not better as she suffered an emotional and physical decline following the murder of her son and grandson. According to Vital Fontes, a server at the Ajuda Palace, she seemed to have *"aged twenty years. Never so great was her pain. She suffered more with the death of her son than the one before with her husband. She did not sleep and had to be made to eat. She would stop in any place, and then stay there an hour or more, talking alone and making gestures like a lunatic."*[45]

The emotional trauma Maria Pia had suffered led to a nervous breakdown, and in her diminished mental capacity she now had one great obsession. Maria Pia believed the flowers on the carpet in her room were sprinkled with the blood of her son and grandson. The Queen Dowager was continually ordering her servants to water the carpet to erase all traces of blood.

The change in this once glamorous, strong-willed Queen into a broken old woman was shocking for all to see. Raul Brandao sadly observed in his memoirs: "[In] *the...Ajuda Palace, among invalids and some ladies-in-waiting...Maria Pia passed days and nights, what a figure of tragedy, watering the flowers of her carpet... counting one...two...three - Of whom does she refer? The brother, the King, the Prince, all assassinated? Seated at the table she would talk to imaginary figures...that were seated to her side: 'Eat Luis. You don't want this dish, Carlos?' – And the return to water one day, another day, always, the flowers that never turn green again of the same carpet in her room...And this was the elegant wife, who had aroused passion and inspired poets, [now] she looks like an old actress, without a contract…full of wrinkles, out of the middle of her epoch…with false teeth and hair died…blond.*"[46]

Although she had retired from almost all official ceremonies and had stopped receiving due to her declining mental and physical state, even at this stage of her life Maria Pia was still capable of charming many of the people that she came into contact with. In her last meeting with her *"dear and unforgettable Queen,"*[47] the Marquesa de Rio Maior could see that Maria Pia was afraid small talk would turn to the recent tragedy, and she had gently led the conversion to the subject of the Queen's two Angora cats, but the Marquesa recalled that despite everything Maria Pia was still extremely affectionate with her.

Fortunately, as the shock of the trauma she endured lessened over time, Maria Pia made strides in regaining her mental faculties. By the end of that fatal year Maria Pia's correspondence shows coherent thought, although sadly much of her letters were written to offer condolences as the old guard at court was dying off. She would be particularly pained by the death of her devoted friend the Duque de Loule in March of 1909. But despite this added grief Maria Pia refused to allow her newfound pain to set her back and she had pulled herself together enough to again begin receiving official visitors of state such as the presidents of Argentina and Brazil.

While Maria Pia saw improvements in her mental condition, sadly her physical health continued to deteriorate. Increasingly, she suffered from trouble with her kidneys and poor circulation, along with migraines, a malady which had plagued her since childhood.

Unfortunately, there were a few in the younger generation at court that sought to take advantage of the Queen Dowager in her altered condition, and soon there emerged a plot to commit Maria Pia to an insane asylum. When Thomaz de Mello Breyner was called to the Ajuda Palace on March 9, 1910 by Dr. Lencastre to confer on Maria Pia's state, he was horrified to learn this doctor was of the opinion she should be committed. *"I have reason to suspect that this is…inspired by the Condessa de Figueiró* [the devoted lady-in-waiting to Queen Amelia] *in order to put the old Queen in an asylum,"* Breyner noted in his diary. *"It does not have my vote. This is a disgrace. From the Ajuda Palace I'll go at once to speak to the King."*[48]

Although Breyner attributed this scheme solely to the Condessa, it appears the conspiracy went even higher up the chain of command. While Lencastre may have set this plan into motion on the orders of the Condessa, he was confident of Amelia's approval. After meeting with Thomaz, Lencastre had immediately telegraphed Amelia, who was in Biarritz, with the report that he'd recommended, *"what you have for years advocated."*[49]

Amelia's long standing recommendation bears examination. While it is true Maria Pia had suffered from periods of depression throughout her life and could be eccentric, she had certainly not displayed signs of certifiable insanity "for years." Only in the previous year could her behavior fall into this category, but even now all evidence pointed towards Maria Pia having fully recovered from her mental breakdown. Amelia's avocation merely shows her continuing rancor for her mother-in-law more than any true concern for her well-being.

Thomaz did indeed complain to the King, but if he had expected Manuel to share his outrage, he would be disappointed. Manuel's reaction can best be described as muted as he was well aware the Condessa and Lencastre were acting in accordance to his mother's sentiments. While Manuel himself found it difficult to go against his beloved mother, the situation also presented the King with other troubling concerns. He didn't want to face the wrath of the Savoys if he carried through with putting his grandmother away, as Victor Emmanuel, Clotilde, and Laetitia had all communicated their indignation when they learned on what Manuel was deliberating. The King also had to take under consideration the reaction of the Portuguese, as Maria Pia was the only member of the Royal Family who remained popular with the people.

Nostalgic for the more stable times in which Luis and Maria Pia had reigned, the Queen Dowager had in the eyes of the populace evolved into a symbol of political neutrality; a non-polarizing figure. A passage written by Joao Chagas, published in a biography on King Manuel by Rocha Martins, describes the reputation Maria Pia had earned through the ages with her dedication in upholding the Portuguese constitution by her refusal to play the country's political parties against one another: *"Queen Maria Pia...could not be corrupted, enticed or bribed in favor of a political party. She didn't divide a nation. While she was* [the reigning] *queen, the Portuguese were all liberal even the church."* He concluded his assessment by comparing Maria Pia's scrupulously upheld promise of political fairness to the behavior of her successors. *"After her queens* [sic] *wreaked havoc in Portugal."*[50]

Clearly committing Maria Pia would have been an act of infamy in the public conscientious, and with this in mind Manuel stalled for time, ordering doctors of the royal court to observe his grandmother for a week before reuniting to vote on a decision. On March 11 the doctors of the Royal Court gathered at the Necissidades Palace to decide Maria Pia's fate. To Breyner's relief in the ensuing vote his colleagues, Feijao, Tavares, Ravara, and Meireles, all joined him in energetically and unanimously rejecting the idea forwarded by Lencastre.[51] Outmaneuvered Lencastre was reduced to covering his tracks and he sent Amelia the self-serving telegraph, *"The Queen is much better. Don't worry."*[52] The hypocrisy of this turn around has inspired Maria Pia's most recent Portuguese biographer to quite reasonably point out that if she were still *"insane"* during this time then her insanity could have hardly been cured within a week![53]

Manuel, himself, wrote to his mother clearly wanting the matter over and done with: *"Grandmother by the grace of God is better, especially her mental state; she said the most extraordinary things you could possibly imagine, that I don't even want to repeat...*[The] *doctors have decided on the treatment Grandmother is currently following which has already resulted in improvements."*[54]

Manuel's refusal to record just what his grandmother said is quite intriguing. It raises the question of whether Maria Pia confronted the conspirators over the plot to have her committed.[55] Did Breyner alert his beloved queen of the conspiracy concocted against her or did the constant supervision from the doctors arouse Maria Pia's own suspicions? While Maria Pia may not have been at her best, she was certainly no fool and perfectly aware of what was going on around her. Unfortunately, this is another shadowy period of Maria Pia's life in which there is little documentation and in the scant paper trail the involved parties did leave behind they were extremely guarded in their choice of words. Historians can only speculate on what all transpired.

What we do know is that for now Maria Pia was allowed to remain in her beloved Ajuda Palace. But there were even more ruthless conspirators to contend with and they were determined to expel the entire Braganza Royal Family from their home.

Chapter XIV

Revolution, Exile and Death

Franco's dictatorship did not survive Carlos's death. Sensitive to the role he had played in the tragedy, Franco offered his resignation, which King Manuel gladly accepted.[1] The remaining Royal Family had never approved of Franco, and the former strongman had left the royal palace in tears. Maria Pia was alleged to have reviled him with the words: "*You promised to release the monarchy from its tomb and all that you have done has been to dig the graves of my son and grandson.*"[2] Years later Franco claimed in his memoirs that Maria Pia had not displayed any hostility toward him after the regicide, and in all probability he was telling the truth. Despite her great pain, Maria Pia was an empathetic enough person to realize that Franco was also suffering. "*I very much pity this man,*" she told the Italian minister at the time of his departure. "[He had] *such good intentions, but so sad an end!*"[3]

The former president of the council, Jose Luciano, who had served both his grandfather and father, quickly appeared to advise the inexperienced young King in forming a substitute government. But Luciano just as quickly ran afoul of the republican contingency. The republican Espregueira accused Luciano of authorizing advanced payments to Maria Pia, who according to Espregueira, was at this juncture mad.[4] Eventually, Luciano would follow the same path as Franco as he too was driven into exile when a bank, of which he was governor, was found guilty of embezzling funds.

Fortunately, Manuel did not rely upon his politicians alone for advice as he had the support of his stalwart mother Amelia. However, Amelia's support would prove to be a double edged sword for the King. While Manuel was able to draw emotional strength from his mother, unfortunately her tutelage was not well received in certain factions at court. Sadly, there remained the divide between Carlos's old party and that of Amelia's as the private diaries of Thomaz Breyner illustrate.

A devoted friend to Carlos, Breyner had also been fond of Manuel as a child, but he soured on him in the role of King as Manuel's dependence on his mother did not inspire confidence in Thomaz. While Breyner admitted there was good in Amelia, he could not bring himself to like her as she continued her political activism against her deceased husband's policies. He was even less tolerant of her circle, especially the Condessa de Figueiró, who did not bother to hide her satisfaction at finally being in control. "*All goes wrong in Portugal,*" Breyner recorded in disgust. "*And they want to attribute all the blame...to poor King Carlos. On the very night of the regicide I heard...the Condessa de Figueria exclaim...now we will start to have order...Poor dear King Carlos. How well he knew treachery.*"[5]

His diary entries became increasingly critical of Manuel and his reign. *"He is weak and without courage,"* Thomaz wrote when complaining of the King's reliance on his mother and her entourage. *"The Condessa de Figueria is treacherous and the Visconde de Lima is sly. And it is these three creatures who give* [advice]*...at this moment. Poor King!"*[6]

Unfortunately, Amelia's public persona was also problematic for her son. Amelia was hated for her piousness by the Republican movement, who portrayed her as a reactionary, and under her guidance Manuel, himself a devout Catholic, was earning the same reputation.

In a calculated move to bolster his image it was planned for Manuel to visit the northern provinces of his country famed for their liberalism, where his grandmother, known for maintaining a strong spirit in this fundamental belief and still remembered for her charitable aid to this region, remained extremely popular. It was hoped Maria Pia's popularity could extend to include the young King.

Manuel spent his nineteenth birthday, his first as King, touring Oporto, and he received a warm reception even from the young idealistic students at Coimbra University, the birthplace of the republican movement. It would seem that all the deliberate planning had paid off. *"I am very grateful my dear daughter for...the good news of the sincere and enthusiastic manifestations Manuel received in Oporto,"* Maria Pia wrote in relief upon learning from Amelia the details of Manuel's favorable reception. *"For me it is my one solace amid the sadness of these times."*[7]

But Manuel's next move to bolster support for the ailing monarchy would not be as easily accomplished. Similar to his grandfather's time the Braganza monarchy was again short on heirs. Manuel's uncle Afonso was declared the Hereditary Prince, but as a lifelong bachelor it was unlikely he would marry. Thus the preservation of the Braganza Dynasty fell entirely upon Manuel's shoulders. Procuring a royal bride was a must for the King.

In order to strengthen his country's ancient alliance with their ally Great Britain, Manuel was determined his bride would be a British princess. There was talk of Princess Patricia of Connaught, originally considered for his elder brother, and now of Princess Alexandra of Fife, King Edward's granddaughter, the eldest daughter of his daughter Louise, the Princess Royal, and Alexander, the Duke of Fife. As Princess Patricia was Manuel's elder by eight years the still teenaged Manuel not unnaturally gravitated towards Princess Alexandra, two years his junior.

When discussing the marriage negotiations with Maria Pia, her lady-in-waiting the Marquesa de Unhao advised, *"Your Majesty, Manuel...must chose...And he can chose after viewing."*[8] But Maria Pia, who had married Luis by proxy without ever meeting him, looked back fondly on her marriage, considering their union a successful one. Thus, she did not think it was absolutely necessary for Manuel to meet the Princesses in order to choose. *"And you think that it is preferable he see them?"*[9] she questioned.

At this stage her grandson very much wanted to view the Princesses, particularly his preference Princess Alexandra. In November of 1909, Manuel traveled to England, to enlist the aid of the Portuguese ambassador, the Marques Luis de Soveral, who was also a close friend of the British sovereigns, in his search for a bride. During the visit, Soveral was unable to obtain an opportunity for his King to meet with Princess Alexandra, and showing his immaturity the disappointed Manuel had left Soveral a departing note jokingly involving the Princess: *"My dear Luis/the Bride and Bridegroom send their best love/Alexandra/Manuel."*[10]

From England Manuel paid a state visit to France, where he found consolation in the arms of the French actress and dancer Gaby Deslys. After Manuel returned to Portugal he recklessly continued the affair, inviting Gaby to Lisbon where he plied her with jewels. Unfortunately, the King's youthful liaison played right into his opponents' hands. According to Republican propaganda Manuel intended to marry Gaby, whom he had already given not only the crown Jewels but also vast sums of money from the Portuguese treasury.[11]

Faced with the constant republican criticism Manuel resumed his search for a wife, no longer considering viewing the princesses a prerequisite for his marriage and his desperation to secure a British princess shows in his new appeal to Soveral. *"Where is the issue of the marriage? To which princess has negotiations led? My dear Soveral you cannot image the anxiety that there is here in the country to have knowledge of the subject and the burning desire that the marriage be with a British princess. I learned recently today that Bernardino Machado* [a republican politician] *said to one of his supporters the following: On the day that the King marries an English Princess the republican party will lay down their arms!"*[12]

Manuel stubbornly persisted, writing to the ambassador his impression of the British sovereigns' preferences for his potential bride. *"King Edward I think is more inclined to the side of Princess Patricia, and Queen Alexandra seems to me to prefer Princess Alexandra of Fife."*[13]

Contrary to the impression King Manuel had received, Queen Alexandra was not enthusiastic at the prospect of her granddaughter becoming Queen of a besieged monarchy, where the former King and Hereditary Prince had been slaughtered in their own streets.[14] Nor would the British Court have supported sending Princess Patricia to Portugal for the very same reason.[15] However, when confronted with the insistent inquiries of Soveral on behalf of his king, Queen Alexandra fell back on the old excuse of difference of religion. Instead, she and her husband produced an alternative candidate with more distant British connections, Edward's great-niece, Princess Louise of Battenberg, a morganatic member of a German Princely House.

King Edward would not, however, play a large role in these new negotiations as he fell ill with bronchitis in early 1910, culminating in his death in May. Although deeply saddened by the death of his father's close friend, Manuel saw King Edward's funeral, scheduled for May 14th, as an opportunity to pursue the hand of Princess Louise. He instantly wrote Soveral requesting an interview with the Princess. *"I beg you tell me it is possible despite the…occasion to take advantage of my stay in London to advance the question of marriage. I would much appreciate being able to see the*

Princess Battenberg to know her and ask her despite her sadness."[16]

In a letter written to his mother from Buckingham Palace on May 15 Manuel left a detailed account of King Edward's funeral and of Queen Alexandra's efforts, despite her bereavement, on behalf of the Braganzas cause:

"In London I was met at the station by the King [George V who had succeeded his father] *and the whole royal family; and there were masses of people on the streets from Victoria station to the Palace. When we arrived here the King introduced me to the whole household and took me straight up to Queen Alexandra. When she saw me she embraced me in tears. Poor darling: I feel so sorry for her... We talked for a while and in the end the King put his arms around me at one side and Queen Alexandra on the other, and the King said to the Queen: 'This is a true friend, who understands our grief better than any of those who have come here.... King Edward's funeral took place yesterday. It was the most wonderful spectacle one could possibly see. I can't even try to describe it. Nine kings, more than sixty princes on horseback followed by their retinues; the Queens and Ladies in all the ceremonial carriages. In the streets, where there were more than 4,000,000 people, the silence and respect were extraordinary. It was terribly hot; there were more than 6,000 cases of sunstroke. The ceremony in St. George's Chapel at Windsor was the most impressive one could imagine. Confidentially, and only for your eyes, I must tell you that Soveral spoke to Queen Alexandra today. In view of their conversation Queen Alexandra is to give a dinner party tomorrow, to which the family "in question" has been invited. We shall see how it goes...How good it is of Queen Alexandra to think of all this in the midst of her tremendous grief! May God help us!!!"*[17]

But Queen Alexandra's efforts and Manuel's hopes were for naught as Princess Louise famously quipped she'd never marry a king or a widower. Ironically, when Louise finally wed Crown Prince Gustav Adolf of Sweden in 1923 her choice of a spouse was a combination of the very two things she swore she didn't want in a man. Manuel returned from King Edward's funeral to Portugal without a bride, and sadly he would soon be without a throne.

The republicans had continued their campaign against the Royal Family, with the former extravagance of Maria Pia a new favorite target. The anti-monarchist press published several articles on the Queen Dowager's debts, revealing that Maria Pia owed a Parisian jeweler a small fortune.[18]

In the meantime, her grandson was trying to get a handle on yet another ministerial crisis as his Prime Minister Veiga Beirao wanted to dissolve the cortes and hold new elections to gain more control. But the King would not repeat his father's mistake and Beirao was forced to resign. However, in refuting Carlos's actions Manuel would make a devastating tactful error of his own. He appointed Teixeira de Souza to the vacant office, a move that would lose the monarchy much of its remaining monarchist support as Souza was regarded as a man of almost Republican tendencies.[19] Clearly, Manuel had hoped this appointment would help recruit more liberals to the side of the monarchy, but he had sadly misjudged the situation. Now, Maunel had lost indispensable support amongst the vital military segment, and there quickly emerged evidence that certain elements of the navy planned to stage a revolution.[20] After consulting with the King and Amelia, Souza ordered the alleged units of the navy to sea, thus only briefly delaying the inevitable.[21]

Shortly afterwards on October 3, 1910 Dr. Miguel Bombarda, a popular republican deputy, who was also on the board of directors of Lisbon's lunatic asylum, was murdered by one of his former patients. Although the murder had not been politically motivated in any way it was just the excuse the republicans needed. On October 4 regiments of the Sixteenth Infantry and the First Artillery mutinied, gaining control of Lisbon within hours.

Manuel bravely tried to make a stand against the rebels by establishing himself in the capital at the Necessidades Palace. But when the warships the Adamastor, the San Raphael, and the D. Fernando, stationed in the Tagus, began to bombard the palace the King was persuaded by his ministers to flee. Manuel drove to the Mafra Palace, an old monastery that was a safe distance from Lisbon, to regroup.

Both Maria Pia and Amelia, who were in Sintra when the revolution broke out, rushed to join the King at Mafra. Here on October 5 they learned that the victorious rebels had declared Portugal a republic. In a hasty family conference it was decided that they would sail for Oporto, still considered loyal to the crown. Manuel and the two Queens would drive to Ericeira, a nearby fishing village, where Afonso would be awaiting them with the Royal yacht Amelia, though the commander of the ship believed the waters at Ericeira were too rough for the remaining Royal Family to try to board the vessel.

Maria Pia, however, it seems was the only member of the Braganzas to question if they were making the right decision as she asked, *"But is it* [necessary] *in order to govern that we leave?"*[22] Despite her reputed mental deficiencies, Maria Pia appears to have been the only one in this instance to fully realize the potential danger for the monarchy of quitting Portuguese soil if even only momentarily. Maria Pia had no intention of leaving Portugal, which had been her home for almost half a century, and she wished to die there as well. She would resist departure until the very last,[23] proclaiming that a Savoy Princess knew how to die beside her husband.

At 4 o'clock that afternoon the Royal Family began their journey for Ericeira. Accompanying Mara Pia was her devoted lady-in-waiting the Marquesa de Unhao. Departure from the royal attendants remaining behind was difficult, but for now the majority of the Braganzas were confident they would be returning. The decision made, Maria Pia, whatever her misgivings, slipped into her role of the correct sovereign never giving a hint to her inner turmoil. Thomaz de Mello Breyner, who had loved and admired Maria Pia since he was a child, faithfully recorded his last meeting with his beloved Queen, touching upon this stoicism that she displayed in the face of uncertainty: *"I saw Queen Maria Pia for the last time in Mafra…when she left for exile. I kissed her hand twice when she got into the automobile and she said to me 'Goodbye Thomaz, many thanks.' I am wretched. How she was my friend. She left for exile with serenity as if she were entering the throne room."*[24]

At Ericeria the two Queens boarded the vessel the Navegador, while Manuel boarded the ship ironically called Bom-Fin, *"the Good End,"* which would take them out to meet the yacht Amelia. As feared the boarding did indeed prove difficult for the aged Maria Pia. Jose Jacob Bensabat, the maritime officer who oversaw the transfer, found the Queen Dowager excessively pale, which he acknowledged was understandable under the circumstances, though he did note that she was unafraid.[25]

Once on board the Amelia the Royal Family would find their plans to sail to Oporto foiled by the commanding officers. These officials feared crossing paths with the rebels, and asserted they had no means of defense. Considering it their first and foremost duty to preserve the lives of the Royal Family they instead set course south for the British colony of Gibraltar, despite the protests of the Queens. *"But it will look as if the King as vanished,"* Maria Pia had objected, emphasizing her point with an expressive gesture.[26] Unbeknownst to the officials, in their caution, would make it impossible for Manuel to reclaim his crown. Maria Pia, said to be the only member of the Royal Family still loved by the people, sailed into exile.[27] Ironically, it was exactly forty-eight years to the day that she had first arrived to the country. On that day Maria Pia had been welcomed to Portugal with a sense of euphoria, now as she sailed away there was only an ominous silence.

At Gibraltar the Royal Family clung with fervor to the hope that Oporto and other regions distant from Lisbon would rally to their cause and counterbalance the insurrectionary success in the capital.[28] But their hopes were in vain as without a King to rally behind the monarchist supporters remained inert. Ultimately, it was Amelia, thus far the only member of the Royal Family to have experienced exile, who sadly concluded, *"One does not return from exile."*[29]

It had never been the Braganzas intention to quit Portugal, and Amelia always strove to correct the impression that they had fled the country in face of adversity. Years later in an interview after Maria Pia's death she asserted: *"The Braganzas did not flee to Gibraltar. They embarked for Oporto. Nor did the yacht sail south because she carried two crying Queens. No! We have to honor Queen Maria Pia's memory and I ask for justice, only justice. We did not cry, we were not afraid!"*[30]

At Gibraltar, Amelia and Manuel accepted the inevitable, making plans to settle in England, Amelia's old home in exile. Maria Pia, however, had no intention of joining them. If she could not live in Portugal then she would return to her old homeland, Italy. Sadly, while Maria Pia would have the companionship of her devoted lady-in-waiting on this journey, she would be without a single member of her family since Afonso, like his brother before him, had never cultivated a closer relationship with the Savoys. Fearing his presence in Italy could create diplomatic difficulties Afonso decided it would be best to go to England to help Manuel and Amelia settle in before joining his mother, who'd have to pave the way for his welcome.

On October 16 Maria Pia was met at Gibraltar by the Italian cruiser *Regina Elena*. Dignified and dressed entirely in black, the Queen boarded the ship amid military honors.[31] Despite everything she had gone through, Maria Pia still knew how to present herself suitably befitting her position. Throughout the short journey to Italy, Maria Pia impressed the Italian crew with her calm demeanor and affability. Maria Pia spoke enthusiastically of her birthplace and expressed the desire to go to Naples as she felt the climate there would be beneficial to her health. On the sensitive subject of the Portuguese revolution Maria Pia generally stayed silent, only once alluding to her pain at having to leave her country of adoption after forty-eight years.[32]

On October 18 the ship anchored offshore Italy at the San Rossore beach. Maria Pia's nephew King Victor Emmanuel III boarded the ship to escort her onto Italian soil. Once safely in the presence of her extended family Maria Pia could finally let down her guard and express her inner anguish: *"How unhappy I am… At my age, not to have family or country."*[33] *"Come, dear Aunt…Elena awaits you,"*[34] her nephew had rallied, expertly giving her into the care of his capable wife, Queen Elena, who was extremely fond of her aunt by marriage.

Maria Pia stayed for a time with Victor and his family at the Racconigi Castle, where she found some comfort in her sadness in the affection of Victor and Elena's young children,[35] then visited with her sister Clotilde at Moncalieri, before arriving at her original destination of Naples. Here she would be joined by Benjamin Pinto, who had been ill at the time of the revolution and thus not by his Queen's side. Once recovered, Pinto with his family devotedly followed her into exile. Maria Pia's other devoted lady-in-waiting the Marquesa de Belas with her son and daughter soon followed.

But the most emotional reunion for the Queen was with her son Afonso who finally arrived in Naples on December 2. Witnesses recall that when Afonso spotted his mother, who was patiently waiting for him at the train station, he had immediately ran for her with his arms wide open to embrace her, while Maria Pia made no effort to hold back her tears of joy.[36]

Sadly, while Maria Pia had the loving companionship of her son and friends, she would have no permanent residence in Italy, only apartments set aside for her at various Savoy palaces. But the Queen Dowager was perhaps not overly perturbed by this situation as she had no plans of staying in Italy permanently. Although described by many as broken in body and mind, Maria Pia still retained some of her old fighting spirit, and she was determined to return to Portugal. Shortly after her arrival in Turin, Maria Pia petitioned the new government to allow her to return to Portugal as a private citizen and, if it felt so inclined, to grant her a small living allowance.[37] Her request was denied: her presence in the country would obviously be of the utmost discomfort to the Republican regime,[38] although the Portuguese Minister of Foreign Affairs did eventually concede in granting Maria Pia an annuity.

While Maria Pia's relations welcomed her with open arms, Amelia and

Manuel arrived in England to a like reception. The Duke of Orleans, Amelia's brother, allowed the Portuguese exiles to settle in one of his estates, Woodnorton Hall, while they looked for a home of their own. Amelia finally settled on a property in Richmond, Abercorn House, a stone's throw from York House, the estate where she was born.

Meanwhile, Maria Pia led a melancholy but comfortable existence in exile assured to her by her newly granted annuity and the benevolence of her Savoy relations. But the Queen Dowager's desire to return to Portugal never waned. The Englishwoman Lady Paget commented on the exiled Maria Pia's continuing loyalty to her adopted country:

> "[At] *present she clings with...fidelity to everything Portuguese, and, indeed, she has returned to a transformed country; instead of Piedmont, she has found Italy, of which she even barely knows the language [it was a common complaint that the elder generation of the Savoys spoke Italian with a strong Piedmontese accent], much less, the habits of the people! They, who know her very well, always said that she was a very fine character...The Portuguese ought to be moved by the sad fate of this Princess, who came to them a mere child and felt so lonely and forlorn during the first years of her stay there that she wrote on the walls of her Palace the pathetic words 'Je m'ennuie!' and who yet has become so passionately attached to the country of her adoption that her exile from it, even after the ghastly events of some years ago, appears a crowning misfortune.*"[39]

In April of 1911, the Enlgish Dowager Queen Alexandra saw Maria Pia in Italy and passed along a message from her to Soveral: *"Queen Maria Pia asked that I tell you your Queen is well but sad."*[40] Tragically, although Maria Pia had attested that she was well, within a mere three months of this visit she would be dead.

Although in ill health for some time, Maria Pia's death would catch everyone by surprise. It was her sister Clotilde's health that was at center stage. After a near fatal brush with pneumonia, it was discovered that Clotilde had cancer. In late June the family began to gather at Moncalieri, and despite her own failing health Maria Pia had hurried to attend her sister's bedside. When Maria Pia arrived, she had bent to kiss Clotilde, who made a supreme effort to speak to her beloved little sister, but she was unable to articulate any intelligible words.[41] Clotilde died on June 25, 1911 in the presence of her children, sister, and sister-in-law Margherita. Maria Pia had immediately kissed her deceased sister's forehead, murmuring softly, *"Clotilde, I will soon follow."*[42]

Truer words were never spoken. Maria Pia did not feel well enough to attend her sister's funeral, and indeed after the death of her sole remaining sibling she appears to have lost all will to live. She had barely returned to her apartments in the Stupinigi Palace, her latest grace and favor residence, when on July 5, 1911 she began to experience a number of uremic attacks.[43] The doctors to the Italian Royal Family acknowledged that she was lost, and sent for her immediate relatives. Maria

Pia's sister-in-law Margherita, her nephew's wife Queen Elena, her niece Laetitia with her son Umberto, the Count of Salemi, and her son Afonso all managed to be with her in the end. Her dying request was to be turned to face her beloved Portugal. At 3:15 that afternoon Maria Pia died between the arms of Queen Margherita and her devoted lady-in-waiting the Marquesa de Belas. At the foot of her bed Afonso and Elena sobbed hysterically. It was exactly ten days after the death of her sister Clotilde.

The death chamber was immediately turned into a chapel. Four candles were lit around the bed, and honoring the deceased's abiding love for beautiful objects, flowers were placed around Maria Pia's remains in abundance. Margherita, who had loved Maria Pia since childhood, took on the heartrending task of responding to the numerous condolences the family received. "*The soul of our adored was already dead,*" she admitted in one reply. "[She] *had suffered too many horrific wounds to withstand this last sorrow* [the death of Clotilde]."[44]

Amelia had not assisted in Maria Pia's final moments, but she would have the final word on the funeral arrangements for her mother-in-law. She and her son Manuel were opposed to Maria Pia's remains being returned to Portugal at this early stage of their exile so it was decided that Maria Pia would rest among her ancestors at Superga for the time being.[45] After a mass on July 8 at Stupinigi Palace, Maria Pia's body was borne to the Church of Gran Madre di Dio, where her remains were given the final rites of absolution in the presence of German Kaiser Wilhelm II, Emperor Franz Joseph of Austria, and Tsar Ferdinand of Bulgaria, before being interned in the burial vault of the Italian Royal Family at Superga.[46]

Maria Pia's will revealed that she had made Afonso her heir, but he immediately renounced all his rights as the beneficiary so as not to bear the responsibility of her debts.[47] Afonso now made his home in Italy, but he was completely lost without his mother's counsel. He was, thus, to everyone's horror easy pickings for Nevada Stoody, a twice-divorced, once-widowed American adventuress. Nevada pursued the Duke of Oporto relentlessly, determined to gain a title, with one of Afonso's friends complaining that she had an "*animal sense of smell*"[48] since she always seemed to know where to find him. That Afonso was in ill health was probably also a factor in his capitulation. Afonso suffered from syphilis like his father, and within a year of their marriage he had almost completely lost his memory and was half paralyzed.

When they learned of his marriage, Manuel and Amelia cut off relations entirely with Afonso, and his Savoy relatives were only slightly more tolerant. Although the Italian King withdrew Afonso's pension, Victor Emmanuel, out of compassion for his cousin's ill health, allowed the Duke of Oporto to continue to live in Italy. In Naples on February 20, 1920 Afonso died, according to some journalists of the period, in poverty asleep atop some old newspapers. If true it was an inglorious end for Maria Pia's last surviving son.

Two years after her death Maria Pia's grandson also married in exile, but his choice of a bride was entirely suitable. Although Manuel had settled in England, he had become resigned to the fact that he would be unable to marry a British princess. He and his mother wisely turned their attention to Catholic princesses, and in 1913 Manuel finally wed his second cousin Princess Augusta Viktoria of Hohenzollern, the granddaughter of his Great Aunt Antonia. Sadly, for the Braganzas and their monarchist supporters their union would remain childless.

Manuel and Augusta Viktoria eventually settled in an estate of their own, Fullwell Park, not far from Amelia's home. Trying times were not far away as the First World War started in August 1914. During the conflict, the Portuguese royal family became deeply involved in hospital and humanitarian work. Queen Amelia visited field hospitals along the Western Front and served as a nurse in a hospital in Whitechapel; Manuel II also provided assistance to Allied hospitals in France, while supporting a hospital in Brighton; Augusta Viktoria served as a nurse in England, even though some were ungrateful to her for being a German.

In 1919, a few months after the end of the Great War, Amelia lost her mother, the Comtesse de Paris. The inheritance Amelia received from her mother certainly improved her own finances. In 1920 Abercorn House was closed down and after spending Christmas with her son and his wife, Amelia relocated to France. There she found a small palace, Château de Bellevue, in Chesnay, near Versailles. This became her home for the last three decades of her life. It was there, in fact, where Amelia received news of her son's untimely death in July 1932. It is said that the expression on the face of her servants was enough to convey to the Queen the awful news. As her butler extended to her a silver tray with a telegram on it, Amelia looked at him and said, *"I know, my son, he is dead!"*[49]

Amelia immediately departed to England to preside, with Augusta Viktoria by her side, over the funeral of her son. The Portuguese government asked that King Manuel return to lay in peace at St. Vicente da Fora. Amelia and her daughter-in-law accepted the request, although neither accompanied the late King on his last journey.

After Manuel's death, Augusta Viktoria returned to Germany. Seven years after Manuel's death, Augusta Viktoria married secondly. Her husband was Count Robert Douglas, an aristocrat ten-years her senior. They settled at Schloß Langenstein, his family's estate near Lake Constance. He died there in 1955. Augusta Viktoria survived her husband by a little more than a decade. She died at Münchhöf, Germany, in August 1966. Not surprisingly, Count Douglas and Augusta Viktoria were childless.

The death of King Manuel in 1932 brought to an abrupt end the ruling line of the Braganza dynasty. He was the last male descendant of Queen Maria de Gloria and King Ferdinand. However, thinking that preparations had to be made for such an eventuality, Manuel as his cousin the Duke of Braganza had settled the succession years before. In a sign of dynastic unity, Manuel and his cousin the Infante Miguel, only son of King Miguel, agreed that the Migueline line would succeed in case of extinction of the Braganza-Coburg line. Hence, in 1932, after Manuel's passing, Miguel's son, Infante Duarte Nuño succeeded his late cousin as head of the Portuguese royal family. Interestingly, Duarte Nuño went on to marry Princess Maria Francisca of Orleans-Braganza, a granddaughter not only of Emperor Pedro II of Brazil, but also of Prince Gaston of Orleans, a first cousin of Queen Amelia's father. It is due to this marriage that the bloodlines of Braganza, Coburg and Orleans find themselves present in the person of the Duke of Braganza, Duarte, eldest son of Duarte Nuño and Maria Francisca. He is the present-day head of the Portuguese royal house.

While Maria Pia's own line died out, her memory lived on in her Savoy relations, particularly with her great nephew Umberto II, who was also driven into exile after his own father Victor Emmanuel's dalliance with a dictatorship. Umberto chose Portugal as his home in exile, confirming in an interview that it was his family history along with his affection for his Great Aunt Maria Pia that prompted his decision:

"Certainly my choice was influenced more or less unconsciously, by the memory of Carlo Alberto, to whose memory, since a boy, I always had a kind of worship (among other things, judging by some portraits I resemble physically). Moreover, apart from Carlo Alberto, others...of the House of Savoy are inextricably linked to Portugal... Three Princesses of the House of Savoy, in fact, were Queens of Portugal. The first was Mafalda, wife of Alfonso Henriques, the first King of Portugal. The second was Maria Francesca di Savoia-Nemours who towards the end of the Seventeenth Century was the wife of King Alfonso VI...(she) later obtained an annulment of marriage for the serious mental state of her husband...(and remained Queen) by her second marriage to King Pedro II, brother of...Alfonso and his successor to the throne. A Princess of Savoy was the first Queen of Portugal. Fate wanted another queen with Savoy blood to assist the tragic decline of the monarchy. This was Maria Pia, daughter of King Victor Emmanuel II...who, on September 27, 1862, married King Louis I of Portugal. Maria Pia was an energetic and intelligent woman. She reigned for many years peacefully and happily, much loved by her subjects. But at the end of her life misfortune fell on her head. In February 1908, when she was already a widow...her son, King Carlos I and her grandson the Crown Prince Luiz Felipe, were slaughtered in a square in Lisbon. The old Queen did not cease to have love for her homeland of her adoption and her people...But two years after the Republican revolution had the upper hand and King Manuel (her remaining grandson) was forced to leave for exile. The old Queen Maria Pia even then did not cease to love her country of adoption; she did not want to leave the castle in Sintra where she led an almost monastic existence. Later, however, events forced her to return to Italy, where in the Stupinigi Castle she died a few months later. Despite the appalling evidence of recent years, her homeland of adoption and her subjects were always foremost in her thoughts and her love. When dying, she wished that her bed to be turned towards Portugal. I saw the Queen Maria Pia only a few times when I was very little, but felt for her, perhaps because I was deeply touched by her tragedy and her great courage, a particular affection and a boundless admiration. It was in tribute to her memory that I wanted to call my first daughter Maria Pia. I remember also, and this is one of my earliest memories of my

childhood, my mother, when I was four or perhaps five, sometimes promising me: 'If you are good you'll be sent to Portugal to your aunt.' Well, you see that I was too good because I have been sent to Portugal forever."[50]

Sadly, Umberto II died in exile and his body was not allowed to return to his homeland for burial. And the great aunt that had served as an inspiration to him still suffers from the same fate.

Maria Pia's wish to return to Portugal has never been fulfilled. While the other exiled Braganzas Manuel, Amelia, Afonso, and even the usurper Miguel and the wife he had espoused in exile have all been returned to St. Vicente da Fora for internment, Maria Pia, the most beloved Portuguese royal of her time, remains inexplicably in exile, interned in the Cathedral of Superga, near Turin, Italy.

Epilogue

Revolution, Exile and Death

The end of the Portuguese monarchy, although tragic, seems to have been unavoidable. While the country's worsening political situation instilled a sense of deep worry, infighting within the royal family did not help matters either. The rivalry between the two queens, Maria Pia and Amelia, was used by antimonarchists to further fuel the rancor already effectively directed against the monarchical institution. King Manuel II was a youngster lacking the political savvy to withstand outside influences that although good meaning, turned out to be detrimental to the success of his reign. There was around the court and country a sense that inevitable was doomed to happen, no matter what monarchists did to avoid the abyss. Hence, when the military rose against their king, the house of cards on which Manuel II's throne sat fell in a matter of hours.

The Duke of Oporto's decision to embark the Royal Family proved to be yet another terrible political and logistical error. Once off the kingdom's territory, once off Portuguese land, the Braganzas were unable to return. This decision has proven in countless example to be erroneous for a monarch facing a revolution ought never to abandon his sacred and constitutional obligation. He who runs, abandons – Manuel II's boarding the royal yacht was therefore seen by his already disheartened supporters as their king conceding defeat.

Once in exile, the Portuguese king was unable to stage a comeback. The shaky regime he led proved its weakness when unable to withstand a challenge that could have easily been extinguished. Yet in Portugal, life was just a tenuous under the new republic for political instability continued unabated. Socialism, anarchism, communism consumed the country and brought unparalleled political instability to a former kingdom that had a challenging time becoming a functional republic. It was not until 1932 when Portugal's political ills came to an end. That year, the shaky republic came under the control of Antonio de Oliveira Salazar, a right-wing politician once was described as one of the most gifted politicians of his generation. Salazar only briefly sat on the presidential chair, but he ruled Portugal with an iron fist for nearly four decades. He founded the Estado Novo (New State), a political entity that relied on Portugal being a beacon of multi-continental Luso civilization – Portugal was the beacon that brought light to the countries African territories, seeing as mere extensions of Portugal itself. Portugal thus became a source of civilization and stability to all its remaining worldwide possessions. His opponents, however, blamed Salazar's strong-arm tactics for the economic stagnation that Portugal suffered during his rule.

A Conservative Catholic, Salazar also reestablished serious contact with the exiled Braganzas. Eventually, Queen Amelia was invited to visit Portugal, while the remains of several Braganzas who died in exile were returned to the motherland and buried in eternal peace at San Vicente de Fora. Queen Amelia hoped to visit Portugal before dying. Her dream came true years later, three and a half decades after the overthrow of her son. Amelia's contacts with the Salazar regime had began in the late 1930s when she approached the Portuguese embassy with her intentions to donate to the country several historical objects in her collection, because she wanted to, *"give the Portuguese Nation, which I love so very much, and of which I had to honor to serve as queen, a testament of my deep tenderness and constant melancholy, wishing that the Portuguese will remember me with the same affection that I continue to have for them."*[1]

When the Second World War started, France fared quite poorly. Before the war's first year had passed, Paris was under German occupation. Concerned about Amelia's well being, the Portuguese embassy in Paris telegraphed Salazar requesting his intervention to secure the queen's safety. Portugal extended Amelia an invitation to return, but she kindly refused to accept it. When the German reached her home in Versailles, the Château de Bellevue, they requisitioned the structure for the use of officers. Amelia vehemently protested this violation of her privacy and left Versailles. However, unable to get far given the precarious state of affairs, she was left with no other options but to return to Bellevue. The officers who lived under her roof remained away from her private apartments, but she was forced for some time to serve as hostess to her beloved France's invaders. This unpleasant situation found a solution when Salazar ordered the Portuguese embassy to raise the national flag over Bellevue. By doing, not only was Amelia returned full control of her home, yet more importantly, she was rid of the German interlopers. One author described the situation as, *"Amelia was once again Queen of Portugal, at least as far as the end of her garden."*[2]

Throughout the years, Amelia and Salazar had maintained an important correspondence, developing a deep admiration and respect for the other. When in 1945 Salazar invited Amelia to visit Portugal, she gladly accepted. She arrived on May 17 and two days later Amelia went to San Vicente de Fora to pay her respects at the tombs of her husband and sons. It was an emotionally charged day for the remaining living member of the old Portuguese Royal Family. Outside San Vicente a large crowd had gathered to witness this historic visit.[3] When Amelia exited the monastery, the crowd broke into a spontaneous cheer celebrating their former queen. Salazar visited Amelia two days later, the day before she traveled to Sintra, site of so many fond memories. She also visited many other localities across Portugal, most reminding her of happier times. At the end of June, after spending nearly six weeks in her former kingdom, Amelia returned to Bellevue.

The return to Portugal accomplished, Amelia could now die in peace. In early 1948 she suffered a debilitating heart attack. Recovery was long and difficult, and she was never the same. Her will made the Duke of Braganza, Duarte Nuño, head of the family's Miguelist line, the heir to an important part of her legacy.

In 1950, both Portugal and France abolished the law that had forced their royal families to live in exile. The Duke of Braganza could now return to settle in Portugal, while the Comte de Paris, Henri, a nephew of Queen Amelia, could depart from his Portuguese estate near Sintra on his return journey to France. Amelia was delighted when informed of the news. *"I can finally,"* she said, *"in the very capital of France, hug my nephew, who is returning to the land of his ancestors."*[4] That July 5, on his forty-second birthday, the Comte de Paris, accompanied by his wife Isabelle, a sister of the Duchess of Braganza, came to Bellevue to pay his respects to his aunt Amelia. Photos taken that day show the joy visible in the old queen's face. Unfortunately, the visit was to be the last flicker of the happiness that had proved so elusive during Amelia's long life. In January 1951, Queen Amelia received news that brought her great affliction – her beloved sister, the Dowager Duchess of Aosta, died at Castellamare di Stabia.[5] Helene had lived since the fall of the Italian monarchy. It was a blow from which Amelia did not recover. More worrisome news arrived a few months later when the Duke and Duchess of Braganza were involved in a terrible automobile accident after attending the wedding of Archduke Otto of Austria and Princess Regina of Saxe-Meiningen. Their recovery took months.

The end approached by October 1951. Augusta Viktoria, now the wife of Count Douglas, arrived from Germany to keep vigil by her former mother-in-law's bedside. Also present were the Comte and Comtesse de Paris, who had settled in a large estate nearby. Present as well were some of Amelia's remaining loyal companions, among them the Visconde de Asseca and his wife, and Dr. Lencastre. Amelia died on October 25, 1951.[6]

Five days later, Amelia's earthly remains were brought to Dreux, necropolis of the Orleans family. A funeral for her earthly remains was celebrated there. Four weeks later, her coffin was taken to Brest, where the *Bartolomeu Dias* awaited to sail Amelia on her final journey to Portugal, where some 400,000 mourners filed past her bier as she lay in state. The government ordered the construction of a mausoleum at San Vicente de Fora, where on March 10, 1952, Queen Amelia's remains were buried. On the outside of large tomb that serves as her last resting place the legend reads: *"Here Rests in God Donha Amelia de Orleans e Braganza, Queen on the Throne, in Charity and Pain."*[7]

After her former mother-in-law's passing, Augusta Viktoria returned to Schloß Langenstein, where she lived in relative obscurity with her second husband. He died in 1955, while Augusta Viktoria survived him by more than a decade. She, a queen who never sat on the throne of her husband the king, passed away at Eigeltingen, in the German state of Baden-Württemberg on August 29, 1966.[8] Augusta Viktoria is buried on the grounds of Schloß Langenstein.

Maria Pia's Savoy relations eventually also lost their throne. During the Great War, Victor Emmanuel III abandoned his Austrian and German allies when bringing Italy on the side of the Allies. In the aftermath of November 1918, Italy gained large territories formerly ruled by the Habsburgs. These territorial gains immersed Rome in the intricacies of Balkan politics for the Savoy kings now saw the Adriatic Sea as another area of Italian influence. Italy's involvement in Balkan politics had dire results for the kingdom, particularly during the Second World War when Italy developed a hunger for further territories in the region.

Expansionism was a hunger that Rome did not satiate just with the Balkans. In due course, the Italians conceived late imperialistic ambitions that brought them to Africa, where they gained Libya, Eritrea and Somalia. Italy's African possessions were to be a deep source of instability for the next few decades. As with many other endeavors, Italy had embarked a few decades too late in the race for empire. Not only were the African possessions the source of great expenditure, but also they eventually brought unnecessary and devastating military campaigns that the Savoy kingdom could hardly afford. One of Queen Amelia's nephews, Prince Amedeo, 3rd Duke of Aosta, served as Viceroy and Governor General in Italian East Africa. When the Second World War ignited, Amedeo was also made commander of Italian forces in the region.[9] He was honorably defeated by the British in 1941 and allowed to surrender with military honors. The Duke of Aosta was interned in a prisoner of war camp. He died of a combination of malaria and tuberculosis in 1942.

Victor Emmanuel III, frustrated by the political instability affecting his kingdom sought a radical solution. In late 1921, bowing to popular demand Victor Emmanuel entrusted Benito Mussolini with the kingdom's government. Overnight, a right-wing dictatorship descended on Italy and democracy was dormant for the next few decades. Mussolini strong-armed the kingdom into submission by whatever means possible, imprisoning and exiling opponents, while manipulating public opinion with nationalism and Italian expansionism along the Mediterranean. For a time the ill-conceived dictatorship seemed to thrive and Italy witness a degree of stability not seen ever before. Yet, the undercurrents of Fascism eroded the Royal Family's prestige. When the situation worsened and Italy, now embroiled along with Nazi Germany in the Second World War, faced defeat both Mussolini and Victor Emmanuel III were held responsible for the ensuing debacle. In July 1943, to the horror of Italians, the Allies began an air bombing campaign over Rome. Six days later in an effort to break away from the tentacles of Nazi Germany, Victor Emmanuel III had Mussolini arrested. The King believed that by following a separate course from Berlin, he would save Italy from utter defeat at the hands of the Allies, who now seemed unstoppable. The damage was done however, and by the time the war ended two years later, the Savoys's days were numbered. The Germans retaliated against Victor Emmanuel by apprehending his daughter Mafalda, wife of Prince Philipp of Hesse, and sending her to a prison camp. She died in Buchenwald in 1944 from injuries she suffered after an Allied air raid.

Defeated, devastated and humiliated, Italy lay in ruins and occupied by Allied forces. Victor Emmanuel III was logically held responsible for Mussolini's abuses of power. In a last ditch effort to save the monarchy, the King abdicated and departed. Two years earlier he had named his only regent, in an effort to distance the monarchy from his mistakes. King Umberto II, who had been less amenable to Mussolini and his regime, succeeded his father. Umberto II's wife, Belgian-born Marie José, daughter of King Albert and Queen Elisabeth, had been an outspoken critic of Mussolini and the Fascists. Supporters of the monarchy believed that Umberto II and his popular wife would be able to prevent the monarchy from crashing against the rocks of political opposition. They were mistaken, for by then the damage was irreparable and the antimonarchist forces rising along the peninsula bode ill for the Savoys. In an effort to obtain clarity, a referendum on the form of government was held in June 1946. Umberto II and Marie José tried their best to save the institution they represented, but their efforts proved fruitless. The monarchy lost the referendum and the Savoys lost the throne they had built and nurtured for nearly a century.

In due time, Umberto II settled in Portugal. There, he acquired a mansion in Cascais, an exclusive seaside resort next to Estoril, another retreat that housed several exiled royals, among them the Count and Countess of Barcelona and King Carol II of Romania. In due time, Umberto II's sister, Queen Giovanna of Bulgaria, Widow of King Boris III, joined the expanding colony of exiles, which also included Archduke Josef and Archduchess Anna Monica of Austria and their large brood. Anna Monica's father was the last King of Saxony, Frederick August III, whose mother was the Infanta Maria Anna of Portugal, one of the sisters-in-law of Queen Maria Pia. Further inland lived the Comte and Comtesse de Paris, while in 1950 the Dukes of Braganza joined the exclusive colony of former royals.[10]

In exile, the tensions that had caused turmoil within the domestic life of Umberto II and Marie José led to an unofficial separation. The last Queen of Italy refused to live in Cascais. She argued that the climate made her vision suffered and instead departed Portugal with considerable trepidation. Marie José settled in Switzerland and was never again to live with her estranged husband. The couple's four children (Maria Pia, Victor Emmanuel, Maria Gabriela and Maria Beatrice) were shuffled between both parents, the instability caused by this unorthodox arrangement become palpable in later years.

Meanwhile, King Vittorio Emmanuel III had died in Alexandria, Egypt, in 1947. Queen Elena, a devoted wife and mother, survived her husband by nearly five years. She died in Montpellier, France, in November 1952. Long gone was Queen Mother Margherita, Maria Pia's cousin and sister-in-law. Margherita had been an enthusiastic supporter of Fascism's rise to power. Mussolini's main supporters even stopped at her home in Bordighera while on their march to Rome. Margherita died at Bordighera on January 4, 1926.[11]

That same year saw the passing of Laetitia, Maria Pia's niece. Widowed since 1890, Laetitia outlived her husband by nearly four decades. Their marriage, which started enveloped by scandal, was her only one. At the time of the announcement of their engagement, news caused a considerable stir at the Italian court for not only was the groom twenty-two years her senior, but the bride was his niece. Amedeo seems to have cared deeply for Laetitia, while it seems that she saw his offer as a way to escape from her mother's oppressive control.

After Papal dispensation was granted, Amedeo and Laetitia were married at the Royal Palace in Turin on September 11, 1888. Interestingly, this was the first marriage between a Bonaparte and a member of a reigning house since 1859 – the last marriage being that of Clotilde and Plon-Plon. In June 1889, Laetitia gave birth to a son, Umberto, Count of Salemi, who died of Spanish flu in October 1918.[12] Laetitia, Dowager Duchess of Aosta, passed away at her home, the Castle of Moncalieri on October 25, 1926.[13]

Maria Pia's Saxon and Hohenzollern in-laws had, perhaps, a somewhat slightly better future in store. Maria Anna's death untimely death in 1884, not only deprived Maria Pia of a well-liked sister-in-law, but also left her husband George a widower with a brood of children. Maria Anna died in Dresden, the Saxon capital, in February 1884, a few months short of celebrating her silver wedding anniversary. George, who was a deeply Catholic, as well as a man of few words, showed no interest in finding a second wife. He lived the rest of his life dedicated to his military duties and the raising of his six motherless children.

The six surviving Saxon children were educated in an oppressive environment ruled by obedience to duty and faith. Princess Mathilde, who lacked the good looks so easily found in the families of both her parents, remained unmarried. Mathilde's two youngest brothers also remained unmarried – one by choice, one not so. Prince Maximilian renounced his rights to the throne in 1896 and entered the priesthood. He lived a long life and died in 1951.[14] He was the only one of Maria da Gloria and Ferdinand of Portugal's grandchildren to become a priest. Prince Albert, whose illness caused the death of their mother, died in 1900 in a traffic accident. His carriage overturned after being hit by a phaeton driven by none other than Miguel, eldest son of the Duke of Braganza, the head of the Miguelist branch of the Portuguese Royal Family. Since Miguel's actions were deemed non-intentional, he escaped a court martial, but was forced to resign his military commission and depart Saxony.

Frederick August, who succeeded as King of Saxony in 1904, was married to the former Archduchess Luise of Austria-Tuscany, whose fun-loving personality was completely unsuited for the conservative and humorless family she married into. To everyone's horror, Luise eloped from Dresden in the company of one of the tutors for her children employed by her father-in-law, by then King George of Saxony. The ensuing scandal was among the most talked about in royal circles, leading to the King passing a decree that divorced his son from his peculiar wife. Luise eventually gave birth to a seventh child, Anna Monica, whom Frederick August III raised along with his other children. The King, a pious, quiet man, who loved nothing more than hunting and his children, believed that Anna Monica was his child. And that was that. Like his father, Frederick August III did not remarry. His reign ended in November 1918 after the fall of the German Empire. When asked by Saxon politicians on the telephone is he would abdicate, the King replied, *"Oh, well, I suppose I'd better."*[15] This approach to life was to stay with him. On another occasion, years after his abdication he was cheered by a large crowd in a railroad station. Surprised by the cheers, he struck his head out of the train's window and yelled, *"You're a fine lot of republicans, I'll say."*[16] While attending his Aunt Antonia's funeral in 1912, not only did he complain to her eldest son that the frigid temperature in the crypt might gain the deceased lady a few companions, but also unceremoniously informed Kaiser Wilhelm II that he ought to wear uniform at all times for he looked *"ridiculous"* in civilian clothes.[17] Frederick August III retired to his vast properties and died at Schloß Sibyllenort in 1932, the same year as his second cousin-once removed King Manuel II.

Then there was Princess Maria Josepha, who in 1886 married the very handsome Archduke Otto of Austria, a nephew of Emperor Franz Josef. Their union proved to be rather inauspicious as Maria Josepha was deeply in love with her husband, while he only saw her as the vessel for his future offspring. The couple had two children, Karl and Maximilian, born in 1887 and 1895 respectively.[18] Karl succeeded his great-uncle Franz Josef in 1916 and ruled for a brief two years, thus becoming the last Austro-Hungarian monarch. Interestingly, his wife Zita was a granddaughter of King Miguel of Portugal, the same man who usurped the throne of Karl's great-grandmother, Queen Maria da Gloria. Otto led a carefree existence that eventually got him in trouble. He died a painful death in 1906. Maria Josepha, a pious woman who devoted herself to her sons and myriad charitable endeavors, outlived her husband by nearly four decades. She died at Schloß Wildenwart, a Bavarian royal property, in 1944.[19]

Infanta Antonia of Portugal's children had a better lot in life than their Portuguese and Saxon cousins. Antonia arrived at Sigmaringen in 1861 and she was going to call this picturesque town home for the next half a century. Once the heady days of her husband Leopold's candidacy to the Spanish throne ended, the couple lived in relative quiet in Sigmaringen, with frequent visits to the imperial court in Potsdam. Antonia's first child, Wilhelm, was born at Schloß Benrath, a property near Düsseldorf her father-in-law had received as a summer residence from his Prussian cousins. Two other children, Ferdinand and Karl Anton, were born to Leopold and Antonia in 1865 and 1868 respectively. Leopold died in Berlin in 1905, twenty years after succeeding his father as head of the Catholic branch of the Hohenzollern dynasty. In widowhood, Antonia remained in Sigmaringen dying there in December 1913, as well as living long enough to witness her granddaughter marry her beloved brother Luis's grandson and heir King Manuel II.

Wilhelm succeeded his father as head of house in 1905. In 1889 he married Princess Maria Theresa of Bourbon-Two Sicilies, by whom he had three children: Augusta Viktoria and twins Friedrich and Franz Josef. Having a weak constitution, Maria Theresa was in constant ill health and died in 1909. Six years later, and during the Great War, Wilhelm remarried, his second wife being Princess Adelgunde of Bavaria, one of the many daughters of King Ludwig III and Queen Maria Theresa, the same Habsburg bride that had once been suggested as a possible bride of King Luis of Portugal. While Adelgunde enjoyed a long life, dying in 1958 aged nearly ninety that was not the case with her husband, who enjoyed smoking and gourmet food far too much. Wilhelm died at Sigmaringen in 1927.[20]

Ferdinand of Hohenzollern was one of three kings who were grandsons of Queen Maria da Gloria and King Ferdinand of Portugal. Yet, at birth, Ferdinand was not destined to wear the purple mantle. However, since his uncle King Carol I of Romania did not have any children, Ferdinand was chosen to be his successor. After having a dalliance with a court lady, Ferdinand was safely married to his cousins Princess Marie of Edinburgh and Saxe-Coburg & Gotha, a granddaughter of both Queen Victoria and Tsar Alexander II. Ferdinand and Marie had a peculiar marriage during which she gave birth to six children, some of whom may not have been Ferdinand's. Yet that is another story. He became King of Romania in 1914 and fought on the Allied side, which caused a serious rift with some of his German relations. Marie, of course, relished her role as queen and today is far better remembered than her cigar-smoking taciturn husband. Their children included King Carol II of Romania, Queen Elisabeth of Greece and Queen Marie of Yugoslavia, among others. Ferdinand died in 1927, while Queen Marie died in 1938 after a very difficult time with her son King Carol II, who had a love-hate relationship with his bombastic mother.

Prince Karl Anton of Hohenzollern is one of the least-known grandchildren of Ferdinand and Maria da Gloria of Portugal. He was born at Sigmaringen and led a quiet life dedicated to his military career and various properties. In 1894 he married Princess Josephine of Belgium, one of the daughters of the Count and Countess of Flanders. Josephine's mother being a sister of Karl Anton's father, the couple were first cousins, besides also being closely related through shared Saxe-Coburg & Gotha descent. Karl Anton served in the Prussian army and the couple's four children were born in either Potsdam or Berlin. He died at Burg Namedy, a large property he owned, in 1919. Josephine, who remained a devout Catholic throughout her long life, eventually entered a religious order. She died in Namur, Belgium, in 1958.

Last, but by no means least, there are the Miguelists.

King Miguel I of Portugal eventually settled in Germany, where he managed the properties of his wife's family. In 1851, nearly aged forty-nine years, Miguel married twenty-year old Princess Adelaide of Löwenstein-Wertheim-Rosenberg. Because he father died young, Adelaide's mother resorted to Miguel for support in handling the family's affairs. It both gave him a purpose, as well as allowing the exiled former king to finally settle down. All of Miguel and Adelaide's children were born at Löwenstein properties, either Kleinheubach or Bronnbach. Between 1852 and 1862, Adelaide had seven children: Maria das Neves (1852-1941), who married the Carlist Infante Alfonso of Spain, Duke of San Jaime (1849-1936); Miguel (1853-1927), Duke of Braganza; Maria Teresa (1855-1944), who married Archduke Karl Ludwig of Austria (1833-1896); Maria José (1857-1943), who married Karl Theodor, Duke in Bavaria 91839-1909); Adelgundes (1858-1946), married to Prince Enrico of Bourbon-Parma, Count of Bardi (1851-1905); Maria Anna (1861-1942), married to Grand Duke Guillaume VI of Luxembourg (1852-1912); and

Maria Antonia (1862-1959), second wife of prolific father Duke Robert I of Parma (1848-1907).[21] King Miguel died at Jagdschloß Karlshöhe, near Bronnbach, in 1866. A century later, in 1967, his remains, along with those of Adelaide, were repatriated to Portugal, where he rests inside San Vicente de Fora. Adelaide's long widowhood, much of which she spent living in monastic simplicity at Saint Cecile Abbey, Isle of Wight, ended with her death in 1909.

Miguel, the only son of King Miguel, settled in Austria, where he lived at Schloß Seebenstein, a property with a long history. He married firstly at Regensburg Princess Elisabeth of Thurn und Taxis, a niece of Empress Elisabeth of Austria. The wedding took place in 1877, but four years later Miguel found himself a widower when Elisabeth died several weeks after giving birth to their third child. The couple's three children were: Miguel (1878-1923), who married morganatically Anita Stewart (1886-1977), daughter of a wealthy American industrialist; Francisco Jose (1879-1919), a complicated man whose homosexual scandals were the talk of royal Europe; and Maria Teresa (1881-1945), who married Prince Karl Ludwig of Thurn und Taxis. (1863-1942). Twelve years after becoming a widower, Miguel married secondly. His choice was Princess Marie Therese of Löwenstein-Wertheim-Rosenberg (1870-1935), a first cousin. With his second wife, Miguel had a further eight children: Isabel (1894-1970), married to Fürst Franz Josef of Thurn und Taxis (1893-1971); Maria Benedita (1896-1971), unmarried; Mafalda (1898-1918), unmarried; Maria Ana (1899-1971), married to Fürst Karl August of Thurn und Taxis (1898-1982); Maria Antonia (1903-1973), married to American Ashley Chandler; Duarte Nuño (1907-1976); and Maria Adelaide (1912-2012), married to Dutchman Nicolaas van Uden (1921-1991).[22]

The fall of the Austro-Hungarian Empire brought difficult time for the Braganzas. In the meantime, Miguel and King Manuel II, whose childlessness left the Miguelists as the direct male heirs to the Portuguese throne, had began a dialogue to bridge the longstanding dynastic conflict that separated both branches. The archive of the Marques de Soveral attested to the fact that Manuel II and Infante Miguel had met and agreed to recognize each other's claims: Miguel accepted Manuel II as his monarch, while Manuel II recognized the Miguelists's claims to the throne. Apparently, there were many among their supporters who expressed their opposition to the pact. Hence it was never officially published.

The parties met again in 1922, when Miguel's advisors met with King Manuel's representatives. The meeting took place in Paris and a new deal was reached. By then Manuel had been married nearly a decade and it was becoming increasingly apparent to him and Augusta Viktoria that they were to remain childless. The last constitution in force when the monarchy was overthrown restricted the succession to descendants of Queen Maria da Gloria, who were also holders of Portuguese nationality. Since that left no one eligible to succeed after Manuel II's death, the succession of the Duke of Braganza was thus challenged by a small number of monarchists. The Pact of Paris sought to provide an avenue through which the claims of the Miguelists would receive the support of King Manuel II if he died without heirs, which ultimately was the case.

Duarte Nuño, on whom the Duke of Braganza renounced his rights in 1920, was educated first at home and later at Catholic schools in Bavaria and France. He completed secondary education in Regensburg, before he attended university in Toulouse, where he obtained a degree in agricultural science. In 1927, at his father's death, Duarte Nuño became the sole male representative of the Miguelist line. Two years later he visited Portugal incognito since the law of exile barred him from legally entering the former kingdom.

When turn came for Duarte Nuño to settle down, he married Princess Maria Francisca of Orleans-Braganza, a granddaughter of the Braganza last Emperor of Brazil, Pedro II. Maria Francisca, born in 1914 at the Château d'Eu, a family property in Normandy, was one of the children of Pedro d'Alcantara, Prince of Grao Pará, and of his wife Elisabeth, née Countess Dobrzensky de Dobrzenicz. Maria Francisca's siblings included Pedro Gastao and Isabelle, who married a niece and nephew of Queen Amelie of Portugal respectively: Pedro Gastao married Princess Maria de la Esperanza of Bourbon-Two Sicilies, daughter of Amelia's sister the Infanta Luisa of Spain, while Isabelle married the Comte de Paris, only son of the Duke and Duchess of Guise.

In due time, Maria Francisca gave birth to three sons, all born in Bern Switzerland, before the law of exile was abrogated in 1950: Duarte Pio, Miguel and Henrique. Unfortunately, Duarte Nuño and his family had to delay their official return to Portugal until 1952 due to the injuries the Duke of Braganza suffered in an automobile accident on his return from the wedding of his cousin the Crown Prince of Austria. Once in Portugal, however, Duarte Nuño was provided a residence by the Fundaçao Casa de Bragança, the organization charged with the administration of the dynasty's properties in Portugal. The vast residence, the Palacio de San Marcos near Coimbra, between Lisbon and Oporto, served as home to the Duke of Braganza until he donated the building to the University of Coimbra in 1974.

While Salazar toyed with the idea of declaring Portugal a kingdom, as General Francisco Franco had done in neighboring Spain, no definitive action was ever taken to settle matters. The dictatorship continued until Salazar suffered a brain hemorrhage in 1968. He died two years and his Estado Novo survived him only four years since in 1974 a non-violent revolution overthrew the Portuguese dictatorship. The uprising is known in Portugal as the Carnation Revolution since almost no shots were fired by the armed forces and instead red carnations were put in the muzzles of rifles and the uniforms of the armed forces. By then, however, Duarte Nuño, who suffered greatly the loss of his wife to cancer in 1968, had retired to the south of Portugal. He died in Lisbon on Christmas Eve in 1976.

Today, headship of the House of Braganza rests on the shoulders of Duarte Pio, Duke of Braganza since his father's death. A likeable man with a welcoming personality, he is frequently seen attending royal events all over Europe. He oftentimes represents Portugal overseas in cultural matters and as such has been received by countless foreign leaders. In 1995 he married a Portuguese aristocrat, Isabel Inês de Castro Curvelo de Héredia, in a ceremony attended by a lengthy roster of European royalty. The Duke and Duchess of Braganza reside in Lisbon, but also have a country estate near Sintra. Their three children (Afonso, Maria Francisca and Dinis) represent the future of the House of Braganza.

Family Trees

The Royal House of Savoy

Charles Emmanuel, Prince of Savoy-Carignan = Maria Christina of Saxony
1770-1800 1779-1851

Charles Albert, King of Sardinia = Maria Theresa of Austria-Tuscany
1798-1849 1801-1855

Victor Emmanuel II,King of Italy = Adelaide of Austria
1820-1878 1822-1855

Clotilde = Jerôme Napoleon
1843-1911 1822-1891

*Laetitia
1866-1926

Umberto I = Margherita
1844-1900 1851-1926

*Laetitia Napoleon = Amedeo, Duke of Acsta =
1866-1926 1845-1890

Umberto, Count of Salemi
1889-1918

Victor Emmanuel III = Elena of Montenegro
1869-1947 1873-1952

Jolanda
1901-1986
= Giorgio Calvi di Bergolo
1887-1977

Mafalda
1902-1944
= Philipp of Hesse
1896-1980

Umberto II
1904-1983
= Marie José of Belgium
1906-2001

Giovanna
1907-2000
= Boris III of Bulgaria
1894-1943

Maria Pia
b. 1934
1)= Alexander of Yugoslavia
b. 1924
2)= Michel of Bourbon-Parma
b. 1926

Victor Emmanuel
Prince of Naples
b. 1937
= Marina Doria
b. 1937

Emmanuel Philiberto, Prince of Venice = Clotilde Courau
b. 1972 b. 1969

2 daughters

Maria Gabriela
b. 1940
1)= Robert de Balkany
b. 1931

Maria Beatrice
b. 1943
= Luis Reyna
1939-1999

Elisabetta = Rainer of Austria
1800-1856 1783-1853

Ferdinando, Duke of Genoa = Elisabeth of Saxony
1822-1855 1830-191

Marie Elisabeth of Bavaria = Tommaso, Duke of Genoa
1863-1924 1854-1931

Dukes of Genoa

a del Pozzo
6

Oddone
1846-1866

Maria Pia = Luis of Portugal
1847-1911 1838-1889

Charles Albert
1851-1854

Victor Emmanuel
b./d. 1855

Maria
914-2001
= Louis of Bourbon-Parma
1899-1967

Emmanuel Philiberto, Duke of Aosta = Helene of Orleans
1869-1931 1871-1951

Victor Emmanuel
1870-1946

Louis Amedeo
1873-1933

Amedeo, Duke of Aosta
1898-1942
= Anne of Orleans
1906-1986

2 daughters

Aimone, Duke of Aosta
1900-1948
= Irene of Greece
1904-1974

Dukes of Aosta

The Royal House of Portugal

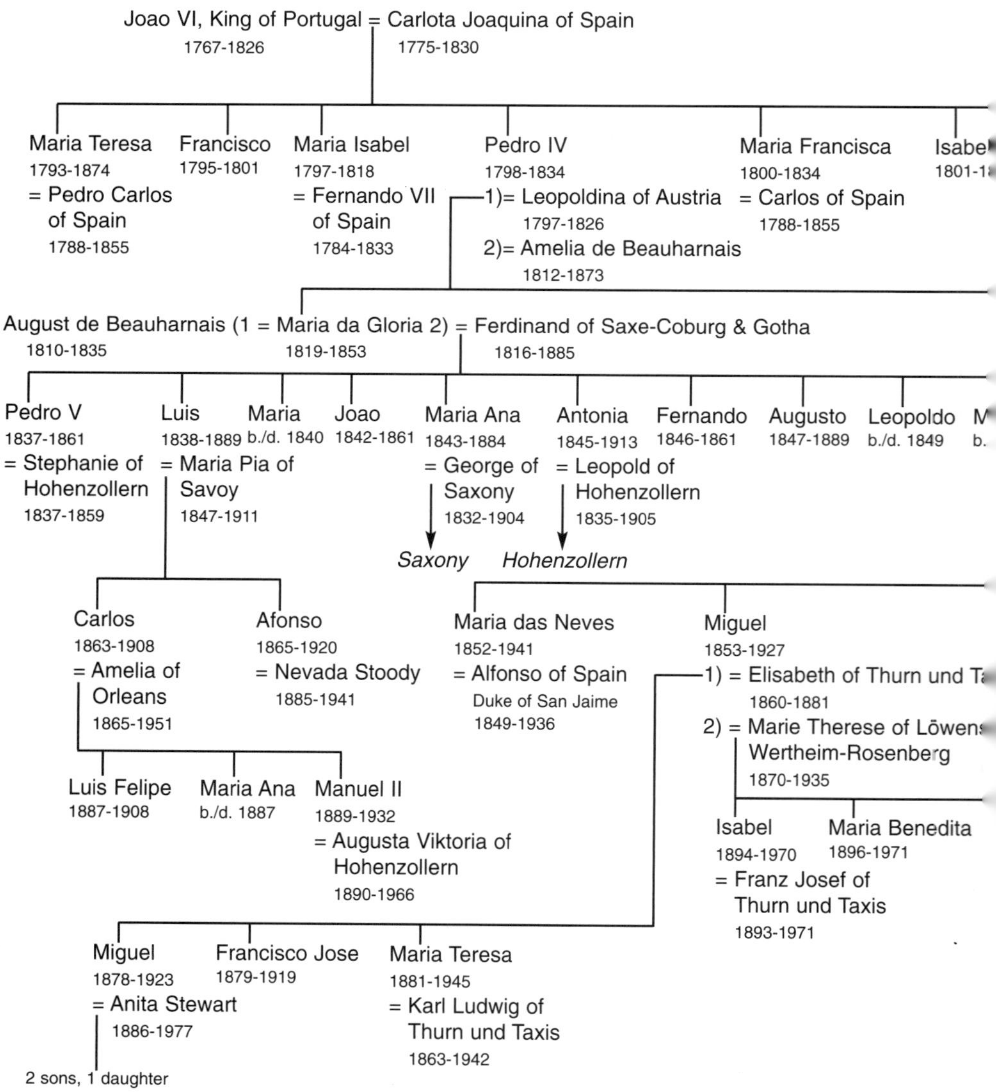

Miguel I
1802-1866
= Adelaide of Löwenstein-Wertheim-Rosenberg
1831-1909

Maria da Assuçao
1805-1834

Ana de Jesus
1806-1857
= Nuño de Mendoza
Duke of Loulé
1804-1875

Pedro II of Brazil = Teresa Cristina of Bourbon-Two Sicilies
1825-1891 | 1822-1889

Isabel = Gaston, Count d'Eu
1846-1921 | 1842-1922

Pedro d'Alcantara = Elisabeth Dobrzensky
1875-1940 | 1875-1951

*Maria Francisca
1914-1968

Eugenio
b./d. 1853

Maria Teresa
1855-1944
= Karl Ludwig of Austria
1833-1896
Liechtenstein

Maria José
1857-1943
= Karl Theodor
Duke in Bavaria
1839-1909
Dukes in Bavaria

Adelgundes
1858-1946
= Enrico
Count of Bardi
1851-1905

Maria Ana
1861-1942
= Guillaume IV of Luxembourg
1852-1912
Luxembourg

Maria Antonia
1862-1959
= Robert I of Parma
1848-1907
Parma

Maria Ana
1899-1971
= Karl August of Thurn und Taxis
1899-1982

Maria Antonia
1903-1973
= Ashley Chandler
1905-1994

Filippa
1905-1990

Duarte Nuño
1907-1976
= Maria Francisca of Orleans-Braganza*
1914-1968

Maria Adelaide
1912-2012
= Nicolaas van Uden
1921-1991

Duarte Pio = Isabel de Heredia
b. 1945 | b. 1966

Miguel
b. 1946

Henrique
b. 1949

Afonso
b. 1996

Maria Francisca
b. 1997

Dinis
b. 1999

Endnotes

Chapter I

1. Monti, Antonio, *La Giovinezza*, page 153.
2. Savoia, page 12.
3. Bolton, page 26.
4, Andreoli, page 47.
5. Casalandra, page 24.
6. Ibid.
7. Ibid, page 25.
8. Andrade, Maria do Carmo Rebello de, page 20.
9. Ibid, pages 20-21.
10. Ibid, page 22.
11. Biancotti, page 5.
12. Cognasso, Volume 1, page 679.
13. Andrade, page 19.
14. Ibid, page 197 (appendix).
15. Ibid, page 18.
16. Ibid.
17. Ibid, page 21.
18. Ibid, page 59.
19. Holt, page 135.
20. Ibid.
21. Crankshaw, page 145.
22. Holt, page 138.
23. Ibid.

Chapter II

1. Bradford, page 31.
2. Howe, page 33.
3. Esher, Volume I, pages 110-11.
4. Nobre, *Paixoes Reais*, page 99.
5. D'Auvergne, pages 139-140.
6. Ashdown, page 85.
7. Esher, page 153.
8. Ashdown, page 84.
9. Maxwell, page 652.
10 .Howe, page 61.
11. Abecasis, http://www.cidadevirtualpt./palacio-ajuda/guidedtour.html, (1-12) page 5.
12. Livermore, page 287.
13. Lemos, page 201.
14. Leitao, *Novos Documentos*, page 310.
15. Nobre, *Paixoes Reais*, page 127
16. Monica, *Correspondencia*, page 41.
17. Rebelo, page 39.
18. Medrano, page 50.
19. Gribble, page 246.
20. Medrano, page 50.
21. Vilhena, *Cartas Ineditas da Rainha D. Estefania*, page 190.
22. Ibid, page 118.
23. Ibid, pages 159-160.
24. Monica, page 308.
25. Ibid, page 309.
26. Nobre, *Casa Real*, page 32.
27. A Visit to Neccesidades Palace. http://www.min-nestrangeiros.pt/mne/visita/engp.html, 4/23/2008 (1-13) page 9.
28. Fulford, *Dearest Child*, page 203.
29. A Visit to Neccesidades Palace. http://www.min-nestrangeiros.pt/mne/visita/engp.html, 4/23/2008 (1-13) page 9.
30. Loring, page 60.
31. D'Auvergne, page 266
32. Benson and Esher, Volume III, page 592.
33. D'Auvergne, page 284
34. AN/TT - CCR, box 7488, folder 1045, doc. s.n. Letter from Luis to Maria Pia, August 30, 1862
35. AN/TT - CCR, box 7366, folder 322, doc. 1 Letter from Queen Victoria to Luis, January 16, 1862
36. AN/TT - CCR, box 7336, folder 322, doc. 13 Letter from Queen Victoria to Luis, March 5, 1862
37. Vilhena, D. Pedro, page 175.
38. AN/TT - CCR, box 7434, folder 915A, doc. 28 Letter from Archduke Albert to Luis June 6, 1862
39. AN/TT - CCR, box 7341, folder 364, doc. 14 Letter from Luis to Victor Emmanuel, June 18, 1862

Chapter III

1. Carvalho, Volume III, page 160.
2. Cognasso, Volume I, page 764.
3. AN/TT - CCR, box 7336, folder 315 Letter from Prince Oscar to Luis, July 23, 1862
4. RA VIC/MAIN/J/64/103
5. AN/TT - CCR, box 7335, folder 302, doc. 1 Letter from Maria Pia to Luis, August 10, 1862
6. Nobre, Paixoes Reais, page 145.
7. AN/TT - CCR, box 7335, folder 302, doc. 5 Letter from Maria Pia to Luis, September 17, 1862
8. AN/TT - CCR, box 7335, folder 302, doc. 4 Letter from Maria Pia to Luis, September 11, 1862
9. AN/TT - CCR, box 7488, folder 1045, doc. s.n. Letter from Luis to Maria Pia, August 23, 1862
10. AN/TT - CCR, box 7488, folder 1045, doc. s.n. Letter from Luis to Maria Pia, August 21, 1862
11. AN/TT - CCR, box 7335, folder 302, doc. 4

Letter from Maria Pia to Luis, September 11, 1862
12. AN/TT - CCR, box 7335, folder 302, doc. 2 Letter from Maria Pia to Luis, August 30, 1862
13. AN/TT - CCR, box 7335, folder 302, doc. 4 Letter from Maria Pia to Luis, September 11, 1862
14. Nobre, Casa Real, page 46.
15. AN/TT - CCR, box 7488, folder 1045, doc. s.n. Letter from Luis to Maria Pia, September 10, 1862
16. AN/TT - CCR, box 7488, folder 1045, doc. s.n. Letter from Luis to Maria Pia, September 12, 1862
17. AN/TT - CCR, box 7335, folder 302, doc. 4 Letter from Maria Pia to Luis, September 11, 1862
18. Bunsen, page 176.
19. Ibid, page 179.
20. Ibid, page 182.
21. Ibid, page 183.
22. Ibid, page 184.
23. Ibid.
24. Ibid, page 185.
25. Saviotti, pages 97-100.
26. Carvalho, Volume III, page 160.
27. Loring, page 175.
28. Martins, page 11; Pallier, page 21.
29. Cidadania Cascais. http://cidadaniacsc.blogspot.com/ 8/2/2007 (1-17) page 4.
30. Ibid.
31. Guimaraes, page 14.
32. Lopes, page 142.
33. AN/TT – CCR, box 7488, folder 1045, Letter from Luis to Maria Pia not dated.
34. Silveira, page 60.
35. Ibid.
36. RA VIC/Main/J/65/1
37. Lopes, page 142.
38. Abecasis, page 8
39. Ramos, page 27.
40. Ibid, page 28.
41. Cognasso, Volume I, page 746.
42. Monti, Antonio. *Donne e Passioni del Risorgimento*. Milano: Corticelli, 1935, p. 132.
43. Cognasso, 807 (vol. II)
44. Monti, *Donne e Passioni*, page 132.
45. Guedes, page 27.
46. Ibid, page 29
47. Lutyens, page 179.
48. Ibid.
49. Ibid.
50. Ibid.
51. Ibid.
52. Oporto, pages 4-5.
53. Monti, *Donne e Passioni*, page 133.
54. AN/TT-CCR, box 7335, folder 302, doc. 4 Letter from Maria Pia to Luis, September 11, 1862
55. Monti, *Donne e Passioni*, page 134.
56. Bolton, page 28.
57. Biancotti, page 36.
58. Monti, *Donne e Passioni*, pages 134-135.
59. Cognasso, Volume II, page 1135.
60. AST/LUII, folder 16, a repeated confidence of Maria Pia
61. Festa, pages 110-11.
62. Paget, page 129.
63. AN/TT-CCR, box 7335 Letter from Joao Jose de Simas to Luis, May 14, 1867
64. Mellano, page 33.
65. AN/TT-CCR, box 7335 Letter from Maria Pia to Luis not dated
66. Casalandra, page 151.
67. Ibid, page 272.
68. Ibid, pages 151-152.
69. Katz, page 50.
70. Ibid.
71. Ibid.
72. Ibid.
73. Gerbore, page 123.
74. Katz, page 51.
75. Cognasso, Volume II, page 1208.
76. Martins, page 18.
77. Bunsen, page 258.
78. AST/LUII, folder 16 Letter from Luis to Victor Emmanuel
79. Cognasso, Volume II, page 1441.
80. Carvalho, Volume III, page 150.
81. Ibid.
82. Ibid.
83. Martins, page 19.

Chapter IV

1. Stern, page 126.
2. D'Auvergne, page 281.
3. Rebelo, page 64.
4. Dias, *Lisboa Desaparecida*, page 202.
5. Ibid, page 204.
6. Ibid (Letter from Antonia to Luis dated November 27, 1873 in AN/TT - CCR)
7. Ibid.
8. AN/TT - CCR, box 7335, folder 305, doc. 53 Letter from Maria Pia
9. Bolton, page 26.
10. Cognasso, Volume I, pages 776-77.
11. Mowlam, From the forward by Francisco de Carvalho Louro.
12. Martins, page 23.
13. AN/TT- CCR, box 7335, folder 310, doc. 43 Letter from Antonia to Luis
14. Stern, page 126.
15. Bonnin, Gooch and Massey, page 9.
16. D'Auvergne, page 284.

17. Gribble, page 251.
18. Ibid, page 253.
19. AST/LUII, folder 31 Letter from Maria Pia to Victor Emmanuel
20. Fulford, *Your Dear Letter*, page 280.
21. Stern, page 129.
22. Bonnin, page 274.
23. Fulford, *Your Dear Letter*, page 282.
24. Ibid, page 284.
25. Holt, page 231.
26. Ibid.
27. Ibid, page 232.
28. Sagrera, page 120.
29. Rebelo, page 81.
30. Festa, pages 121-22.
31. Holt, page 237.
32. Sagrera, page 120.
33. Holt, page 237.
34. Kertzer, page 84.
35. Sagrera, page 121.
36. RA VIC/MAIN/J/65/27
37. Lopes, page 190.
38. Salva Galan, page 337.
39. Whitehouse, page 205.
40. Bergamini, page 273.
41. Ibid.
42. Speroni, page 169.

Chapter V

1. Mowlam, from the forward by Francisco de Carvalho Louro.
2. Oporto, page 10.
3. Ibid, page 18.
4. Ibid.
5. Gribble, page 255.
6. Ibid, pages 255-56.
7. Noronha, page 179.
8. Oporto, page 18.
9. Ibid.
10. Cancio, page 348.
11. Ibid, page 348.
12. "July 5, 1911 – Death of Maria Pia of Savoy, Queen of Portugal. Unofficial Royalty. http://www.unofficialroyalty.com/july-5-daily-featured-royal-date. 2/12/2014 (1-3) page 2.
13. Ibid.
14. Breyner, *Memorias*, pages 87- 88.
15. Ibid, pages 86-87.
16. Martins, page 41.
17. AN/TT – CCR, box 7335, folder 302, doc. 22 Letter from Maria Pia to Luis
18. Guedes, page 110.
19. Cancio, page 356.
20. Guedes, page 110.
21. Oporto, page 9.
22. Guedes, page 63.
23. AST/LUII, folder 16 Letter from Luis to Victor Emmanuel
24. Benevides, Volume II, page 342.
25. Carvalho, Volume III, page 143.
26. Byron, page 20.
27. Southey, page 178.
28. http://www.oldandsold.com/articles04/europe6.shtml. Cintra-Portugal. 2/2/2006 (1-7) page 2.
29. Ibid.
30. Ibid.
31. Ashton, page 34.
32. Oporto, page 19.
33. Ibid.
34. Guedes, page 65.
35. AN/TT – CCR, box 7335, folder 302 doc. 16 Letter from Maria Pia to Luis, February 13, 1875
36. Teixeira, page 217.
37. Abecasis, page 9.
38. Lopes, page 128.
39. Mowlam, from the forward by Francisco de Carvalho Louro.
40. Oporto, page 3.
41. Abecasis, page 6.
42 .Colaco, page 172.
43. Abecasis, page 5.
44. RA VIC/MAIN/J/65/61
45. RA VIC/MAIN/J/65/61
46. Oporto, pages 23-24.
47. Oliveira, Domingos. "Perfil de Uma Rainha." www.prof2000.pt/users/adcostina/PerfildeUmaRainha/Perfil. 7/17/2006 (1-10) page 2
48. Ibid, page 8.
49. Breyner, pages 90-91.
50. Mowlam, from the forward by Francisco de Carvalho Louro.
51. Carvalho, page 154.
52. Prince Michael of Greece, page 115.
53. Corpechot, page 96.
54. http://estandosentido.blogs.sapo.pt/699615.html. 11/18/2010
55. http://www.arqnet.ptdictiionario/mariapia.html. 3/6/2006 (1-4) page 3.
56. Oliveira, Domingos. "O Anjo da Caridade." http://www.prof2000.pt/users/adcostinha/OAnjoDa. 7/17/2006 (1-8) page3.
57. Ibid.
58. Oliveira, *Perfil*, page 1.
59. Colaco, page 175.
60. Ibid, page 178.
61. http://www.it.wikipedia.org/wiki/Maria_PiaPdi_Savoia. 6/27/2008

62. http://www.arqnet.pt/dicionario/mairapia.html. 3/6/2006 (1-4) page 3.
63. Guimaraes, page 14.
64. D'Auvergne, page 282.
65. AN/TT – CCR, box 7335, folder 302, Letter from Maria Pia to Luis
66. AN/TT – CCR, box 7335, folder 305, doc. 20 Letter from Ferdinand to Luis, March 3, 1873
67. AN/TT – CCR, box 7335, folder 305, doc. 20 Letter from Ferdinand to Luis, March 3, 1873
68. Rebelo, page 66.
69. AN/TT – CCR, box 7335, folder 310, doc. 48 Letter from Antonia to Luis, January 5, 1886
70. Lopes, page 201.
71. Ibid.

Chapter VI

1. Katz, page xv.
2. Ibid.
3. Ibid, pages xv-xvi.
4. Ibid, page xvi.
5. *Memorie del re galantuomo*, page 118. Victor Emmanuel II. Memorie del re galantuomo. Milano: F. Garbini, 1882.
6. Katz, page xvi.
7. *Memorie del re galantuomo*, page 118.
8. Kertzer, page 124.
9. Ibid, page 128.
10. Katz, page 45.
11. Ibid, page 46.
12. Kertzer, page 131.
13. Katz, page 45.
14. Lucas, page 46.
15. The Times, London, January 13, 1878 (quoted from Katz, page 48).
16. Paget, page 157.
17. Breyner, page 219.
18. Katz, page 48.
19. Andreoli, page 105.
20. Lucas, page 48.
21. Holt, page 258.
22. Ibid.
23. Ibid.
24. Martins, page 100.
25. Colaco, page 186.
26. Ibid.
27. Benevides, page 362.

Chapter VII

1. D'Auvergne, page 292.
2. Gribble, page 244.
3. Zeepvat, page 161.
4. Ibid.
5. Gribble, page 244.
6. Ibid.
7. Staatsarchiv Sigmaringen, Signaturen: FAS HS 1-80 T 8 R 53, 13 Nr. 34 Letter from Luis to Leopold, April 8, 1885
8. Nobre, *Casa Real*, page 35.
9. Fulford, *Dearest Child*, page 86.
10. Ibid, page 87.
11. Ibid.
12. Nobre, *Casa Real*, page 35.
13. Vilhena, page 148.
14. Leitao, *Cartas de D. Pedro*, page 201.
15. Fellmann, page 183.
16. Dias, page 211.
17. Fellmann, page 183.
18. AN/TT - CCR, box 7335, folder 302 Letter from Maria Pia to Luis
19. Gribble, page 244.
20. Nobre, Casa Real, page 135.
21. Silveira, page 89.
22. Ibid.
23. RA VIC/MAIN/J/65/107a
24. AN/TT - CCR, box 7335, folder 310, doc. 47 Letter from Antonia to Luis, December 31, 1885
25. AN/TT - CCR, box 7335, folder 310, doc. 48 Letter from Antonia to Luis, January 5, 1886
26. AN/TT - CCR, box 7335, folder 310, doc. 48 Letter from Antonia to Luis, January 5, 1886
27. AN/TT - CCR, box 7335, folder 310, doc. 45 Letter from Antonia to Luis, April 11, 1885
28. AN/TT - CCR, box 7335, folder 310, doc. 48 Letter from Antonia to Luis, January 5, 1886
29. Nobre, Casa Real, page 86.
30. AN/TT - CCR, box 7335, folder 310, Letter from Antonia to Luis
31. Nobre, *Casa Real*, page 86.

Chapter VIII

1. AN/TT - CCR, box 7335, folder 310, doc. 44 Letter from Antonia to Luis
2. Ibid.
3. Ibid.
4. Ibid.
5. Corpechot, page 31-32.
6. Cockfield, page 62.
7. Ibid.
8. Ibid.
9. Corpechot, page 68.
10. Catinot-Crost, page 51.
11. Ibid.
12. Corpechot,page 69.
13. Ramos, page 47.

14. Nobre, *Paixoes Reais*, page 167.
15. Corpechot, page 74.
16. Ibid.
17. Ibid, page 75.
18. Ibid.
19. Diesbach, page 276.
20. Colaco, page 194.
21. Ibid.
22. Ibid.
23. Ibid, page 195.
24. Ibid, page 196.
25. Ibid, page 197.
26. Catinot-Crost, pages 56-57.
27. Ibid, page 62.
28. Corpechot, page 84.
29. MacColl and Wallace, page 257.
30. Corpechot, page 85.
31. Colacco, page 212.
32. Ibid.
33. Nobre, *Amelia Rainha de Portugal*, page 45.
34. Colacco, page 217.
35. Ibid.
36. Corpechot, pages 86-88.
37. Ibid, pages 89-90.

Chapter IX

1.Godinho, page 273.
2. AN/TT - CCR, box 7336, folder 315, Letter from Oscar to Luis, October 29, 1864
3. AN/TT - CCR, box 7341, folder 364, doc. 12 Letter from Luis to Oscar
4. AN/TT - CCR, box 7336, folder 321, doc. 7 Letter from Empress Eugenie to Luis, July 8th year uncertain
5. Lopes, page 269.
6. Fontes, page 21.
7. Ibid, page 17.
8. Ibid, page 19.
9. Bartoli, pages 21-22.
10. Oliveira, Domingos. "Perfil de uma Rainha." http://www.prof2000.pt/users.adcostinha/PerfilDeUmaRainha?Perfil. 7/17/2006 (1-10) page 4.
11. Cancio, page 328.
12. Calaco, page 185.
13. Ibid.
14. Nobre, *Amelia*, page 54.
15. Ibid, page 56.
16. Ibid, page 57.
17. AN/TT – CCR, box 7335, folder 310, doc. 59 Letter from Antonia to Luis, July 1, 1887
18. Nobre, Amelia, page 58.
19. AN/TT – CCR, box 7335 Letter from Maria Pia to Luis (quoted from Lopes, page 282)
20. Ibid.
21. Ibid, page 284.
22. AN/TT – CCR, box 7335, folder 302, doc. 46 Letter from Maria Pia to Luis, December 14, 1887
23. Lopes, page 285.
24. Ibid.
25. Nobre, *Amelia*, page 59.
26. Ibid.
27. Ibid.
28. Ibid.
29. Prince Adalbert of Bavaria, page 184.
30. AN/TT – CCR, box 7335, folder 302, doc. 39 Letter from Maria Pia to Luis, September 11, 1886
31. AN/TT – CCR box 7342, Letter from Amelia to Maria Pia, January 16, 1889
32. Silveira, page 99.
33. Ibid.
34. Ramos, page 50.
35. Ibid.
36. AN/TT – CCR, box 7335, folder 310, doc. 51 Letter from Antonia to Luis, October 26, 1886
37. Silveira, page 77.
38. Ibid.

Chapter X

1. Carvalho, page 164.
2. Ibid.
3. Ibid.
4. Cancio, page 341.
5. Carvalho, page 162.
6. Ibid.
7. Dias, *Do Desafio a Debandada*, page 109.
8. Silveira, page 111.
9. AN/TT – CCR, box 7488, folder 1045, doc. s.n.
10. AN/TT – CCR, box 7335, folder 302, doc. 4 Letter from Maria Pia to Luis, September 11, 1862
11. AN/TT – CCR, box 7335, folder 310, doc. 42 Letter from Antonia to Luis, August 2, 1883
12. AN/TT – CCR, box 7335, folder 310, doc. 62 Letter from Antonia to Luis, October 26, 1887
13. Silveira, page 112.
14. Ibid.
15. Ibid.
16. Bern, page 96.
17. Silveira, page 111.
18. Carvalho, page 163.
19. Fontes, page 40.
20. Breyner, pages 316-17.
21. Howe, page 79.
22. Ibid.
23. Oporto, page 37.
24. Ibid, page 27.

25. Ibid, page 28.
26. Sherwood, pages 303-04.
27. Ibid, page 305.
28. Silveira, page 103.
29. Ibid.
30. Ibid, page 104.
31. Moreira, page 268.
32. Silveira, page 104.
33. Ibid.
34. Ibid.
35. Ibid.
36. Ibid, page 105.
37. Ibid.
38. Ibid, page 104.
39. Ibid, page 105.
40. Ibid.
41. Nobre, *Amelia*, page 67.
42. Almeida, *Os Gatos, Volume I*, page 153.
43. Lopes, page 189.
44. Fontes, page 24.
45. Norontha, page 93.
46. Oliveira, Domingos. "Perfil de uma Rainha." http://www.prof2000.pt/users/adcostinha/PerfilDeUmaRainha/Perf. 7/17/2066/ (1-10) page 7.
47. Ibid.
48. Silveira, page 113.
49. Ibid.

Chapter XI

1. Silveira, page 258.
2. AN/TT - CCR, box 7335, folder 302, doc. 21 Letter from Maira Pia to Luis, August 12, 1876
3. AN/TT - CCR, box 7335, folder 302, doc. 46 Letter from Maria Pia to Luis, December 14, 1887
4. AN/TT - CCR, box 7335, folder 310, doc. 57 Letter from Antonia to Luis, July 20, 1887
5. Silveira, page 259.
6. Ibid.
7. Nobre, *Amelia*, page 64.
8. Loring, page 60.
9. Ibid, page 36.
10. Ibid.
11. Ibid, pages 39-40.
12. Ibid, page 53.
13. Moreira, page 271.
14. Ibid.
15. Ramalho, page 38.
16. Loring, page 76.
17. Silveira, page 260.
18. Noronha, page 237.
19. Ramalho, page 38.
20. Ibid.
21. Ibid, page 39.
22. Silveira, page 262.
23. Loring, page 60.
24. Ibid.
25. AN/TT – CCR, box 7335, folder 310, doc. 20 Letter from Antonia to Luis, September 25, 1889
26. Fontes, page 23.
27. Silveira, page 262.
28. Fontes, page 23.
29. Ibid.
30. Loring, page 79.
31. Staatsarchiv Sigmaringen, Signaturen: FAS HS 1-80 T 8 R 53, 13 Nr. 35 Letter from Maria Pia to Leopold, May 28, 1890
32. Nobre, *Casa Real*, page 111.
33. Andrade, *Cascais*, page 326.
34. Loring, pages 80-84.
35. RA VIC/MAIN/Z/77/113
36. RA VIC/MAIN/Z/77/113
37. Howe, page 69.
38. Lopes, page 192.
39. AN/TT, ACR box 7342
40. Staatsarchiv Sigmaringen, Signaturen: FAS HS 1-80 T 8 R 53, 13 Nr. 35 Letter from Maria Pia to Leopold, May 28, 1890

Chapter XII

1. Lopes, page 316.
2. Nobre, *Amelia*, page 76.
3. AN/TT-CCR, box 7354 Letter from Maria Pia to Carlos
4. A Visit to Necessidades Palace. http://www.min-nestrangeiros.pt/mne/vista/engp.html. 4/23/2008 (1-13) page 10.
5. Nobre, Casa Real, page 114.
6. Benton, page 10.
7. Ibid.
8. Ibid, page 11.
9. Nobre, *Casa Real*, page 115.
10. RA VIC/ADDU/307
11. Benton, page 12.
12. Nobre, *Casa Real*, page 115.
13. Nobre, *Amelia*, page 78.
14. Fontes, page 36.
15. Benton, page 22.
16. Ibid.
17. Lopes, page 337.
18. Nobre, *Amelia*, page 92.
19. Ibid, page 93.
20. Ibid.
21. Ibid.
22. Benton, page 22.
23. Nobre, *Amelia*, page 94.

24. Ramos, page 219.
25. http://archives.ned.edu/calendar/c1892.htm. 05/31/2008 (1-9) page 3, Notre Dame Archives: Calendar X-3-n- A.L.S. – 4pp. – 12mo. – {6} Letter from Sister Mary Magdalene MacDonnell to Father Daniel E. Hudson, C.S.C. 1892.
26. Ibid.
27. ANTT/ACR, box 7342
28. Corpechot, page 267.
29. Walters, http://postpoems.com/cgi=bin/displaypoem.cgi?pid=353833. 08/04/2007 (1-23) page 8.
30. Ramos, page 297.
31. Gribble, page 264.
32. Young, page 275.
33. Singleton, pages 2780-81.
34. Catinot-Crost, page 126.
35. Lucas, page 132.
36. Lopes, page 330.
37. Ibid, page 332.
38. AN/TT box 7342
39. AN/TT box 7343
40. Lopes, page 321.
41. Ramos, page 274.
42. Lopes, page 321.
43. Ibid.
44. Crisipi, pages 238-39.
45. Regolo, page 228.
46. Fairni, page 1052.
47. Ibid.
48. Regolo, page 228.
49. Andreoli, page 198.
50. Ibid.
51. Ibid.
52. Regolo, page 252.
53. Bartoli, page 63
54. Salazar, page 147.
55. Bartoli, page 63.
56. Katz, page 148.
57. Bordeux, page 189.
58. Ibid.
59. Casalegno, page 183.
60. Katz, page 150.
61. Oporto, page 86.
62. Fontes, page 29.
63. Vicente and Vicente, page 23.
64. Bartoli, page 52.
65. Steed, page 168, part I.
66. Halstead, page 78.
67. The New York Times. August 1, 1901.
68. The New York Times. August 2, 1901.

Chapter XIII

1. Ramos, page 152.
2. AST/LUII, folder 16 letter from Antonia to Maria Pia
3. Almeida, *Memorias*, page 38.
4. Frankland, page 236.
5. Almeida, page 52.
6. Ibid, page 54.
7. Nobre, *Amelia*, page 88.
8. Ibid, page 139.
9. Vicente and Vicente, page 78.
10. Benton, page 28.
11. Ibid.
12. Ibid, page 31.
13. Ibid, page 26.
14. Martins, pages 483-84.
15. Benton, page 32.
16. Howe, page 81.
17. Benton, page 33.
18. Howe, page 81.
19. Corpechot, page 185.
20. Howe, page 83.
21. Williams, page 176.
22. Ibid.
23. Howe, page 83.
24. Breyner, *Diario de um Monarquico 1908-1910*, page 26.
25. Almeida, page 54.
26. Williams, page 179.
27. Bartoli, page 63.
28. Corpechot, page 185.
29. Almeida, page 98.
30. Ibid.
31. Ibid, pages 98-99.
32. Baena, pages 48-52.
33. Ibid, page 52.
34. Ibid.
35. Williams, page 186.
36. Baena, page 53.
37. Brandao, page 127.
38. Ramos, page 322.
39. Howe, page 85.
40. Taylor, page 19.
41. Howe, page 85.
42. Brook-Shepherd, page 316.
43. Colaco, page 248.
44. Ibid.
45. Fontes, page 49.
46. Brandao, Volume I, page 175.
47. Colaco, page 249.
48. Breyner, *Diario de um Monarquico 1908-1910*, page 245.
49. AN/TT-ACR box 7448
50. Martins, page 401.

51. Breynor, *Diario de um Monarquico 1908-1910*, page 247.
52. AN/TT-ACR box 7448
53. Lopes, page 381.
54. Ibid.
55. Ibid.

Chapter XIV

1. Benton, page 48.
2. Gribble, page 288.
3. Sa, page 424.
4. Fontes, page 51.
5. Breyner, *Diario de um Monarquico 1908-1910*, page 280.
6. Ibid, page 282.
7. AN/TT-ACR, box 7426
8. Guimaraes, page 27.
9. Ibid.
10. Nobre, *Amelia*, page 150.
11. Benton, page 79.
12. Nobre, *Amelia*, page 150.
13. Ibid.
14. Ibid, page 151.
15. Ibid.
16. Ibid.
17. Howe, page 197.
18. Ibid, page 103.
19. Benton, page 87.
20. Ibid, page 88.
21. Ibid.
22. Monteiro, page73.
23. Benton, page 114.
24. Breyner, *Diario de um Monarquico 1911-1913*, page 54.
25. Bensabat, page 9-12.
26. Sousa, pages 488-490.
27. Monica, *Queda da Monarquia*, page 28.
28. Benton, page 117.
29. Ibid, page 114.
30. Almeida, page 173.
31. Regolo, page 461.
32. Lopes, page 389.
33. Oliveira, Domingos. "Os Ultimos Anos." http://www.prof2000.pt/users/adcostinah/OsUltimosAnos/OsUltimosAnos.htm. 7/17/2006 (1-3) page 2.
34. Regolo, page 461.
35. "Gave All to Portugal." New York Times. November 6, 1910.
36. Lopes, page 391.
37. Benton, page 137.
38. Ibid, page 138.
39. Paget, pages 129-130.
40. Nobre, *Amelia*, page 153.
41. Casalandra, page 279.
42. "Maria Pia di Savoia Regina del Portogallo." www.tricolore-italia.com. 10/16/2006 (1-12) page 11.
43. Benton, page 143.
44. L'Illustrazione Italiana Anno XXXVIII - N.29 - 16 Luglio 1911, page 50.
45. Benton, page 143.
46. Ibid.
47. Ibid.
48. Garcia, page 157.
49. Nobre, *Amelia*, page 165.

Interview with Umberto II by Louis Cavicchioli, 1960, at http://64.233.179.104/translate_c?hlen&langpair-htp:/www.diesis.com/ph. 4/27/2008 (1-14) pages 9-11.

Epilogue

1. Nobre, *Amelia*, page 167.
2. Ibid.
3. Ibid, page 168.
4. Ibid., page 176.
5. Enache, Nicolas.,*La descendance de Marie-Thérèse de Habsburg, Reine de Hongrie et de Bohême*, page 205.
6. Ibid., page 655.
7. Nobre, *Amelia*, page 185.
8. Enache, page 69.
9. Tourtchine, Jean-Fred, *Le Royaume d'Italie, Volume III*, page 61.
10. Mateos Sáinz de Medrano, Ricardo, *Estoril - Los Anõs Dorados*, page 57.
11. Enache, page 201.
12. Ibid., page 207.
13. Ibid., page 205.
14. Ibid., page 434.
15. Miller, Ilana D. & Arturo E. Beéche, *Royal Gatherings, Volume II*, page 172.
16. Ibid.
17. Ibid.
18. Enache, page 32.
19. Ibid.
20. Ibid., page 83.
21. http://www.angelfire.com/realm/gotha/gotha/portugal.html
22. Ibid.

Index

A

Almeida Neves, Antonio d' 49
Alvito, Marques de 122
Andrade, Governor Rafael de 107
Andrade Corvo, Minister 42, 73
Anzino, Father Valerio 59, 60
Aires Pacheco, Canon 122
Asseca, Visconde de 121, 122, 123
AUSTRIA
Albert, Archduke of 18, 24, 32, 61, 81
Anna Monica, Archduchess of (née Saxony) 144, 145
Elisabeth (née Bavaria), Empress of 55, 114, 148
Elisabetta (née Savoy), Archduchess of 1
Franz Ferdinand Archduke of 72, 123
Franz Josef, Emperor of 33, 89, 136, 146
Josef, Archduke of 144
Karl, Emperor of 66, 146
Karl Ludwig, Archduke of 147
Ludwig Victor, Archduke of 33
Maria Theresa, Archduchess of 17
Maria Theresa, Archduchess of, Princess of Este 32
Mathilde, Archduchess of 32, 33
Maximilian, Archduke of 146
Otto, Archduke of 66, 146
Otto, Crown Prince of 142, 149
Rainer, Archduke of, Viceroy of Lombardy 1
Regina, Archduchess of (née Saxe-Meiningen) 142

B

BADEN
Marie, Princess of 38

Bandeira, Marques da 17
Barros Gomes, Henrique de 90, 96
BATTENBERG
Louise, Princess of (later Queen of Sweden) 130, 131

BAVARIA
Karl Theodor, Duke in 147
Leopold, Prince of 90
Ludwig II, King of 53
Ludwig III, King of 146
Ludwig Ferdinand, Princess of (née Spain, Infanta María de la Paz of) 83
Maria Theresa, Queen of (née Austria-Este) 146

Belas, Marquesa de 134, 136
BELGIUM
Albert, King of the Belgians
Clementine, Princess of 91
Elisabeth, Queen of Belgium (née Bavaria) 143
Leopold I, King of the Belgians 11, 16, 18, 91
Marie, Countess of Flanders (née Hohenzollern) 147
Philippe, Count of Flanders 91, 147

Bensabat, Jose Jacob 133
BEAUHARNAIS
Augusta, Duchess of Leuchtenberg (née Bavaria) 11
Augustus, Prince de, Duke of Leuchtenberg, Prince Consort of Portugal 10, 11
Eugene, Duke of Leuchtenberg 10
Maximilian, Duke of Leuchtenberg 11

Beauvoir, Marquis de 73
Beckford, William 51
Bilbroth, Dr. 65
Bismarck, Otto, Prince von, German Imperial Chancellor 38, 41, 71
Bolton, Glorney 29
Bombarda, Dr. Miguel 132
Bossa, Dr. 122
Brandao, Raul 123, 124
BRAZIL
Amelia, Empress of (née Beauharnais) 10, 11, 28, 103
Elisabeth, Princess of Grao Pará (nee Dobrzensky de Dobrzenicz) 149
Maria de la Esperanza, Princess of Orleans-Braganza (née Bourbon-Two Sicilies) 149
Pedro II, Emperor of 10, 11, 103, 138, 149
Pedro d'Alcantara, Prince of Grao Pará 149
Pedro Gastao, Prince of Orleans-Braganza 149
Teresa Christina, Empress of Brazil (née Bourbon-Two Sicilies)

Brederode, Fernando de 47
Bresci, Gaetano 112
Brito Capelo, Vice Admiral Guilherme de 122
Bruno, Lorenco 59
Buica, Manuel 119, 120
BULGARIA
Alexander, Prince of (né Battenberg) 71
Boris III, King of Bulgaria 144
Ferdinand, King of 136

Bunsen, Madame Charles de 21, 22, 34
Burnay, Conde de 115
Byron, Lord 51

C

Campos, Luis de 85
Carreira, Conde da 21
Caervalho de Vasconcelos, Senhor (Portuguese diplomat) 111
Castro, Luciano de 90, 97
Catalania, Senhor (Italian diplomat) 85
Catinot-Crost, Laurence 83
Cavour, Count Camillo 7
Cesali, Lieutenant Colonel 62
Chagas, Joao 126
Chandler, Ashley 148
Corpechot, Lucien 83
Costa, Alfredo 119, 120
Crispi, Francesco 111
Crosio, Felicita (Countess of Villafranca-Soissons) 36
Cunha, Augusto Jose da 49

D

Dacdi, Guillermo 63
Damasceno, Rosa 79
Daupias, Countess of 47
Desiderj, Father Pietro 59
Deslys, Gaby 130
Douglas, Count Robert 137, 142
Dragonetti, Signor 43

E

Espregueira, Senhor 128
Esteve, Pedro 114

F

Feijao, Senhor 126
Fernandes Costa, Senhor (Poet) 85
Ferronays, Countess Ferdinand de la 72
Fialho d'Almeida, Senhor (Author) 115
Fife, Alexander, Duke of 129
Figueiró, Conde de 121, 122
Figueiró, Condessa de 121, 125, 126, 128, 129
Finot, Jean 108
Fontes de Melo, Antonio Maria de 85
Foras, Camille de 6
FRANCE
Bonaparte
Eugenie, French Empress iv, 7, 43, 55, 78
Jerome ("Plon-Plon"), Prince Bonaparte 6, 31, 32, 41, 42, 145
Laetitia, Duchess of Aosta 62, 84, 90, 100, 126, 136, 144, 145
Napoleon I, French Emperor 9, 10
Napoleon III, French Emperor 6, 7, 16, 28, 35, 37, 41, 42

Orleans
Antoine, Duke of Montpensier 35, 37, 99, 100
François, Prince of Joinville 11
Françoise, Duchess of Chartres 74
Gaston, Count d'Eu 138
Henri, Comte de Paris 142, 144, 149
Isabel, Comtesse de Paris 76, 137
Isabelle, Duchess of Guise 109, 149
Isabelle, Comtesse de Paris (née Orleans-Braganza) 142, 144, 149
Jean, Duke of Guise 149
Louis, Duke of Nemours 11
Louis-Philippe, King of the French 11, 35
Louis-Philippe, Comte de Paris 72, 73, 77
Louis-Philippe, Duke d'Orléans 135

Franco, General Francisco 149
Franco, Joao (Portuguese politician) 115, 118, 119, 128

G

Galliotti, Signor (Anarchist) 114
Gama, Vasco da 99
Gerbaux de Sonnaz, Carlo Alberto 111
Gomes da Costa, Captain 107
Grant, Ulysses S. 64
Grant, Mrs. Ulysses S. 64
GREECE
Elisabeth, Queen of (née Romania) 147
Gribble, Francis 108
Grobles, Mr. 69

H

Halvey, Ludovic 34
Hensler, Elise (Countess of Edla) 13, 35, 36, 37, 42, 52, 57, 58, 64, 67, 68, 69, 70, 95, 96, 98
HESSE
Philipp, Landgrave of 143

HESSE AND BY RHINE
Alice, Grand Duchess of (née United Kingdom) 17
Louis IV, Grand Duke of 17

Hintz, President of the Ministry 109, 115, 118
HOHENZOLLERN-SIGMARINGEN
Adelgunde, Princess of (née Bavaria) 146
Franz Josef, Prince of 146
Friedrich, Prince of 146
Josephine, Princess of (née Baden) 37
Josephine, Princess of (née Belgium) 147
Karl Anton, Prince of 38
Karl Anton, Prince of 146, 147
Leopold, Prince of 15, 37, 38, 41, 65, 87, 101, 115
Maria Theresa, Princess of (née Bourbon-Two Sicilies) 146
Marie, Princess of (Countess of Flanders) 17
William, Prince of 99, 101, 146

J

Junot, Marshal Jean-Andoche 9

L

Lavradio, Marques de 116, 117, 121, 123
Lencastre, Dr. Antonio 122, 125, 126, 142
Lima, Visconde de 129
Lopes, Maria Antonia 110
Lorinig, George Bailey 96, 99, 101
Loulé, Duke of (previously a Marques) 16, 22, 39, 85, 125
Lucas. Matilda 60, 109
Luciano, Jose 128
LUXEMBOURG
Guillaume IV, Grand Duke of 147

Luynes, Duchess de 77
Lytton, Robert 28

M

MacDonell, Sister Mary Magdalene 107, 108
Machado, Bernardino 130
Magalhaes Coutinho, Dr. 25, 79
Malherio Dias, Carlos 86
McKinley, William (US President) 114
Meireles, Senhor 126
Mensdorff-Pouilly, Count Albert von 123
Mello Breyner, Thomaz de 47, 48, 53, 54, 61, 88, 119, 123, 125, 126, 127, 128, 129, 132, 133
Mirafiori, Count Emmanuel Albert 60

MONTENEGRO
Nicholas, King of 113

Moreira Jr., Dr. 122
Mossamedes, Viscount of 48
Motta, Marina 79
Mussolini, Benito 143, 144

N

NETHERLANDS
Sophie, Queen of (née Württemberg) 43
Netto, Cardinal Patriarch JNose Sebastiao 76

O

Oldoini, Marquis 39, 40
Oliveira, Maria 14
Oliveira Feijao, Dr. 98

P

Paget, Lady Walburga 31, 60, 135
Panizzardi, Virginia 6, 26, 28, 29, 30
PARMA
Enrico, Prince of, Count of Bardi 147
Robert I, Duke of 148

Pereira, Miguel Angelo 13
Pes di Villamarina, Marchesa ("Nona Pes") 2, 4, 5, 6, 22
Pinto, Joao Benjamin 108
PORTUGAL
Adelaide, Queen of (née Löwesntein-Wertheim-Rosenberg) 147, 1348
Adelgundes, Infanta of (Duchess of San Jaime) 147
Afonso, Infante of, Duke of Oporto 27, 28, 39, 46, 47, 49, 52, 53, 58, 88, 89, 90, 91, 92, 93, 96, 105, 106, 107, 111, 113, 120, 129, 132, 133, 134, 136, 139, 140
Afonso, Infante of 150
Afonso VI, King of 19, 51, 97, 138
Afonso Henriques, King of 19, 138
Amelia, Queen of (né Orleans) 72, 73, 74, 75, 76, 77, 80, 81, 82, 83, 84, 87, 88, 92, 103, 105, 107, 108, 109, 110, 116, 117, 119, 120, 121, 122, 123, 125, 126, 128, 129, 132, 133, 135, 136, 137, 138, 139, 140, 141, 142, 143
Ana de Jesus Maria, Infanta of 16
Antonia, Infanta of, Princess of Hohenzollern-Sigmaringen 12, 15, 36, 37, 38, 58, 66, 68, 69, 71, 74, 81, 83, 84, 86, 87, 88, 89, 93, 95, 99. 101, 104, 105, 115, 137, 146
Augusta Viktoria, Queen of (née Hohenzollern) 137, 142, 148
Augusto, Infante of 12, 15, 16, 17, 26, 35, 68, 69, 85, 95, 96, 98
Carlos, King of iv, 25, 31, 33, 34, 39, 45, 46, 47, 48, 48, 49, 52, 54, 58, 61, 62, 70, 71, 72, 73, 74, 75, 76, 77, 80, 81, 82, 83, 87, 88, 89, 91, 92, 93, 99, 100, 103, 104, 105, 106, 107, 109, 110, 111, 114, 115, 116, 117, 118, 119, 120, 121, 122, 123, 124, 128, 131
Carlota, Queen of (née Spain) 9
Dinis, Infante of
Duarte Nuño, Duke of Braganza 138, 141, 142, 148, 149
Duarte Pio, Duke of Braganza 138, 149, 150
Elisabeth, Duchess of Braganza (née Thurn und Taxis) 148
Ferdinand, King Consort of (né Saxe-Coburg & Gotha) 11, 12, 13, 14, 16, 26, 31, 35, 36, 37, 39, 40, 41, 42, 52, 57, 58, 64, 65, 67, 68, 69, 70, 71, 137, 145, 146, 147
Fernando, Infante of 12, 15, 16
Francisco Jose, Infante of 148
Henrique, Infante of 149
Isabel, Infanta of (Princess of Thurn und Taxis) 148
Isabel Inés, Duchess of Braganza (née de Castro Curvelo de Heredia) 150
Joao, Infante of 12, 15, 16, 17
John V (Joao), King of 54
John VI (Joao), King of 9, 16, 110
Jose I, King of 120
Luis, King of 8, 12, 14, 15, 16, 17, 18, 19, 20, 21, 22, 23, 24, 25, 26, 27, 32, 33, 34, 35, 36, 39, 40, 46, 50, 51, 53, 57, 58, 66, 68, 71, 72, 73, 74, 75, 78, 79, 80, 83, 84, 85, 86, 87, 88, 89, 90, 91, 92, 93, 94, 95, 96, 97, 98, 99, 100, 101, 102, 103, 104, 105, 146
Luis Filipe, Prince of Beira 80, 81, 82, 103, 104, 113, 116, 117, 118, 119, 120, 121, 122, 123, 124, 138
Mafalda, Queen (née Savoy) of 19, 138
Mafalda, Infanta of 148
Manuel I, King of 51
Manuel II, King of 54, 103, 117, 119, 120, 121, 122, 123, 126, 128, 129, 130, 131, 132, 133, 135, 136, 137, 138, 139, 140, 146, 148, 149
Maria Adelaide, Infanta of (Mrs van uden) 148
Maria Anna, Infanta of, Princess of Saxony 12, 15, 53, 65, 66, 67, 69, 71, 74, 82, 83, 144, 145
Maria Anna, Infanta of (Grand Duchess of Luxembourg) 147
Maria Anna, Infanta of (Princess of Thurn und Taxis) 148
Maria Antonia, Infanta of (Duchess of Parma) 148
Maria Antonia, Infanta of (Mrs Chandler) 148
Maria Benedita, Infanta of 148
Maria da Gloria, Queen of 9, 10, 11, 12, 39, 65, 67, 137, 145, 146, 147, 148
Maria das Neves, Infanta of 147
Maria Francesca, Queen of (née Savoy) 19, 51, 138
Maria Francisca, Duchess of Braganza (née Orleans-Braganza) 138, 142, 149
Maria Francisca, Infanta of 150
Maria José, Infanta of 147
Maria Pia, Queen of, (née Savoy) iii, iv, 1, 2, 3, 4, 5, 6, 7, 8, 15, 17, 18, 19, 20, 21, 22, 23, 24, 25, 26, 27, 28, 29, 30, 31, 32, 33, 34, 36, 37, 38, 39, 40, 41, 43, 44, 45, 46, 47, 48, 49, 50, 51, 52, 53, 54, 55, 56, 57, 58, 61, 62, 63, 66, 67, 69, 72, 73, 74, 75, 76, 78, 79, 80, 81, 82, 83, 84, 85, 86, 87, 88, 89, 90, 91, 92, 93, 94, 95, 96, 97, 98, 99, 100, 101, 102, 103, 104, 105, 106, 107, 108, 109, 110, 111, 112, 113, 114, 115, 116, 117, 122, 123, 124, 125, 126, 127, 128, 129, 131, 132, 133, 134, 135, 136, 137, 138, 139, 140, 142, 144, 145
Maria Teresa, Infanta of (Archduchess of Austria) 147
Maria Teresa, Infanta of (Princess of Thurn und Taxis) 148
Marie Therese, Duchess of Braganza (née Löwenstein-Wertheim-Rosenberg) 148
Miguel, King of, Duke of Braganza 9, 10, 11, 17, 137, 139, 146, 147, 148
Miguel, Duke of Braganza 137, 145, 146, 147, 148
Miguel, Infante of 30
Miguel, Duke of Viseu 145, 148
Miguel, Infante of 149
Pedro II, King of 19, 138
Pedro III, King of 51
Pedro IV, King of 9, 10
Pedro V, King of 7, 12, 13, 14, 15, 16, 17, 26, 36, 65, 67, 74, 117
Stephanie, Queen of (née Hohenzollern-Sigmaringen) 6, 13, 14, 15, 17, 31, 65, 67, 75

Pretti, Pedro 79
Prim, Juan, Spanish General, Count of Castillejos 35, 38
PRUSSIA

Eitel Frederick, Prince of 123
Frederick III, German Emperor, King of Prussia 33, 61
Wilhelm I, German Emperor, King of Prussia 38, 41, 89
Wilhelm II, German Emperor, King of Prussia 89, 109, 110, 115, 116, 123, 136
Victoria, German Empress, Queen of Prussia 41, 89
Victoria ("Moretta"), Princess of 71

R

Rapallo, Niccolo Marquis 36
Ratazzi, Princess 33, 49
Ravara, Senhor 126
Rio Maior, Condesa de 25, 53
Rio Maior, Marquesa de 53, 56, 74, 76, 77, 79, 94, 124, 125
Rocha Martins, Senhor 126
Roden, Lord 61
Roh- Guerriero, Maria Pia 29
Roh, Virginia 29
ROMANIA
Carol I (né Hohenzollern-Sigmaringen), King of 38, 147
Carol II, King of 147
Ferdinand, King of 146, 147
Marie, Queen of (née Edinbjurgh & Saxe-Coburg & Gotha) 147

Rui Ramos, Senhor (Portuguese historian) 110
RUSSIA
Alexander II, Tsar of 33, 112, 147
Nicholas Mikhailovich, Grand Duke of 72

S

Salazar, Antonio de Oliveira 140, 141, 149
Sabugosa, Conde de 123
Saldanha, Joao Carlos de, Duke of Saldanha 38, 39, 86
SAVOY (Italy)
Amedeo, Duke of Aosta, King of Spain 1, 23, 26, 27, 29, 30, 31, 32, 42, 43, 44, 51, 57, 61, 84, 89, 90, 100, 104, 110, 144
Amedeo, 3rd Duke of Aosta 143
Charles Albert, King of Sardinia and Piedmont 2, 26, 138
Charles Albert, Prince of 1, 20, 22
Clotilde ("Kekina"), Princess of, Princess Napoleon 1, 2, 3, 4, 5, 7, 26, 29, 30, 31, 32, 37, 42, 43, 61, 62, 67, 78, 84, 126, 134, 135, 136, 145
Elena, Queen of (née Montenegro) 111, 116, 134, 136, 144
Elisabeth, Duchess of Genoa (née Saxony) 7, 36
Eugene, Prince of Savoy-Carignan ("Barba") 11, 21, 26, 27, 36
Ferdinand, Duke of Genoa 4, 20
Giovanna, Princess of (Queen of Bulgaria) 144
Helene, Duchess of Aosta (née Orleans) 142
Jolanda, Princess of 116
Luigi, Prince of Savoy-Aosta 44
Mafalda, Princess of (married Hesse) 143
Margherita, Queen of Italy iv, 22, 32, 61, 83, 111, 112, 113, 135, 136, 144
Maria Beatrice, Princess of 144
Maria Gabriela, Princess of 144
Maria Pia, Princess of married Yugoslavia and later Bourbon-Parma) 144
Maria Vittoria, Duchess of Aosta Queen of Spain (née dal Pozzo della Cisterna) 31, 44
Marie Adelaide (née Austria), Queen of Piedmont 1, 3, 4, 20
Marie José, Queen of (née Belgium) 143, 144
Oddone, Prince of 1, 7, 28, 29, 32
Tommaso, Duke of Genoa 113
Umberto I, King of Italy 1, 3, 5, 7, 21, 22, 23, 29, 32, 33, 61, 104, 110, 111, 112, 113, 120
Umberto II, King of Italy 138, 139, 143, 144
Umberto, Count of Salemi 136, 145
Victor Emanuel II, King of Italy 1, 2, 3, 4, 6, 7, 17, 18, 19, 22, 26, 27, 28, 29, 30, 31, 33, 34, 42, 43, 44, 45, 58, 59, 60, 61, 62, 63, 85, 138
Victor Emmanuel III, King of 61, 111, 112, 113, 115, 116, 126, 134, 136, 138, 142, 143, 144
Victor Emanuel, Prince of 3, 4
Victor Emanuel, Count of Turin 110
Victor Emmanuel, Prince of Naples 144
SAXONY
Albert, Prince of 66, 145
Elisabeth Albertine, Princess of 66
Frederick August III, King of 66, 144, 145
George, King of 15, 65, 66, 67, 69, 145
George, Prince of 66
Johan George, Prince of 66
John, King of 33
Luise, Crown Princess of (née Austria-Tuscany) 145
Maria Johanna, Princess of 66
Maria Josepha, Princess of (Archduchess Otto of Austria) 66, 67, 71, 146
Mathilde, Princess of 66, 67, 69, 145
Maximilian, Prince of 66, 145

SAXE-COBURG & GOTHA
Antonia, Princess of (née Kohary) 11
Ernst II, Duke of 35
Ferdinand, Prince of 11

Seisal, Marques de 73
Sherwood, M.E.W. 90
Sousa Rosa, Thomas de 86, 93
Southey, Robert
Soveral, Marques Luis de (Portuguese diplomat) 130, 148
SPAIN
Alfonso, Infante of, Duke of San Jaime 147
Alfonso XII, King of 45
Alfonso XIII, King of 117
Enrique, Infante of, Duke of Seville 35
Francisco, King of 35
Isabella, Queen of 35, 45
Juan, Count of Barcelona 144
Luisa, Infanta of (née Orleans) 149
Maria Christina, Queen of (née Austria) 45
Maria de las Mercedes, Countess of Barcelona 144
Philip II, King of 38
Victoria Eugenia, Queen of (née Battenberg) 117

Steed, Henry Wickham 113
Stewart, Anita 148
Stoody, Nevada 136
SWEDEN
Gustav Adolf VI, King of 131
Oscar II, King of 17, 19, 25, 78, 89, 95

T

Tavares, Senhor 126
Teixeira de Souza, Antonio (Portuguese politician) 131
THURN UND TAXIS
Franz Josef, Prince of 148
Karl August, Prince of 148

Karl Ludwig, Prince of 148

TUSCANY
Carolina, Archduchess of Austria, Princess of 91
Ferdinand, Grand Duke of 90

TWO SICILIES
Francesco II, King of (aka King of Naples) 18

V

Vale de Reis, Conde de 85, 86
VATICAN
Leo XIII (Cardinal Pecci), Pope 62
Pius IX, Pope 1, 33, 43, 62

Veiga Beirao, Antonio da (Portuguese politician) 131
Vercellona, Rosa ("Rosina") 2, 3, 36
Vila Real, Condesa 25
Vilhena, Marquis Julio de 79
Vital Fontes, Senhor 93, 106, 124

W

Waddington, Major Antonio 122
Werfen, General 99
Worth, Charles Frederick 75

U

Uden, Nicolaas van 148
Unhao, Marquesa de 129, 132
UNITED KINGDOM
Albert, Prince Consort (né Saxe-Coburg & Gotha) 12, 13, 14, 15, 17, 65
Alexandra, Queen of (née Denmark) 123, 130, 131, 135
Alexandra, Princess of Fife 129, 130
Alfred, Duke of Edinburgh and Saxe-Coburg & Gotha 33, 99
Arthur, Duke of Connaught 116
Edward VII, King of 13, 116, 123, 129, 130, 131
George V, King of 131
Leopold, Duke of Albany 64, 65
Louise, Princess Royal, Duchess of Fife 129
Margaret, Princess of 116, 117
Marie, Duchess of Edinburgh (née Russia) 33
Mary Adelaide, Princess of Cambridge 7
Patricia, Princess of 116, 117, 129, 130
Victoria, Queen of 10, 11, 13, 14, 15, 16, 17, 18, 19, 24, 33, 40, 41, 43, 53, 61, 64, 65, 68, 71, 78, 105, 147

Y

Marie, Queen of (née Romania) 147

Z

Zicaloh, Count of 74

Bibliography & Sources

Archival Sources

Materials utilized in this book draw on both published and unpublished sources. Archival abbreviations used within the Source Notes are listed below.

1. AN/TT: The Institute of National Archives: Torre do Tombe, Italy
2. AST: Turin State Archives, Turin: Legato Umberto II
3. RA: The Royal Archives, Windsor Castle
4. Staatsarchiv Sigmaringen, Germany

Books

Almeida, D. Jose e Luiz de (Lavradio). Memorias do Sexto Marques de Lavradio. Lisbon: Editoria Nova Atica. 3rd Edition, 2004.
Almeida, Fialho de. Os Gatos. Volume I. Lisbon: Classica Editora, 1958.
Andrade, Ferreira de. Cascais Vila da Corte-Olto Seculos de Historia. Cascais: Editores, 1964.
Andrade, Maria do Carmo Rebello de. Maria Pia de Saboia. Lisbon: Institutto dos Museus da Conservacao, Palacio Nacional de Ajuda, 2011.
Andreoli, Claudio Alberto. Umberto I di Savoie: Un Regno Tra un Attentatao el Alto. Florence: Libri, 2002.
Ashdown, Dulcie. Victoria and the Coburgs. London: Robert Hale, 1981.
Baena, Miguel de Sanches. Diario de D. Manuel e Estudo Sobre o Regicidio. Lisbon: Alfa, 1990.
Bartoli, D. La fine della Monarchia. Milan: A. Mondadori, 1947.
Bavaria, H.R.H. Prince Adalbert of. Through Four Revolutions, 1862-1933. London: John Murray, 1933.
Beéche, Arturo E. The Coburgs of Europe – The Rise and Fall of Queen Victoria and Prince Albvert's European Family. East Richmond Heights, CA: Eurohistory, 2013.
Benevides, Francisco da Fonseca. Rainhas de Portugal: Estudo Historico com muitos Documentos. 2 Volumes. Lisbon: Typographia Castro Irmao, 1879.
Bensabat, Jose Jacob. A Verdade dos Factos: Occorridos na Villa da Ericeria na Occassiao da Implantacao da Republica. Lisbon: Impr. Africana, 1929.
Benson, Arthur Christopher, and Viscount Esher. The Letters of Queen Victoria: A Selection From Her Majesty's Correspondence Between the Years 1837 and 1861. 3 Volumes. New York: Longmans, Green, and Co., 1907.
Benton, Russell E. The Downfall of a King: Dom Maneul II of Portugal. Washington: University Press of America, 1977.
Bergamini, John D. The Spanish Bourbon: The History of a Tenacious Dynasty. New York: G. P. Putman's Sons, 1974.
Bern, Stephane. Eu, Amelia, Ultima Rainha de Portugal. Porto: Editora Civilizacao, p. 1997.
Biancotti, Angiolo. Maria Clotilde di Savoia. Turin: Societa Editrice Internazionale, 1955.
Bolton, Glorney. A Roman Century: A Portrait of Rome as the Capital of Italy, 1870-1970. New York: The Viking Press, 1970.
Bonnin, Georges, Dr. G. P. Gooch, and Dr. Isabella Massey. Bismarck and the Hohenzollern Candidature for the Spanish Throne. London: Chatto & Windus, 1957.
Bordeux, Vahdah Jeanne. Margherita of Savoy. London: Hutchinson & Co., 1914.
Bradford, Sarah. Portugal. New York: Walker and Company, 1973.
Breyner, Thomaz de Mello. Memorias do Professor Thomaz de Mello Breyner 4th Conde de Mafra, 1869-1880. Lisbon: Pareceria Antonio Maria Pereira, 1930.
___ Diario de um Monarquico 1908-1910. Oporto: Lisboa Rocha, 1993.
___ Diario de um Monarquico 1911-1913. Oporto: Ramos dos Santos, 1994.
Brook-Shepherd, Gordon. Uncle of Europe: The Social and Diplomatic Life of Edward VII. New York: Harcourt Brace Jovanovich, 1975.
Bunsen, Madame Charles de. In Three Legations: Turin, Florence, The Hague. New York: Charles Scribner's and Sons, 1909.
Byron, George Gordon. Letters of Lord Byron. London: Dent, 1962.

Cancio, Francisco. O Paço da Ajuda. Lisbon: Imprensa Barreiro, 1955.
Carvalho, Joao Pinto de. Lisboa de Outrora. 3 Volumes. Lisbon: Amigos de Lisboa, 1938.
Casalandra, Estelle. Nuptials Without Love: The Life of Princess Clotilde of Savoy. New York: P. J. Kennedy & Sons, 1963.
Casalegno, Carlo. La Regina Margherita. Turin: G. Einaudi, 1956.
Catinot-Crost, Laurence. Amelie de Portugal, Princesse de France. Biarritz: Atlantica, 2000.
Cockfield, Jamie H. White Crow: The Life and Times of the Grand Duke Nicholas Mikhailovich Romanov, 1859-1919. Westport, Connecticut: Praeger, 2002.
Cognasso, Francesco. Le Lettere di Vittorio Emanuele II. 2 Volumes. Turin: Palazzo Carignano, 1966.
Colaco, Branca de Gonta. Memorias da Morquesa de Rio Maior. Lisbon: Parceria A. M. Pereira, 2nd Edition, 2005.
Corpechot, Lucien. Memories of Queen Amelia of Portugal. London: Eveleigh Nash, 1915.
Crankshaw, Edward. The Fall of the House of Habsburg. London: Papermac, 1963.
Crisipi, Francesco. Questioni internazionali. Milan: Treves, 1913.
D'Auvergne, Edmund B. The Coburgs: The Story of the Rise of a Great House. New York: James Pott & Company, 1911.
Dias, Marina Tavares. Lisboa Desaparecida. Volume 8. Lisbon: Quimera, 2003.
Dias, Carlos Malheiro. Do Desafio a Debandada: Cheque ao Rei. Lisbon: Livraria Classica Editora, 1912.
Diesbach, Ghislain de. Secrets of the Gotha. New York: Meredith Press, 1968.
Enache, Nicolas. La descendande de Marie-Thérèse de Habsburg, Reine de Hongrie et de Bohême. Paris: L'Intermédiaire des Chercheurs et Curieux, 1996.
Esher, Viscount. The Girlhood of Queen Victoria: A Selection From Her Majesty's Diaries Between the Years 1832-1840. 2 Volumes. New York: Longmans, Green & Co., 1912.
Fairni, Domenico. Diario di fin Secolo. Rome: Bardi, 1961-1962.
Fellmann, Walter. Sachisens Konige 1806 bid 1918. Munich & Berlin: Koehler & Amelang, 2000.
Festa, Hilda Montesi. Clotilde di Savoia. Rome: S.A.L.E.S., 1943.
Fontes, Vital. Servidor de Reis e de Presidentes. Lisbon: Editora Maritimo-Colonial, LDA., 1945.
Frankland, Noble. Witness of a Century. London: Shepheard-Walwyn, 1993.
Fulford, Roger. Dearest Child: Letters Between Queen Victoria and the Princess Royal, 1858-1861. New York: Holt, Rinehart and Winston, 1964.
___ Your Dear Letter: Private Correspondence of Queen Victoria and the Crown Princess of Prussia 1865-1871. New York: Charles Scribner's Sons, 1971.
Garcia, Emidio. O Infante D. Afonso de Braganca. Lisbon: Parceria Antonio Maria Perira, 1939.
Gerbore, P. Dame e Cavalieri del Re. Milan: Longanesi & Co., 1952.
Godinho, Isabel Silveira. D. Luis I: Duque de Porto e Rei de Portugal. Lisbon: Palacio National da Ajuda, 1990.
Prince Michael of Greece. Crown Jewels of Europe. New York: Harper & Rowe, 1983.
Gribble, Francis. The Royal House of Portugal. New York: Kennikat, 1970.
Guedes, Carmina Correia and Isabella Silveira Godinho. Growing Up a Prince at Ajuda Palace 1863-1884. Lisbon: Ajuda National Palace, 2004.
Guimaraes, Luis de Oliveira and Jose Ribeiro dos Santos. Senhoras Conhecidas. Lisbon: Editora Maritimo Colonial, LDA., 1945.
Halstead, Murat. The Illustrious Life of William McKinley our Martyred President. Lansing, MI: P. A. Stone, 1901.
Holt, Edgar. Plon-Plon: The Life of Prince Napoleon. London: Michael Joseph, 1973.
Howe, Malcom. The Braganza Story: A Visit to the Royal Pantheon of Portugal. London: The British Historical Society, 1999.
Katz, Robert. The Fall of the House of Savoy. New York: The Macmillan Company, 1971.
Kertzer, David. Prisoner of the Vatican: The Pope's Secret Plot to Capture Rome From the New Italian State. Boston: Houghton Mifflin Company, 2004.
Leitao, Ruben Anderson editor. Cartas de D. Pedro ao Principe Alberto. Lisbon: Portugalia Editora, 1954.
___ Novos Documentos dos Arquivos de Windsor. Coimbraa: MCMLVIII, 1958.
Lemos, Ester de. D. Maria II: A Rainha e a Mulher. Lisbon: Fundacao da Casa de Braganca, 1954.
Livermore, H.V. A New History of Portugal. London: Blackie and Son, Ltd., 1966.
Lopes, Maria Antonia. Rainhas Que O Povo Amou. Lisbon: Circulo de Leitores e temas e Debates, 2013.
Loring, George Bailey, MD. A Year in Portugal 1889-1890. New York: G. P. Putnam's Sons, 1891.
Lucas, Matilda. Two Englishwomen in Rome. London: Methuen & Co. Ltd., 1938.
Lutyens, Lady Emily editor. The Birth of Rowland: An Exchange of Letters in 1865 Between Robert Lytton and his Wife. London: Rupert Hart-Davis, 1956.
MacColl, Gail and Carol McD. Wallace. To Marry an English Lord: Or, How Anglomania Really Got Started.

New York: Workman Publishing, 1989.
Martins, Rocha. D. Carlos: Historia do seu Reinado. Lisbon: Academia das Sciencias de Lisboa 1926.
Mateos Sáinz de Medrano, Ricardo. Estoril, los Años Dorados. Madrid: La Esfera de los Libros, 2012.
Maxwell, Sir H., editor. Creevey Papers. London: John Murray, 1904.
Mellano, Maria Franca. I Principe Maria Clotilde e Amedeo di Savoia e il Vatican (1870-1890). Turin: Centro Studi Piemontesee, 2000.
Miller, Ilana D. & Arturo E. Beéche. Royal Gatherings, Volume II: 1914-1939. East Rihmond Heights, CA: Eurohistory 2015.
Monica, Maria Filomena. A Queda da Monarquia, Portugal na Viragem do Seculo. Lisbon: Publicacoes D. Quixote, 1987.
Monica, Maria Filomena. Correspondencia Entre D. Pedro V e Seu Tio Principe Alberto. Lisbon: ICS/Quetzal Editores, 2000.
Monteiro, Fernando Amaro. Salazar e a Rainha. Advento de Republicia. Restauracao da Monarquia? Lisbon: Capa, 2006.
Monti, Antonio. La Giovinezza di Vittorio Emanuele II (1820-1849). Milan: A. Mondiadori, 1939.
Monti, Antonio. Donne e Passioni del Risorgimento. Milan: Corticelli, 1935.
Moreira, Fernando Jose Grave. Jose Luciano de Castro: Correspondencia Politica (1858-1911). Lisbon: Quetzal, 1998.
Mowlam, Kay. A Rainha D. Maria Pia: Iconografia. Lisbon: Palacio Nacional da Ajuda, 1987.
Nobre, Eduardo. Paixoes Reais. Lisbon: Quimera, 2002.
___Casa Real. Lisbon: Quimera Editores, 2003.
___Amelia Rainha de Portugal. Lisbon: Quimera, 2006.
Noronha, Eduardo de. Reinado Florescente. Lisbon: Joao Romano Torres & C. Editores, 1982.
Oporto, H. R. H. The Duke of. Memories. London: George Rutledge & Sons, Limited, 1921.
Paget, Lady Walburga. Scenes and Memories. New York: C. Scribner's and Sons, 1912.
Pallier, Jean. Charles I: Roi de Portugal. Biarritz: Atantica, 2000.
Ramalho, Margarida de Magalhaes. Uma Corte e Beira-Mar 1870-1910. Cascais: Quetzal Editores, 2003.
Ramos, Rui. D. Carlos, 1863-1908. Lisbon: Circulo de Leitores, 2006.
Rebelo, Teresa. Condessa d'Edla: A Cantora de Opera, Quasi Rainha de Portugal e de Espanha (1836-1929). Lisbon: Aletheia Editores, 2006.
Regolo, Luciano. Jelena: Tutto il racconto della Vita della Regina Elena di Savoia. Milan: Simonelle Editore, 2002
Sa, Aires de. Principe Real D. Luiz Filipe. Lisbon: Parceria Antonia Maria Pereira, 1929.
Sagrera, Ana de. Amadeo y Maria Victoria. Palma de Mallorca: Alcover, 1959.
Salazar, Fanny Zampini. Margherita of Savoy: First Queen of Italy Her Life and Times. London: Mills and Boon, Limited, 1914.
Salva Galan, J. La Historia de Espana Contada para Escepticos. Barcelona: Ed. Planeta, 1995.
Saviotti, Gino. Italia e Portogallo. Florence: Vallechi Editore, 1941.
Savoia, Maria Gabriella di Savoia and Romano Bracalini. Casa Savoia. Diario di una Monarchia. Milan: Arnoldo Monadori Editore, 1996.
Sherwood, M. E. W. An Epistle to Posterity: Being Rambling Recollections of Many Years of My Life. New York: Harper & Brothers Publishers, 1897.
Silveira, Luis Nuno Espinha da and Paulo Jorge Fernandes. D. Luis. Lisbon: Circulo de Leitores, 2006.
Singleton, Esther, editor. The World's Greatest Events: An Indexed History From Around the World. Volume 9. New York: P. F. Collier & Son, Company, 1916, (from Jean Finot, "The Lisbon Assassination.").
Sousa, Antonia Teixeira de. Para a Historia da Revolucao. 2 Volumes. Coimbra: Moura Marques & Parisos, 1912.
Southey, Charles editor. The Life and Correspondence of Robert Southey. London: Longman, Brown, Green, and Longmans, 1855.
Speroni, Gigi. Amedeo d'Aosta: Re di Spagna. Milan: Rusconi, 1986.
Steed, Henry Wickham. Through Thirty Years, 1892-1922, a Personal Narrative. New York: Doubleday, Page & Company, 1925.
Stern, Fritz. Gold and Iron: Bismarck, Bleichroder, and the Building of the German Empire. New York: Alfred A. Knopf, 1977.
Taylor, Edmond. The Fall of Dynasties: The Collapse of the Old Order, 1905-1922. New York: Doubleday & Inc., 1963.
Teixeira, Jose. D. Fernando II: Rei-Artista, Artista-Rei. Lisbon: Fundacao da Casa de Braganca, 1986.
Tourtchine, Jean-Fred. Le Royaume d'Italie, Volume III. Cercle d'Etudes des Dynasties Royales Européenes, , 1994.
Victor Emmanuel II. Memorie del re galantuomo. Milan: F. Garbini, 1882.
Vilhena, Julio de. D. Pedro Veo seu Reinado: Novos Documentos. Coimbra: Impresna da Universidade, 1922.

Vilhena, Julio de editor. Cartas Ineditas da Rainha D. Estefania. Coimbra: Imprensa da Universidade, 1922.
Vicente, Ana and Antonio Pedro Vicente. O Principe Real Luiz Filipe de Braganca (1887-1908). Lisbon: Edicoes Inapa, 1998.
Whitehouse, H. Resen. The Sacrifice of a Throne. New York: Bonnell Silver Co., 1897.
Williams, John. Heyday for Assassins. London: William Heinemann Ltd., 1958.
Young, George. Portugal Old and Young: An Historical Study. Oxford: At the Claredoon Press, 1917.
Zeepvat, Charlotte. Prince Leopold: The Untold Story of Queen Victoria's Youngest Son. London: Sutton Publishing, 1998.

Websites

Abecasis, Maria Isabel Braga, Maria Manuela d'Oliveira Martins, and Maria do Carmo Rebello de Andrade. Trans. Elizabeth Plaisteer. "Ajuda Palace". http://www.cidadevirtualpt./palacio-ajuda/guidedtour.html. 8/18/2001 (1-12) p. 5.
http://archives.ned.edu/calendar/c1892.htm. 05/31/2008 (1-9) p. 3. Notre Dame Archives: Calendar X-3-n-A.L.S. – 4pp. – 12mo. – {6} Letter from Sister Mary Magdalene MacDonnell to Father Daniel E. Hudson, C.S.C. 1892.
http://www.arqnet.ptdictiionario/mariapia.html. 3/6/2006 (1-4) p. 3.
A Visit to Neccesidades Palace. http://www.min-nestrangeiros.pt/mne/visita/engp.html. 4/23/2008 (1-13) p. 9.
Cidadania Cascais. http://cidadaniacsc.blogspot.com/. 8/2/2007 (1-17) p. 4.
"July 5, 1911 – Death of Maria Pia of Savoy, Queen of Portugal. Unofficial Royalty. http://www.unofficialroyalty.com/july-5-daily-featured-royal-date. 2/12/2014 (1-3) p. 2.
Oliveira, Domingos. "Os Ultimos Anos." http://www.prof2000.pt/users/adcostinah/OsUltimosAnos/OsUltimosAnos.htm. 7/17/2006 (1-3) p. 2.
Oliveira, Domingos. "O Anjo da Caridade." http://www.prof2000.pt/users/adcostinha/OAnjoDa. 7/17/2006 (1-8) p.3.
Oliveira, Domingos. "Perfil de Uma Rainha." www.prof2000.pt/users/adcostina/PerfildeUmaRainha/Perfil. 7/17/2006 (1-10) p. 2.
http://estandosentido.blogs.sapo.pt/699615.html. 11/18/2010
Interview with Umberto II by Louis Cavicchioli, 1960. http://64.233.179.104/translate_c?hlen&langpair-htp:/www.diesis.com/ph. 4/27/2008 (1-14) p. 9-11.
"Maria Pia di Savoia Regina del Portogallo." www.tricolore-italia.com. 10/16/2006 (1-12) p. 11.
http://www.oldandsold.com/articles04/europe6.shtml. Cintra-Portugal. 2/2/2006 (1-7) p. 2.
"Walters, David Arthur." "1908 Lisbon Assassinations." http://postpoems.com/cgi=bin/displaypoem.cgi?pid=353833. 08/04/2007 (1=23) p. 8.
http://www.it.wikipedia.org/wiki/Maria_PiaPdi_Savoia. 6/27/2008

Articles and Periodicals

Ashton, Janet. "A Soup of Many Souls: Maria da Gloria, Fernando II and the Paço de Pena." European Royal History Journal. Issue L Volume 9.2 (April 2006): 21-38.
L'Illustrazione Italiana Anno XXXVIII – N.29 – 16 Luglio 1911.
Mateos Sáinz de Medrano, Ricardo. "An Ill Fated Romance." Royalty Digest, Volume IV No. 2 (August 1994): 50-53.

Newspapers

The New York Times
The Times, London

The Coburgs of Europe

A royal biography of the Saxe-Coburg & Gotha dynasty and all its branches in Great Britain, Belgium, Portugal, Bulgaria and Coburg.

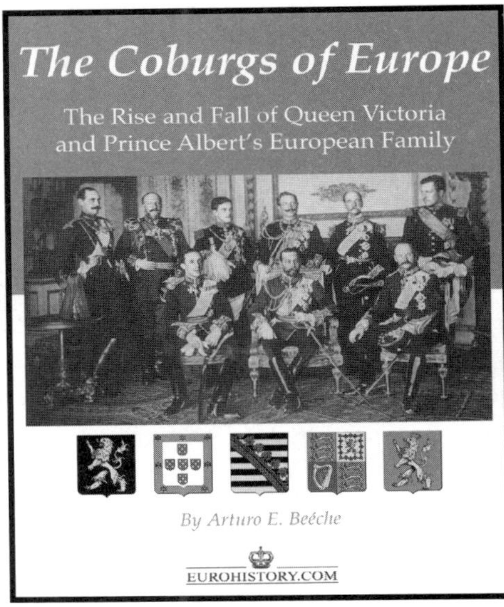

Queen Victoria and the Prince Consort were both Coburgs and they feature prominently in the storyline of each of the dynasty's branches.

It includes more than 500 photos of the various Coburg branches.

The price of this hardback book is: USA price: $48.95 + shipping ($8 in the USA – $24.00 overseas). WE SHIP WORLDWIDE!

To order by phone: (510) 236-1730 or email: books@eurohistory.com

---

APAPA

King Christian IX of Denmark and His Descendants

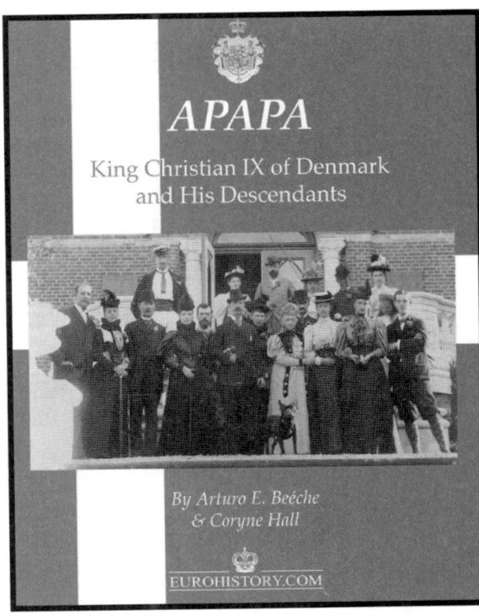

The history of King Christian IX of Denmark, the Father-in-law of Europe, and his descendants. Covering the last 150 years of the royal and imperial houses of: Denmark, Norway, Great Britain, Greece, Romania, Russia, Hanover, Baden, Mecklenburg-Schwerin and many other related dynasties and princely houses.

The authors have handsomely documented their writings with nearly 450 exquisite and rare photos of King Christian IX and his wife Louise and their descendants.

USA price: $48.95 plus shipping ($8.00 in the USA – $24.00 overseas).

Royal Gatherings

Who is in the Picture? – Volume I

Inspired by a very popular feature inside the pages of EUROHISTORY, Ilana D. Miller and Arturo E. Beéche wrote a book on royal gatherings that happened between 1859-1914. Spanning many of Europe's royal families, Royal Gatherings tells the story behind 38 group photos of royals from King Francesco II of the Two Sicilies, to the wedding of Prince Heinrich of Prussia, and the Assassination of Archduke Franz Ferdinand of Austria.

Royal Gatherings' 176 pages are filled with more than 250 unique photographs, most of them from the Eurohistory Archive and some from private royal collections.

The book sells for $43.95 plus shipping ($8.00 in the USA – $24.00 overseas). Order by Phone: 510-236-1730 or email at: books@eurohistory.com

---

Russia and Europe – Dynastic Ties

Authored by Galina Korneva and Tatiana Cheboksarova, it includes nearly 600 photos, an overwhelming majority among them collected from the main archives of Russia and several European countries. The moment captured by these original photos is able, often times, to tell the reader far more about the unique world of royalty and aristocracy than countless pages of text. The authors also relied on important information obtained from Russian and foreign periodicals, memoirs and scientific literature. The English-language version of this book was expanded with contributions written by Arturo Beéche, founder and publisher of Eurohistory.

The price of this hardback book is: USA price: $49.95 + shipping ($8 in the USA – $24.00 overseas). WE SHIP WORLDWIDE!

To order by phone: (510) 236-1730 or email: books@eurohistory.com